MASTER JAPANESE

HOW TO LEARN JAPANESE THROUGH ANYWHERE IMMERSION

JOHN FOTHERINGHAM

MASTER JAPANESE

HOW TO LEARN JAPANESE THROUGH ANYWHERE IMMERSION

JOHN FOTHERINGHAM

COPYRIGHT

Print Edition: 1.1

Digital Edition: 9.3

ISBN: 978-0692181188

DEDICATION

To my wife Rosemary

Thank you for believing in me no matter what, reading my work, and making me laugh until my stomach hurts. You are the most loving, supportive, hilarious, vivacious woman that a man could ever ask for. No matter what you say, *I* am the one who married up.

To my parents Vern and Beverly

Thank you for teaching me to question, think creatively, and march to the beat of my own drum. You have shown me what it means to be an entrepreneur, an artist, and a good human being who does what is right (whatever the cost) and lives in service to others.

To my siblings Brooke, Graham, and David

Thank you for your unwavering support throughout my crazy travel adventures and entrepreneurial endeavors. You are all creative, innovative, and funny in wonderfully unique ways, and I am incredibly proud to be your brother.

ACKNOWLEDGMENTS

Special thanks to:

- **ITOU Katsuhiro (伊東克洋):** My first—and by far my favorite—Japanese teacher who had an infectious passion for languages.
- **Edward Vajda:** My first linguistics professor who made languages so interesting that I switched majors in my third year of university!
- **Dr. James Heisig:** The author of *Remembering the Kanji* who made learning Chinese characters fun and easy.
- **Dr. Jay Rubin:** The author of *Making Sense of Japanese* whose wit and wisdom made learning Japanese all the more enjoyable.
- **Khatzumoto:** The man behind the *All Japanese All the Time* blog who showed me the power of immersion and fun in language learning.
- **Benny Lewis:** The creator of the *Fluent in 3 Months* blog who has been a generous mentor in the world of blogging and publishing.
- **Olly Richards:** The creator of *I Will Teach You a Language* who has always been a friendly ear and supporter.
- **Santiago Madrigal:** A skilled Japanese learner and Spanish translator who has provided priceless feedback and support.

ABOUT THE AUTHOR

John Fotheringham is a linguist, teacher, author, and entrepreneur from Seattle. After studying Linguistics, Japanese, and TESOL (Teaching English to Speakers of Other Languages) at Western Washington University, he began a decade-long adventure in East and South Asia, teaching English at a rural Japanese high school, working as a translator and interpreter for the Japanese government, consulting for a telecom startup in Bangladesh, and teaching business English, learning Mandarin, and studying Wing Chun and Baguazhang in Taiwan.

John now lives in Washington State where you can find him cooking healthy meals with his wife, making corny puns, doing improv comedy, or exploring single track on his bike.

For more about John, visit **LanguageMastery.com/About**.

CONTENTS

START HERE

"One language sets you in a corridor for life. Two languages open every door along the way." —Frank Smith

---

Today, you embark on a journey that will forever change your life. Japanese ability will create a richer travel experience, enable new friendships, and unlock countless employment opportunities. It will deepen your appreciation of the Japanese culture and even your *own*. It will keep your mind sharp as you age and boost your brain power along the way. But above all, it will open doors you never knew existed.

Introduction

Master Japanese is four books in one:

- One part how-to manual.
- One part resource guide.
- One part "choose your own adventure" book.
- One part manifesto.

The primary goal of *Master Japanese* is to provide the tools, methods, materials, and psychological shifts you need to **maximize your active time in Japanese**. By choosing the right resources and adopting the right attitude, you will significantly increase your Japanese input and output, and give your brain the signals it needs to create new neural connections and ever-thicker layers of *myelin*, the neural insulation that drives skill acquisition; that is, it makes our learning "stick." (Myelin is a skill supercharger we'll talk about more later in the book).

The more deep, deliberate practice you get, the better your Japanese becomes. It's not a secret. It's not magic. If you show up and do the work, you *will* reach fluency.

WHAT YOU WILL LEARN

By the time you finish the book, you will be able to:

- Build an environment that enables you to acquire Japanese no matter where in the world you live.
- Learn by *doing* instead of *studying*, and by *communicating* instead of *procrastinating*.
- Optimize your memory to make Japanese words and structures stick.
- Overcome your fears, build discipline, and stay motivated.
- Choose resources that fit your unique interests, goals, and learning style.

HOW THE BOOK IS ORGANIZED

Master Japanese is divided into the following five chapters:

Start Here

You will learn how to use this book, get answers to frequently asked questions, learn the basic principles of Anywhere Immersion and the prerequisites for success, and get a preview of the journey ahead.

Master Your Day

You will learn how to learn *more* in *less* time by creating effective goals and daily systems, optimizing your time *and* timing, developing powerful habits instead of relying on willpower, leveraging the power of social and financial stakes, tracking your progress, and measuring what matters.

Master Your Mind

You will learn to see through the most common myths, how to face your fears, how to increase and sustain motivation, and how to develop diamond-tough discipline.

Learn How To Learn

You will learn how to learn a language, including how to maximize your exposure to Japanese through Anywhere Immersion, how to learn through fun activities and resources *you* pick, how to improve all four language skills (listening, speaking, reading, and writing), how to maximize your myelin (remember, that's the neural insulation that drives skill acquisition) through deep, deliberate practice, how to optimize memory through mnemonics, spaced repetition, and effective note-taking, and how to optimize brain function and health through nutrition, sleep, and movement.

Choose Your Weapons

In the final chapter, you will select your "weapons," the tools and resources you will use to build your *Anywhere Immersion* environment and learn Japanese the fun, effective, natural way. You will learn where to find Japanese reference tools, podcasts, music, video games, anime, TV shows, movies, books, eBooks, audiobooks, comics, newspapers, magazines, and more.

WHY MASTER JAPANESE IS NOT A TEXTBOOK

Master Japanese is NOT a traditional lesson-based textbook or language course. This is by design. Why? There are four reasons.

Traditional Approaches Are Ineffective

The traditional textbook-focused approach to learning languages rarely leads to fluency despite years or decades of study. But despite its poor track record, the traditional way of teaching languages persists in most courses, classes, and textbooks. Why? Momentum. As Thomas Paine wrote in *Common Sense*:

> "...a long habit of not thinking a thing wrong, gives it a superficial appearance of being right..."[1]

You Can't Learn a Language by Reading About It

"You don't learn to walk by following rules. You learn by doing, and by falling over." —Richard Branson

---

You can't master a language by reading about it. And no book or course can "get a language into your head." This is not *The Matrix*, Neo-san. Only *you* can acquire Japanese by getting enough **exposure and practice in meaningful contexts**.

Reading *about* Japanese will do little to help you actually *understand* and *use* the language. To reach fluency, you have to actually hear, read, speak, and write the language. A lot.

This is precisely what *Master Japanese* will show you how to do. Instead of trying to force facts into your head, you will instead learn how to acquire the language naturally through a fun, self-guided approach that I call *Anywhere Immersion.*

"Imagine me teaching you soccer through books. I insist you memorize the physics of each possible shot, over 1–2 years, before we get on the field. How will you do? Well, first, you'll likely quit before you ever touch a ball. Second, when you get on the field, you'll have to start from scratch, turning that paper knowledge into practical knowledge."
—Tim Ferriss, *The 4-Hour Chef*

Those with the "Upholder" tendency, detailed in Gretchen Rubin's book *The Four Tendencies*, may do well with the formal structure and clear expectations afforded by textbooks *in conjunction with* the methods I recommend. Those of the other three tendencies (Questioner, Obliger, and Rebel), however, will likely do better with more organic, self-guided, immersion-based approaches. Find out which you are here: bit.ly/mj4tend

See the *Leverage Your Tendency* section for more on the "Four Tendencies" and how to apply them in language learning.

It's Better To Focus on *How* Than *What*

We all have different interests, learning styles, and reasons for learning a language. So instead of trying to teach *what* you need to learn, it's much more effective and efficient to show you *how* to learn. Once you learn how to fish, you can then go out and catch whichever specific "seafood" you want. Moreover, you can then apply the core principles from *Master Japanese* to learn *other* languages, too!

See *There is No One Way to Learn* for more on why one size never fits all.

Plenty of Textbooks Exist Already

While most Japanese textbooks are boring and ineffective, there *are* a few good ones that can be a useful addition to your Japanese toolbox. They can provide sample sentences, high-frequency vocabulary, and a basic overview of how the language works, all of which can speed up your path to fluency. The key is ensuring these tools *supplement*—not *replace*—the activities that *actually* fuel language acquisition.

And speaking of how the language works, don't miss the *How Japanese Works* bonus guide I created for you. The 300+ page PDF explains the patterns, words, and sounds that make Japanese tick.

While *Master Japanese* focuses on the *why* and the *how* of learning Japanese, the companion *How Japanese Works* guide covers the *what*. I believe that *both* resources will be helpful in your language learning journey, but make sure to focus on finishing *Master Japanese* first.

Download the *How Japanese Works* PDF here:
bit.ly/howjapaneseworks

How To Use This Book

TIPS & SIDEBARS

I've sprinkled the following extra bonuses throughout the book to make your Japanese journey as smooth as possible:

Recommended Resources

A big part of *Anywhere Immersion* is choosing Japanese resources, materials, and tools that make learning more fun and effective. I have scoured the interwebs to find the very best online goodies, which are shown using call-outs like this:

Simply type the **bit.ly** links in your browser or click/tap them in the digital edition. **Note:** the links are case sensitive!

Cross-References

To save you time finding related sections and relevant information, I've included cross-references as follows:

Related sections elsewhere in the book are indicated with this bookmark icon.

Action Steps

A major focus of Master Japanese is learning through ***doing*** instead of ***studying***. To that end, I've included action steps whenever possible to help you translate the tips in the book to actual progress in the real world.

 TAKE ACTION!

1. Read the action list.
2. Actually *do* the actions!
3. Seriously, don't just read them. **DOOOO** them!

Notes, Exceptions & Pro Tips

While mistakes are an important, essential part of the learning process, I've done my best to help you avoid some of the most common missteps by pointing out exceptions and unintuitive patterns with call-outs like this:

 NOTE!

Japanese has fairly consistent rules, but like all languages, there are exceptions, rogue patterns, and arbitrary historical changes to be aware of. Keep a look out for these sidebars to avoid the most common pitfalls.

Mindset Mantras

Your thoughts and feelings about the Japanese language—and your ability to learn it—make a massive impact on the pace and pleasure of your learning journey. To help lift your spirits and keep you going when the going gets tough, I've provided a number of *Mindset Mantras* in the book. Say these aloud, write them down, and post them somewhere you will see them every day. The mantras look like this:

***Attitude* trumps *aptitude*.** Say the following aloud three times:

1. I **want** to learn Japanese.
2. I **can** learn Japanese.
3. I **will** learn Japanese.

Print-Ready Worksheets & Cheatsheets

I've created a number of print-ready PDF worksheets and cheat sheets to help you save time and take action.

When you see this icon, make sure to download the print-ready PDFs using the links shown.

Culture Corners

A fun part about learning the Japanese *language* is that you also learn about Japanese *culture*. I've sprinkled a number of *Culture Corner* sidebars throughout the book to help create context, increase understanding, and make your learning journey more meaningful. They look like this:

 **CULTURE CORNER**

"A language is not just words. It's a culture, a tradition, a unification of a community, a whole history that creates what a community is. It's all embodied in a language." —Noam Chomsky

PRESENTATION OF JAPANESE TERMS & NAMES

Presentation of Japanese Words

To aid learners of all levels, all Japanese terms include the Romanized spelling (i.e. English letters), the word in native Japanese script, and an English translation:

- First, the Romanized spelling—called *roumaji* (ローマ字, ろうまじ)—is presented in *italics*.
- Second, the Japanese script is presented within

parentheses, with *kanji* (Chinese characters) first, followed by the word's pronunciation in *hiragana* (one of Japanese's two "syllabic" alphabets; Japanese is made of syllables—consonant-vowel combinations—instead of separate consonants and vowels like English). For words written in *katakana* (the other syllabic alphabet used for foreign words), I repeat the word in *hiragana* to help you get used to both systems.

- Third, an English translation is provided within quotes when relevant. Sometimes a literal translation will be used, in which case I will include the term *lit.* before the translation.

For example, I would present the word "Japanese language" as follows:

---

nihongo (日本語, にほんご, lit. "Japan language")

As another example, the word for "draft beer" would be written as:

---

biiru (生ビール, なまびいる, lit. "raw beer")

In *katakana*, long vowels are indicated with a dash (ー). In the *roumaji* and *hiragana* equivalents, I simply duplicate the vowel (e.g. *ii* as above).

Presentation of Implied Words

Japanese often leaves out certain words (e.g. subjects and objects) that must be stated explicitly in English. When this happens, I place the omitted words within brackets in the English translation.

For example, in the following sentence, the subject is left out of the Japanese version:

Ureshii desu. (嬉しいです, うれしいです, "[I] am happy.")

Note that without context, you wouldn't actually know *who* the above sentence refers to (it could just as easily be "You are happy" or "He/She is happy").

Presentation of Family Names

To prevent potential confusion and ambiguity, all Japanese names are presented in the original Japanese order:

FAMILY NAME + Given Name

For example:

NATSUME Souseki (夏目漱石, なつめそうせき)

You will also notice that I always write the Romanized version of family names in CAPITAL LETTERS to further reduce potential ambiguity.

For more about naming conventions, see *Japanese Proper Nouns* in *How Japanese Works*. **bit.ly/howjapaneseworks**

Frequently Asked Questions

WHY DID I CREATE MASTER JAPANESE?

"We do not need more language courses. We need courses on how to learn languages." —Steve Kaufmann

---

This book is designed to show you *how* to learn Japanese, not to directly teach you the language. Why? Because nobody can actually "teach" you a language. Not Japanese teachers.

Not Japanese courses. Not Japanese textbooks.

Languages are "acquired" only if we get enough exposure to them—and enough practicing using them—in meaningful contexts.

The incorrect belief that a teacher, course, or textbook will get a language into your head is one of the major reasons why traditional language courses *don't work*. Consider how much you remember from your two years of high school Spanish! On top of the fact that these methods don't work, they tend to bore the heck out of learners, convince them they aren't good at languages, and the methods completely ignore how our brains evolved to learn, process, and produce language. There's a better way, and it's called Anywhere Immersion.

WHAT IS ANYWHERE IMMERSION?

Anywhere Immersion is a fun, effective way to expose yourself to Japanese no matter where you happen to live. Living in Japan is great, but it's no longer a requirement for language immersion thanks to the internet, modern devices, and worldwide media distribution.

For more details on Anywhere Immersion, see:
Learn How to Learn > Learn Through Immersion

WHY SHOULD YOU TRUST MY ADVICE?

"The top 1% often succeed *despite* how they train, not *because* of it. Superior genetics, or a luxurious full-time schedule, make up for a lot. Career specialists can't externalize what they've internalized. Second nature is hard to teach." —Tim Ferriss, *The 4-Hour Chef*

When first starting out in languages, I made just about every possible mistake. I used terribly inefficient methods, slogged through boring materials I wouldn't wish upon my worst enemy, and almost gave up more than a few times. But this is good news for *you*: struggling so much in the beginning and later correcting course makes me a much better language coach. You never want to learn from a "natural" who picks up new skills easily:

- They will not know how to explain what they did and how they did it.
- They will not be able to empathize with people who are struggling along in the dark.

I know *your* pain because *I've* felt it, too. I struggled along in languages just like most folks until I figured out that the traditional "tried and true" methods and materials used in most schools are anything *but* true.

I don't have all the answers, but I *do* know the way up

"Japanese Mountain." I've written this guide to show you the way. I can't promise you an easy climb, but I *can* guarantee that you'll reach the top if you follow the tips, tools, and strategies laid out in this guide.

I also have an academic background in linguistics and a professional background in language teaching and writing. I will translate complex ideas and technical jargon into more comprehensible prose and applicable, bite-sized steps for you. I've read the linguistics textbooks and research journals and will distill that content down for you, so you don't have to!

WHAT DO I MEAN BY "MASTERY"?

First of all, "mastery" (and for that matter, "fluency") does not mean "perfection." Such a thing doesn't exist in languages, or any other natural system. And even if perfection *did* exist, it would not be a "S.M.A.R.T. goal" (covered later in the guide), and is therefore irrelevant to our purposes. So if "mastery" does not equal "perfection," what does it mean? I define "mastery" as follows:

The ability to use a language well for *your* communicative purposes.

That's it.

Mastery is completely relative to *your* personal and professional needs:

- If you want a meaningful social life, then "mastery" might mean being able to understand and contribute to casual conversations at a quiet tea shop in Kyoto or a loud Tokyo dance club.
- If you are a film fanatic, then "mastery" for you might mean being able to understand your favorite flick without relying on English (or even Japanese) subtitles.
- If you are a hitherto monolingual Japanese-American, perhaps "mastery" entails finally being able to communicate well with your relatives in their native language.
- If you are a professional who works in Japan or with a Japanese company, then your version of mastery will involve business-related terms and cultural norms.
- If you are dating or married to someone from Japan, your version of mastery will require the communication of thoughts, feelings, likes, dislikes, etc.

In any of these scenarios, "mastery" does not entail learning every last word you may hear or read. Even native Japanese speakers come across vocabulary they don't know, or encounter kanji that they have forgotten how to write or pronounce. The key is to know enough Japanese that you can ask about the meaning of an unfamiliar word and then actually understand the answer.

Strive to constantly expand your vocabulary, improve your pronunciation, and polish your grammar, but remember that the focus should always be on *quality* over *quantity*. Just as in sports or martial arts, having lots of fancy moves is not as important as mastering a small set of core techniques.

"When something goes wrong in a big way—a once great sports team loses to a no-name underdog or a successful business goes under—it's almost always for the same reason. At some point during their rise, everyone quit paying attention to the fundamentals. They advanced so far and started spending so much time trying to perfect the fancy stuff they lost sight of the basics. And when the basics crumble, the fancy stuff doesn't matter any more." —Tyler Tervooren, founder of *Riskology: Leadership for Introverts*

HOW LONG WILL IT TAKE TO LEARN JAPANESE?

This is one of the most common questions I get from new learners and also one of the hardest to answer. First of all, it all depends on what you mean by "learn." Are you referring to conversational fluency and basic literacy or native-like proficiency? In the case of the former goal, a dedicated learner should be able to master enough core words and structures to have basic—but flowing—conversations in just three to six months. From there, most learners can probably reach level B1 or B2 in the CEFR system in about one to three years.

CEFR stands for *Common European Framework of Reference for Languages*, which is called *Youroppa Gengo Kyoutsuu Sanshou Waku* (ヨーロッパ言語共通参照枠, ようろっぱげんごきょうつうさんしょうわく) in Japanese. The system was developed by the Council of Europe to standardize proficiency assessment and testing, but is now used widely all over the world. It includes the following 6 levels:

- **A1 – Beginner:** Can communicate basic ideas and concepts and give a basic self-introduction.
- **A2 – Elementary:** Can communicate within routine contexts, and discuss their background and immediate surroundings.
- **B1 – Intermediate:** Can communicate within familiar contexts (e.g. work, school, travel, etc.).
- **B2 – Upper-Intermediate:** Can communicate in a clear, flowing way, and discuss both concrete and abstract topics.
- **C1 – Advanced:** Can communicate all social, academic and professional needs in a fluent, flexible manner.
- **C2 – Mastery:** Can communicate with extreme precision, and can easily understand nearly everything heard or read.

Most experienced language learners and polyglots tend to aim at B2 since this level allows them to accomplish the vast majority of day-to-day needs in the language. You can, of course, keep learning and improving from there, but the *law of diminishing returns* starts to kick in quickly. While it may take you only a year to reach B2, reaching C1 or C2 could very well take five or more trips around the sun. As Tim Ferriss puts it:

"To understand 95% of a language and become conversationally fluent may require 3 months of applied learning; to reach the 98% threshold could require 10 years. There is a point of diminishing returns where, for most people, it makes more sense to acquire more languages (or other skills) vs. add a 1% improvement per 5 years."

WHEN IS THE BEST TIME TO START?

"The best time to plant a tree was twenty years ago.
The next best time is now." —Chinese Proverb

There will never be a perfect time to start, so you might as well start now. It's tempting to put off our Japanese journey until a supposedly better time in the future. We tell ourselves, "I'll start *after* the holidays," or, "I'll start as soon as I finish this big project at work." Of course, the holidays come and go, and that work project has long since been replaced by another, and yet we still haven't begun learning.

Or to employ another Tim Ferriss-ism:

> "For all of the most important things, the timing always sucks. Waiting for a good time to quit your job? The stars will never align and the traffic lights of life will never all be green at the same time. The universe doesn't conspire against you, but it doesn't go out of its way to line up the pins either. Conditions are never perfect. 'Someday' is a disease that will take your dreams to the grave with you. Pro and con lists are just as bad. If it's important to you and you want to do it 'eventually,' just do it and correct course along the way."[2]

WHY SHOULD YOU LEARN JAPANESE?

If you've bought this book and read this far, you probably *already* have some pretty strong motivations for learning Japanese. But if you need more convincing, here are eight reasons why acquiring the language is well worth your time.

Japanese is a "Top Ten" Language

With 125,000,000 native speakers, Japanese is the 9th most widely spoken language in the world. If you learn to speak the language, you will be able to converse with 2% of the world's population! Although 99% of first-language Japanese speakers live in Japan, people of Japanese descent, known as *nikkeijin* (日系人, にっけいじん), can be found across the globe. Also, more than a million Japanese citizens are currently living abroad, according to Japan's Ministry of Foreign Affairs.

CULTURE CORNER

First generation *nikkeijin* are referred to as *issei* (一世, いっせい), while second, third, and fourth generations are knows as *nisei* (二世, にせい), *sansei* (三世, さんせい), and *yonsei* (四世, よんせい) respectively. The largest communities of Japanese speakers outside of Japan can be found in the following countries:

COUNTRY	APPROX. # OF NIKKEIJIN
Brazil	1,500,000
United States	1,200,000
Philippines	120,000
United Kingdom	100,000
Peru	90,000
Canada	80,000

For more info, see the *Geographic distribution* section of the *Japanese language* Wikipedia entry: **bit.ly/mjwikjpgd**

Make Travel in Japan More Enjoyable

"Americans who travel abroad for the first time are often shocked to discover that, despite all the progress that has been made in the last 30 years, many foreign people still speak in foreign languages."
—Dave Barry

I would have a small fortune if I had a nickel for every time I heard somebody say, "Why bother learning a foreign language? Everyone speaks English!" It's true that many people in the world *study* English, but that is no guarantee that they will actually *speak* the language or *understand* it when it's spoken to them at the rapid-fire speed used by native speakers. Outside of tourist hotspots, very few people you encounter in Japan will have the skills or confidence to speak English with you. Therefore, if you wish to travel off the beaten path—which I highly recommend you do while traveling in Japan—it's useful to learn at least a modicum of travel-specific Japanese. Speaking the local language will make your trip more enjoyable, more meaningful, less stressful, and less expensive.

Increase Your Income

Speaking of money, learning a foreign language can seriously increase your job prospects and potential salary. Not only will foreign language skills set your résumé apart from monolingual candidates vying for the same job, but bilingualism may one day be a requirement to even get your foot in the door! According to a report from *New American Economy*, a bipartisan research and advocacy organization, the number of job postings requiring a second language doubled from 2010 to 2015, ballooning up from 240,000 to 630,000 job postings![3]

Fluency in a second language can also improve your negotiating position, and potentially lead to a higher salary if you play your linguistic cards right.

Increase Your Tolerance for Ambiguity

As you work your way from "zero" to "hero" in Japanese, you will encounter a great deal of ambiguity. There will be numerous situations in which you don't know exactly what is happening, what someone is saying, or even what *you* just said. This can be particularly uncomfortable for adults who have become accustomed to the crystal-clear understanding and precise speaking skills their highly trained adult brains enable. While this can be stressful in the short-term, the good news is that 1) clarity will eventually come with enough practice, and 2) learning to tolerate ambiguity is a superpower you can apply throughout your life:

- It will increase your patience.
- It will increase your stress tolerance.
- It will help you be a better businessperson and negotiator.

Increase Your Empathy

What is the easiest way to spot someone who has never learned a foreign language? Watch how they interact with someone who has a thick accent or broken English. If they are impatient, rude, or condescending, you can bet good money that they have never mastered a foreign tongue themselves. On the flip side, those who have put in all the work, time, effort, and money it takes to master a foreign language will be far more patient and empathetic with those learning their native tongue. Having walked the path ourselves, we cannot help but feel a profound sense of empathy for other learners on their journey to fluency.

Improve Your Brain

Learning a foreign language has been linked with numerous cognitive and neurophysiological benefits, including:

- **A bigger brain:** Learning a language literally changes the size and structure of your brain! Participants in a 2012 Swedish study, for example, experienced increased cortical thickness and hippocampal volumes after three months of intense language study.[4]

- **Improved memory:** A 2003 study published in the *Scandinavian Journal of Psychology* showed stronger *episodic memory* (autobiographical events) and *semantic memory* (general knowledge) in bilingual participants over their monolingual counterparts.[5]

- **Slowing neurological decline:** While a cure for aging has yet to be developed, multilingualism *does* appear to help offset certain age-related losses in cognitive function[6] and protect against the onset of dementia.[7]

Prerequisites for Success

Using the tips and methods detailed in *Master Japanese*, anyone can learn a foreign language no matter their age, income, or zip code.

- You don't need to take expensive classes.
- You don't need to use boring materials.
- You don't need to have learned any Japanese before.
- You don't need to have done well at languages in school.
- You don't need to move to Japan.

But there *are* some prerequisites to learn Japanese in the way detailed in this book:

- You need a strong "WHY" for learning Japanese.
- You need the discipline and courage to keep showing up.
- You need to believe that success depends more on personal effort and choice than external factors.
- You need the willingness to experiment, try things out, and risk making mistakes.
- You need access to online tools and resources.

A POWERFUL, PERSONAL WHY

Why does having a WHY matter so much? Because as Friedrich Nietzsche famously put it:

"If you know the *why*, you can live any *how*."

He or she with a strong enough WHY will:

- Find the time to study Japanese no matter how busy their schedule.
- Find the money to buy resources no matter how tight their budget.
- Find the courage to practice speaking with native speakers no matter how terrifying it might be.

Need proof of WHY's power? Consider the observations of Victor Frankl, an Austrian neurologist and psychiatrist interned in Nazi concentration camps during World War II. Despite the most horrid circumstances imaginable, he noted that those with a strong enough reason to carry on outlived those who could find no meaning in their suffering.

Obviously there is a big difference between maintaining the will to *live* and simply maintaining the will to *learn a language*, but the same basic principle applies in both domains.

For more about Frankl's experience, read his powerful book *Man's Search for Meaning*. **bit.ly/mjmsfm**

To succeed in your Japanese journey, it's essential that you take time to define an effective WHY. You will then be able to handle the HOWs and WHATs you choose.

So what should your WHY look like? First, let's look at some examples of weak, flabby WHYs to avoid:

"It would fun to speak Japanese someday."

"Japanese *might* be useful in my career."

"I feel like I *should* learn a language."

"I'm required to learn a language to graduate."

"I heard that languages make you smarter."

Can you feel the half-hearted shrug behind each of these? No, your WHY has to be far *stronger* than these. Far more *emotional.* Far more *immediate.* And far more personally *meaningful.* Here are some better examples:

"I am going to propose to my Japanese girlfriend in three months *in Japanese.* Next month, I am going to visit her parents and ask for their blessing, and they don't speak any English."

"I will be taking an intensive Aikido course next summer in Tokyo, and it's only offered in Japanese. Martial arts are my life, and I really want to understand the instructors and connect with the students."

"I am moving to Japan next year to teach English, but will be placed in a rural area far from other foreigners. Speaking Japanese will be my only way to socialize and have a life outside of work."

NOTE!

Knowing one's personal WHY is especially important for those with the "Questioner" tendency detailed in Gretchen Rubin's book *The Four Tendencies.* See the *Leverage Your Tendency* section for more about the Questioner tendency and how to best apply it in language learning.

TAKE ACTION!

It's time to define your own powerful, personal WHY for learning Japanese. Block out at least 15 minutes of focused time to answer the following questions:

1. What about the Japanese culture or language excites you?

    ____

    ____

    ____

2. What do you want to be able to do in Japanese?

    ____

    ____

    ____

3. What will make all of the time and effort worth it?

    ____

    ____

    ____

A WARRIOR'S SPIRIT

"Warriors do not waste time in making decisions. There is little hesitation, hemming, hawing, or hedging. Warriors do not await perfect circumstances to begin the long march to victory; they do not stop when tired or frightened; they do not shy away from a needed fight; they do not apologize for boldness or strength."
—Brendon Burchard, *The Motivation Manifesto* [8]

There's a reason I use martial arts icons, images, and analogies throughout this book. Beyond just thinking ninjas are cool, I include swords, throwing stars, nunchakus, etc. to remind the reader that mastering a language means mastering one's mind and body. And that is precisely what a warrior does.

No, you don't need to wield a literal *katana* to speak Japanese, but you *do* have to properly wield your mind, your time, and your energy. Like a warrior, you have to:

- Develop sufficient discipline and courage.
- Take responsibility for your learning, goals, and choices.
- Believe you can succeed.
- Pursue what you want *most*, not what you want *now*.

Warriors Have Discipline & Courage

"Eighty percent of success is showing up." —Woody Allen

Though the language learning journey can be difficult at times, the truly challenging elements are not usually what new learners expect.

Most learners assume that the hard part of learning Japanese is making sense of complex grammar rules and memorizing thousands of words and characters. These elements certainly *can* be challenging at times, but the reality is that your brain will do most of the heavy linguistic lifting *automatically* if you give it the input and practice it needs.

The *real* challenge of learning a language is having the **discipline** to show up every day and the **courage** to face discomfort.

Many learners struggle to reach fluency because they stick to the safe, comfortable realm of input, and rarely venture into the messy, scary world of output. The reality, however, is that you can't *study* your way to fluency. Instead, you have to get enough practice actually communicating with native speakers in meaningful contexts, an activity that requires repeatedly stepping outside your comfort zone and enduring a significant amount of uncertainty and ambiguity. You have to risk making mistakes and making a fool of yourself. You have to prepare yourself for not understanding and not being understood. All of these can be terrifying to the adult brain which sees mistakes as failure, instead of the proof of progress they really are! Fortunately, there are a number of concrete tools and techniques you can use to increase your discipline and overcome your fears.

See the *Master Your Mind* chapter for more on increasing discipline and overcoming your fears.

Warriors Have an Internal Locus of Control

"I am not a product of my *circumstances*. I am a product of my *decisions*."
—Stephen Covey

In the 1950s, the American psychologist Julian B. Rotter developed the *locus of control* theory, a cornerstone of personality psychology. Julian divided individuals into two main groups based on the degree to which they believed they had control over what happened in their lives:

- **External Locus of Control:** Those with a strong *external* locus of control believe they have little power over much of what happens in their life. They attribute success and failure to *external* factors such as luck, fate, privilege, God, one's environment, the economy, etc. They tend to blame the outside world instead of taking personal responsibility to change their lives.

- **Internal Locus of Control:** Those with a strong *internal* locus of control believe they have power over much of what happens in their life. They attribute success and failure to *internal* factors such as personal effort and choice. They take responsibility for their decisions and take action to improve their circumstances.

When it comes to language learning, these two groups have significantly different—and highly predictable!—outcomes:

EXTERNAL LOCUS	INTERNAL LOCUS
"I'm too old to learn a language."	"I can learn a language at any age if I put in the effort."
"I'm not good at languages. I just don't have the language gene."	"I can learn anything I put my heart and mind into."
"I can't learn because I can't afford classes or learning tools."	"There are tons of free resources and language exchanges available."

While external factors certainly *are* important and we cannot control everything that happens to us, we *can* decide how we respond to what happens to us. No matter your age, no matter your grades in school, no matter where you live, and no matter your income level, you *can* learn Japanese. But you have to want it enough to make tradeoffs. You have to *choose* Japanese over other easier alternatives. And most importantly, you have to *believe* that you can.

Warriors Believe They Can Succeed

"...the most powerful Faith in the world is the humble variety that says, 'I believe in my ability to learn and figure things out. With enough focus, time, effort, and dedication, I believe I can learn to do what must be done and become who I must become to achieve my dreams.'"
—Brendon Burchard, *The Motivation Manifesto*

Warriors know that if they put in the time and effort, they *will* eventually reach their goals and master their craft. They have faith in themselves and the learning process, but this faith is a matter of *mathematics*, not *magic*. They know that greatness is grown through repetition and hard work.

Even if genes and luck afford some advantages, warriors know that these factors alone will only get them over the first foothills of their journey.

Warriors Choose Expertise Over Expediency

"If you will live like no one else, later you can live like no one else."
—Dave Ramsey

Warriors know that mastery takes time—*lots* of time. They know that one of the true challenges of mastering a skill is not learning the skill *itself*, but the fortitude and discipline to constantly choose practice over other enticing alternatives. But the warrior persists day in and day out, choosing what they want *most* over what they want *now*.

If you struggle to see yourself as a "warrior," consider adopting an alter ego or "channeling" someone who you *do* see as a warrior. As Todd Herman details it in *The Alter Ego Effect: The Power of Secret Identities to Transform Your Life*,[9] many of the world's top athletes, performers, and leaders reached their full potential by first creating alter egos, warriors who had the confidence and competence to achieve their dreams. But this is not about self-delusion or arrogant aggrandizement. As Todd puts it, "The Alter Ego Effect is not about creating a false mask—it's about finding the hero already inside you. It's a proven way of overcoming the self-doubt, negativity, and insecurity that hold you back, and empowering you to ultimately become your best self."

ACCESS TO ONLINE TOOLS & RESOURCES

The final prerequisite to acquiring Japanese through Anywhere Immersion is access to **online tools and resources**. While you certainly can learn the language using purely analog methods, you will progress much more quickly if you are able to access modern online media, work with online tutors, get free crowdsourced feedback on your writing, and the like.

Below, you will find two lists: one for "strongly recommended tools" that will allow you to progress as quickly and efficiently as possible, as well as some "nice to haves" which further increase convenience and decrease frustration.

STRONGLY RECOMMENDED	NICE TO HAVE
A high-speed internet connection	A smartphone or media player
A computer with a webcam	A Hulu, Netflix, or Prime account
A library card	A VPN

See the *Choose Your Weapons* chapter for more on using a VPN and how to stream Japanese videos on Hulu, Netflix, etc.

Master Japanese Principles

"As to methods there may be a million and then some, but principles are few. The man who grasps principles can successfully select his own methods. The man who tries methods, ignoring principles, is sure to have trouble." —Ralph Waldo Emerson

---

The following eight principles form the foundation for the *Anywhere Immersion* approach and hold the key to Japanese mastery. If ever you find yourself spinning your wheels or not progressing as fast as you like, return to this list.

1. Learning should be as fun as possible.
2. Learning should be an adventure.
3. Learning requires sacrifice, patience, and making mistakes.
4. There is no one way to learn.
5. Active practice beats passive learning.
6. Long-term marginal gains beat short-term sprints.
7. Perfectionism is the enemy of progress.
8. Time and attitude are more important than talent and aptitude.

LEARNING SHOULD BE AS FUN AS POSSIBLE

"Why do so many frown so sternly at the idea of having fun? Perhaps out of fear that it connotes you aren't serious. But best we can tell, there is no correlation between appearing to be serious and actually being good at what you do. In fact, an argument can be made that the opposite is true." —Steven Levitt & Stephen Dubner, *Think Like a Freak*[10]

During my time studying linguistics and languages at university, teaching English to adults, and working in a variety of businesses, one peculiar theme has stood out to me:

Most people believe that one has to be *serious* to be *effective.*

For whatever reason, the majority of adults believe that having fun is reserved for children. We grownups, they argue, have little time nor need for playfulness. If Dr. Seuss were to describe their position, he might say:

We have families to feed.
Mortgages to pay.
There's no time for games.
No need for play.

While most adults certainly *do* have more responsibilities than most children, who ever said that being *responsible* requires being *serious*? The truth is that fun, play, and curiosity lead to a *higher* level of performance and effectiveness in almost every endeavor. According to Dr. Stuart Brown, founder of The National Institute for Play:

"Nothing fires up the brain like play."

Play not only makes learning more *enjoyable*, but it also makes it more *effective*, to boot.

Play Gives You a Better Brain

Play improves brain function, neural plasticity, adaptability, creativity, and memory, making new words, structures, and concepts become far "stickier." In short, the more you play, the better you learn.

Play Increases Motivation

If you love the process of learning a language, you'll want to do more of it. It will be the first thing you think about when you open your eyes in the morning, and the last thing you think about when closing your eyes at night. Spending time immersed in Japanese will become a *treat* instead of a *chore*.

As Gretchen Rubin puts it in *Outer Order, Inner Calm*:

"To get it done, make it fun."

LEARNING SHOULD BE AN ADVENTURE

"It is fatal to know too much at the outset. Boredom comes as quickly to the traveler who knows his route as the novelist who is over certain of his plot." —Paul Theroux

---

True adventures are difficult.

They're risky.

You won't always know where you're going.

And even when your destination is *clear*, you won't always know *how* you will get there or *whether* you will arrive. If you *do* have such certainty, then you are on a *trip*, not an adventure.

It's important to have aims and goals, but part of the joy of learning a language is embracing the inevitable uncertainty and wonderful serendipity that the journey presents.

LEARNING REQUIRES SACRIFICE, PATIENCE & MISTAKES

Learning Requires Sacrifice

"You can do *anything* but you can't do *everything*." —David Allen

---

Though learning Japanese can be a wonderfully enjoyable and meaningful adventure, it's important to know that mastering any skill requires sacrifice. It requires continually choosing Japanese over other—often easier and more immediately rewarding—activities. You have to decide for yourself if learning Japanese is worth the time, effort, money, and sacrifice it will require.

Learning Requires Patience

Patience is one of the sharpest tools in the language learner's toolbox, and this is perhaps more true in Japanese than any language given the paramount importance of reserve, self-control, and emotional endurance in Japanese culture. Losing your patience with yourself or others while communicating will not only cause you and those around you to "lose face" (experience public disgrace), but it will also increase the anxiety of both parties, making it even more difficult to understand and produce Japanese.

If you start getting frustrated, just take three deep, conscious breaths, making sure that your *belly* expands, not just your chest. If done correctly, this will create a cascade of positive psychological and physiological effects that will put you at ease and help you better communicate.

For extra help staying calm and collected, check out the Headspace app: **bit.ly/mjheadspace**

Learning Requires Making Mistakes

"If you don't make mistakes, you're not working on hard enough problems. And that's a big mistake." —Frank Wilczek, 2004 Nobel Prize winner in physics

---

The journey to fluency in a foreign language can be loads of fun at times, but it also includes inevitable challenges and setbacks.

- You will misunderstand and be misunderstood.
- You will make cultural gaffes.
- You will accidentally mispronounce people's names.
- You will use the wrong level of formality.

- You will butcher grammar.
- You will mispronounce and misspell words.
- You will order the wrong food and get on the wrong bus.

But as frustrating or painful as these mistakes can be, it's critical to understand that they don't block the path to mastery. They *are* the path to mastery.

Screwing up and figuring out where we went wrong is an inevitable, mandatory part of the leaning process. As Carlson Gracie, Sr. once said about Brazilian Jiu Jitsu:

"There is no losing in jiu jitsu. You either win or you learn."

The exact same thing is true of learning a language. The only true mistake is the one we don't learn from. So accept your mistakes. Nay, *embrace* them! See each stumble or gaffe as one step further up Japanese Mountain.

Also, realize that what you screw up *today*, you'll probably get right *tomorrow*, especially if the mistake is particularly embarrassing. My favorite example of this comes from the author Tim Ferriss. The year was 1993, and 16-year-old Tim had recently arrived in Japan for a year-long exchange program. Before going to bed one night, he tried to enlist his host mother's help to get up in time the next morning.

He had *meant* to say:

Ashita hachi-ji-ni ***okoshite****-kudasai.*
明日八時に起こして下さい
"Please wake me up at 8 tomorrow."

But he *accidentally* said:

Ashita hachi-ji-ni ***okashite****-kudasai.*
明日八時に犯して下さい
"Please rape me at 8 tomorrow."

The host mother was as confused as Tim was embarrassed. But instead of letting the mistake deter him, he let the humor of this—any many other gaffes—fuel his Japanese journey:

"I ALWAYS try. At the very least, it's comedic relief, totally breaks the ice, and you can all have a laugh."

THERE IS NO ONE WAY TO LEARN

In 2015, I got certified as a Nutritional Therapy Practitioner (NTP). One of the most important lessons in the 9-month certification course is the principle of *bioindividuality.*

Though there are certain health principles that *tend* to be beneficial for the vast majority of people—drinking enough water, eating enough protein and healthy fats, moving your body, and getting enough sleep—when it comes to the *specifics,* one size *never* fits all. This is why most health paradigms fail. Somebody finds a diet or workout routine that works for *them* and assumes it will work for *everyone.* It won't.

The same is true in language learning. Most books, blogs, YouTubers, and teachers assume that if *you* do what *they* did, you will get the exact same results. You *might,* but you will make much more progress and have a lot more fun if you experiment with different methods and materials until you find what works best for *you.*

You also have to be willing to change your approach as *you* change. Just as nutrition will vary for infants, teens, and adults, so too will resources vary for beginner, intermediate, and advanced learners.

ACTIVE PRACTICE BEATS PASSIVE LEARNING

"*Directness* is the practice of learning by directly doing the thing you want to learn. Basically, it's improvement through active practice rather than through passive learning . . . Passive learning creates knowledge. Active practice creates skill." —James Clear, Forward to Scott H. Young, *Ultralearning*[11]

Learning something directly seems obvious, but in practice, very few people do. Why? Directness often requires stepping out of one's comfort zone and into uncertainty and ambiguity.

This is certainly the case for most language learners. Whether studying in a traditional classroom or using modern apps, the vast majority of time is spent passively acquiring knowledge instead of actively acquiring skill. One thinks they are "learning Japanese," when in fact, they're learning *about* the language *in* their native language. Instead of immersing oneself in authentic content and practicing communicating with native speakers, time is spent memorizing and procrastinating.

The truth is that you can't reach fluency in Japanese unless you actually *use* it. While a little grammar or vocab study can be a helpful supplement, there is no substitute for hearing, speaking, reading, and writing the language.

Take an honest look at how you really spend your time each week. How many minutes or hours are directly, actively practicing the language, and how many are spent in passive pseudo-study?

MARGINAL GAINS BEAT SHORT SPRINTS

> "It is so easy to overestimate the importance of one defining moment and underestimate the value of making small improvements on a daily basis. Too often, we convince ourselves that massive success requires massive action." —James Clear, *Atomic Habits*

We humans love a good story, and one of our favorite narratives is following a hero or underdog as they struggle to overcome a personal weakness or evil foe. Such stories often include a climactic scene where all of the hero's previous training and experience are put to a final test, a single, decisive moment that makes or breaks the character.

While learning Japanese is indeed a hero's journey that will test your heroic mettle at times (more on this later in the book), it's important to understand that language acquisition is fueled by small, steady, incremental steps, not heroic leaps.

Such gradual progress can be really hard to notice—and is not exactly fodder for a good blockbuster movie plot!—but it *does* add up to impressive results over a long enough timespan. As James Clear notes in his book *Atomic Habits*:

"...if you can get 1 percent better each day for one year, you'll end up **thirty-seven times better** by the time you're done."

In fact, such compounding is the secret to long-term growth and progress in *every* worthwhile endeavor, from learning Japanese, to financial investing, to competitive sports. You may not perceive much progress in your Japanese skills, wealth, or physical skills on any given day, but if you keep at it, you will be amazed how high your "marginal gains" will stack up over time.

See the *Track Your Progress* section for tips on how to monitor your progress and make your "marginal gains" more visible.

PERFECTIONISM IS THE ENEMY OF PROGRESS

"Perfectionism is the voice of the oppressor, the enemy of the people. It will keep you cramped and insane your whole life." —Anne Lamott

---

Striving for perfection may *seem* like a noble goal in life, but as a recovering perfectionist, I can assure you it's not. The pursuit of "perfect" leads to:

- **Procrastination instead of progress:** We put off starting our Japanese journey until the "right" time. We wait to start learning until we find the "ideal" resource or method. And we put off communicating with native speakers until we feel "ready."

- **Stress instead of success:** We hyper-focus on the small mistakes we make in our speech or writing instead of celebrating the hundreds of words and structures we get right. We beat ourselves up for our imperfect pronunciation and non-native accents, forgetting what a miracle it is that we can transmit our thoughts and feelings wirelessly through the air using only the vibrations of vocal cords!

I am not saying that we should not strive to *do* and *be* our best. We certainly should! But setting the threshold for action at perfection is a recipe for inaction and frustration.

***Imperfect action* is far better than *perfect procrastination*.**

Or as is often attributed to Voltaire, *Le mieux est l'ennemi du bien* ("Perfect is the enemy of good.")

TIME & ATTITUDE ARE MORE IMPORTANT THAN TALENT & APTITUDE

"Attitude puts aptitude on steroids." —Peter Guber

When I tell someone that I speak Japanese, I almost always hear the same response: "Wow, that's a really hard language. You must be good at languages!" While I know that their intentions are good, I find this comment frustrating for two reasons:

- **There is no such thing as a "hard" language.** Sure, Japanese is quite *different* from English, but that doesn't mean it's inherently *difficult*.
- **You don't need to be "good at languages" to learn them:** Every human (with rare exceptions) acquires their first language by simply getting enough exposure and practice. The same is true for learning foreign languages as an adult.

Does learning a language take a lot of time and effort? Absolutely. Does it take a positive attitude? You bet. Does it take special skills or advanced cognitive abilities? Nope! In fact, it's so easy that babies do it every day!

See *Master Your Mind > Bust the Myths* for more about these false beliefs and cognitive distortions.

The Road to Mastery

"...start with the fundamentals, get a solid foundation fueled by understanding the principles of your discipline, then expand and refine your repertoire, guided by your individual predisposition, while keeping in touch, however abstractly, with what you feel to be the essential core of the art." —Josh Waitzkin, *The Art of Learning* [12]

No two paths to mastery are the same. But there *are* some universal guideposts to show you the way.

The following section will show you where to focus your efforts today—based on your current level—and what adventures lie ahead as you continue to improve.

Happy trails!

CHOOSE YOUR *OWN* ADVENTURE

Choice Lets You Follow Your Bliss

One of the most valuable benefits of *Anywhere Immersion* is that it gives you the freedom to choose your *own* adventure and "follow your bliss," as comparative mythologist Joseph Campbell (1904—1987) famously called it. Instead of following the rigid, impersonal rules and structures of traditional language education, you get to sit in the driver's seat of your own learning adventure. You get to decide *where* you're going and *how* you will get there. As Campbell said:

"My general formula for my students is, 'Follow your bliss.' Find where it is, and don't be afraid to follow it."

"Follow your bliss and the universe will open doors where there were only walls."

By "bliss," Campbell meant the deep fulfillment that comes from pursuing difficult, meaningful endeavors with one's entire being. It's the feeling we get when we heed the "call to adventure," the first step in the "hero's journey."

Learning Japanese Is a Hero's Journey

The "hero's journey," also known as the "monomyth," is a universal cycle first popularized in Campbell's 1949 book *The Hero with a Thousand Faces.*[13] He argued that though the details may vary, one can see the same basic heroic archetypes and narrative structures in every world religion, every mythological system, every great novel, and every epic movie.

From Odysseus, to Neo, to Harry Potter, to Moana, to Iron Man, to Captain Marvel, *all* heroes encountered a similar cycle of trials, tribulations, losses, and victories in their heroic journeys. Though these are all *fictional* characters, they act as composites of deeply, profoundly *true* human ideals and capabilities. And *you* can tap into that same truth when you realize that learning Japanese is a hero's journey, too.

You Are Luke Skywalker

Just like the fictional heroes of literature and film and the real life heroes of history, *you* too are a hero about to embark on an adventure that will change your life forever. The path is steep and you will encounter challenges that will make you want to quit, but you can harness these heroic tales to keep you going and show you the way forward. Perhaps one of the best examples of the hero's journey—and one of the easiest to apply in language learning—is the story of Luke Skywalker in *Star Wars: A New Hope.*

SPOILER ALERT!

The following section contains *Star Wars* spoilers! If you have been living in a *wampa* cave and have yet to watch the movies, please skip ahead to the next section or go watch *Star Wars Episode IV* (*in Japanese* of course!) and then continue the book.

Here now are the basic steps of the hero's journey, with specific examples from *Star Wars: Episode IV*. The naming conventions for each step are based on *The Writer's Journey: Mythic Structure For Writers* by Christopher Vogler.[14] The basic structure follows that detailed by Joseph Campbell, but is adapted to better fit modern movies and fiction.

Departure

- **Ordinary World:** The hero-to-be is minding their own business, living an ordinary, boring, unfulfilling life. In the movie *Star Wars*, Luke Skywalker's "ordinary world" is moisture farming with his aunt and uncle on the desert planet of Tatooine.

Luke: "If there's a bright center to the universe, you're on the planet that it's farthest from."

- **Call to Adventure:** An unexpected message or invitation arrives, calling the hero to embark on an adventure into uncharted territory. For Luke, this was seeing the recording within R2-D2 from Princess Leia:

Leia: "Help me, Obi-Wan Kenobi. You're my only hope."

- **Refusal of the Call:** Before the true adventure begins, the hero must first overcome their doubts, fears, and desire to stay in the Ordinary World. Luke initially refuses Obi-Wan's offer to join the Rebellion and journey with him to Alderaan.

Luke: "I can't get involved! I've got work to do!"

- **Meeting with the Mentor:** When the hero finally musters the courage to heed the call, they encounter a guide who will show them the way. As the saying goes, "When the student is ready, the teacher appears." After returning home to find his aunt and uncle murdered, Luke decides to join Obi-Wan and leave Tatooine behind.

Luke: "I want to come with you to Alderaan.
There's nothing for me here now."

- **Crossing the Threshold:** The hero then departs the "Ordinary World" and enters a new, mysterious realm. Luke travels to Mos Eisley space port with Obi-Wan, where they encounter a slew of space-hardened adventurers, including Han Solo and Chewbacca.

Obi-Wan: "You'll have to sell your speeder."
Luke: "That's okay, I'm never coming back to this planet again."

Initiation

- **Tests, Allies & Enemies:** As the hero enters the unknown, they are tested by evil forces but helped along by friends and allies. Imperial Stormtroopers nearly capture Luke and his droids, but they manage to escape Tatooine with the help of Han, Chewbacca, and the Millennium Falcon.

Stormtrooper: "Stop that ship! Blast them!"

- **Approach to the Innermost Cave:** The hero then approaches the most dangerous part of the journey. In Star Wars, this is when the Millennium Falcon is captured by the Death Star.

Luke: "I have a *bad* feeling about this!"

- **The Ordeal:** The height of the adventure arrives and the hero must endure their greatest challenge yet. When Luke discovers that Princess Leia is being held on the Death Star, he and his allies mount a rescue attempt.

Luke: "The princess? She's here?"

- **The Reward:** If the hero manages to survive the "ordeal," slay the dragon, or defeat the darkness, they leave with a great reward, treasure, or insight. Luke and his allies escape the Death Star with the schematics the Rebellion can use to destroy the weapon and save other planets from the same fate as Alderaan.

Han: "What's he carrying? What's so important?"
Leia: "The technical readouts of that battle station."

Return

- **The Road Back:** The hero has survived the pivotal showdown with evil, and can now return to the ordinary world if they so desire. Han invites Luke to flee with him, but Luke is becoming a true hero and decides to join the Rebel attack on the Death Star.

Han: "What good's a reward if you ain't around to use it? Besides, attacking that battle station ain't my idea of courage. It's more like suicide."

- **The Resurrection:** The hero undergoes a literal or metaphorical "death" and "rebirth." At the pivotal point in *A New Hope*, with the odds against the Rebel forces, numerous pilots already killed, and Darth Vader in hot pursuit of Luke's X-Wing, Obi-Wan's spirit encourages Luke to relinquish control and trust in the Force. He makes a one in a million shot and destroys the Death Star.

Obi-Wan: "Use the Force, Luke! Let go, Luke."

- **Return with the Elixir:** In the final phase, the hero returns to the ordinary world with a gift, skill, or insight that will improve his or her society. In Luke's case, he returns with knowledge of the Force and proof that the Rebels can indeed prevail over the Empire.

A Hero's Journey in Japanese

Here are the same steps of the hero's journey, with Japanese learner examples for each:

STAGE	JAPANESE LEARNER EXAMPLES
Ordinary World	You have no interest in learning Japanese or don't think it's a real possibility for you.
Call to Adventure	You make your first Japanese friend, take your first class, or get hooked on your first *anime* (アニメ) series.
Refusal of the Call	You doubt your ability to learn Japanese or believe that you "aren't good at languages."
Meeting with the Mentor	You find a great tutor or teacher or a polyglot you admire.
Crossing the Threshold	You have your first Japanese tutoring session or read your first *manga* (漫画, まんが, "comic book").
Tests, Allies & Enemies	You encounter both negative naysayers and positive allies online.
Approach to the Innermost Cave	You see the mountain of work ahead and realize fluency is going to take lots of time, effort, and discipline.
The Ordeal	You commit yourself to learning every single day, even when it's not easy or convenient.
The Reward	You reach conversational fluency and start to have authentic conversations.
The Road Back	Now that you can communicate, you consider calling it quits, but then decide to keep working toward mastery.
The Resurrection	You emerge as a new bilingual being, able to fully understand and communicate with another culture.
Return with the Elixir	You reach advanced fluency in Japanese, inspiring other learners to do the same.

A completely new world awaits you, but only if you heed the call first...

Interestingly, Joseph Campbell *himself* began learning Japanese while staying in Japan for five months in 1955, as detailed in his posthumously published journal titled *Sake and Satori*.[15]

You Can't Skip the "Suck"

While learning a language can be a marvelous adventure, it's critical to understand that there is no pain-free path to fluency. If you follow your bliss, you will be blessed with fun and fulfillment. But you will also face challenges and setbacks. You will sometimes want to quit. And you will have to slay psychological dragons.

Campbell joked later in his life that he should have said "follow your *blisters*" since so many mistook his advice as a suggestion to take the easy road in life. As he put it in the *Power of Myth* series on PBS:

> "The adventure is its own reward—but it's necessarily dangerous, having both negative and positive possibilities..."

The good news is that—though hardship is inevitable on any hero's journey—this book will arm you with tools and strategies to overcome the most treacherous patches, sidestep the quicksand, and slay the most intimidating psychological foes.

But just like a lightsaber, you have to actually *use* this book to unleash its power.

THE 4 STAGES OF LANGUAGE LEARNING COMPETENCE

The journey to full fluency in a foreign language can be roughly divided into what psychologists call ***the four stages of competence***:

- Unconscious Incompetence
- Conscious Incompetence
- Conscious Competence
- Unconscious Competence

You can think of progress through the stages like climbing up a mountain peak all the way from sea level:

Stage 1: Unconscious Incompetence

You start out at the sea level of *Unconscious Incompetence*, at which point you don't know *what you don't know*. You haven't learned a lick of the language and think it all sounds like random noise. Monolinguals remain at this stage their entire lives. And most of us remain at this level for most languages, even if we may progress through the other stages for other languages.

Stage 2: Conscious Incompetence

If you decide to learn a language, you soon progress to the next level, the foothills of "Conscious Incompetence." You begin to familiarize yourself with the language's basic sounds, vocabulary, and structures. You realize just how much of the language you don't know. For many learners, this is the most difficult phase, especially on an emotional level. The initial excitement of learning the language begins to wear off, and many "fair weather learners" call it quits. Fortunately, dedicated learners can overcome this hump by:

- Choosing fun materials.
- Committing to daily practice.
- Having a strong enough WHY.

Stage 3: Conscious Competence

The third stage in the learning journey is the long climb through "Conscious Competence." By this phase, you can communicate a fair amount in the language, but it still takes significant conscious effort and it's hard to speak or understand the foreign language while doing anything else. This level of competence is sufficient for many language learner's needs (e.g. short travels abroad) and most stop their journey here.

Stage 4: Unconscious Competence

"A skill, once gained, feels utterly natural, as if it's something we've always possessed." —Daniel Coyle, *The Talent Code*[16]

Truly dedicated language learners eventually reach the fourth stage of learning, the summit of *Unconscious Competence*. You can now communicate effortlessly in the language, saying what you want to say, and understanding almost everything you hear or read. This is the level native speakers operate in when using their first language, and most take their language skills for granted since they operate at a subconscious level. As you would expect, reaching this level of fluency takes significant time and effort, but it's well worth the investment for those who wish to live abroad long-term, work in the target language, etc.

Take a moment to assess what stage you are currently at in your target language or languages. How far up the mountain do you want to climb? Keep in mind that it's perfectly fine to stop at *Conscious Incompetence* or *Conscious Competence* for some languages, reserving *Unconscious Competence* for just your native language or one or two foreign languages. There are no awards for reaching the peak, but there are countless rewards for those who keep climbing.

How do you get started? How do you keep going when the going gets tough? The answer is the same for both: keep putting one foot in front of the other.

BEGINNERS: MASTER THE BASICS

"I do not fear the 10,000 kicks you have thrown once; I fear the one kick you have thrown 10,000 times." —Bruce Lee

---

If you are just starting out in Japanese, start with mastering the basics. The more time and effort you spend building a strong foundation at this stage, the easier it will be to learn more advanced Japanese later.

Just as I've observed in martial arts, new language learners are often too eager to skip what they perceive as "easy" or "simple" and jump ahead to the flashy stuff. Don't make the newbie mistake of waiting until you get kicked in the face to realize how important the fundamentals are!

So where should you start? In phase one of your Japanese journey, you will get the most long-term benefit from focusing all of your time and energy on three primary objectives:

- Mastering Japanese pronunciation.
- Mastering the most common 1,000 words in Japanese.
- Mastering Japanese's basic patterns and structures.

Master Pronunciation

Proper pronunciation and intonation is the single most important skill in language learning. Even with broken grammar and few words, you can often make yourself understood if you have clear, accurate pronunciation. Moreover, it is extremely difficult to *unlearn* bad pronunciation habits. Better to get things correct from the beginning.

There are five key ways to learn native-like pronunciation:

- Learn the International Phonetic Alphabet (IPA).

- Watch videos demonstrating proper mouth positions.
- Listen to authentic Japanese every chance you get.
- Speak with native speakers as much as possible.
- Record yourself and have a tutor review the recordings.

Each of these topics are covered in detail here:
Learn How to Learn > Improve Your Speaking Skills

Master Common Words & Phrases

I recommend the following tools for mastering common words and phrases:

- **Buy a good Japanese phrasebook:** Even if you don't intend to travel in Japan anytime soon, I still recommend getting a phrasebook. Why? Because they are one of the best sources of authentic, common language that you will need on a daily basis. Another advantage is that they are small and can easily fit in your pocket so you always have some Japanese input on hand.

I recommend the *Lonely Planet Japanese Phrasebook & Dictionary*: **bit.ly/mjlpphrase**

- **Use the Drops app:** Drops helps you master new vocabulary through play, intelligent gamification, swipe-based learning (like Tinder, but for languages!), beautiful design, visual learning instead of translations, professionally curated wordlists, and crystal-clear audio recorded by professional voice actors.

Download Drops here: **bit.ly/mjdrops**

PRICE: FREE W/ IN-APP UPGRADES | **PLATFORMS:** IOS & ANDROID

- **Complete the free Duolingo Japanese course:** Duolingo is now one of the most popular language learning platforms in the world. In fact, according to their site, "there are more people learning languages on Duolingo in the US than there are people learning foreign languages in the entire US public school system." Until the fall of 2019, Duolingo's Japanese course was short and barebones. But with their most recent update, it now has many more levels of content to work through, each with extensive explanations (just tap the lightbulb icon in each lesson to reveal useful information about vocabulary, grammar, etc.). I especially like Duolingo's gamification features (e.g. achievements badges, leaderboards, relative rankings with friends, etc.) that help increase motivation for the more competitive among us. Duolingo is free (with in-app upgrades to remove adds and unlock premium features), and can be accessed via their great iOS or Android apps, or in any web browser.

Download Duolingo here: **bit.ly/mjduolingo**

PRICE: FREE W/ IN-APP UPGRADES | **PLATFORMS:** IOS & ANDROID

- **Study the highest-frequency words first:** The most frequent 100 words in Japanese account for over 50% of all written materials, while 1,000 words takes you to over 75%! Learning these high-frequency terms first will accelerate your Japanese journey, allow you to better enjoy authentic listening and reading content, and empower you to speak on a wide range of topics.

Download the *Most Common 1,000 Words in Japanese* PDF here: **bit.ly/mj1000words**

Master Basic Patterns & Structures

Grammar study is one of the most hotly debated topics among language teachers, applied linguists, polyglots, bloggers, and, unfortunately, internet trolls.

- On the one extreme, devout grammar mavens claim that you must formally study a language's grammar lest you forever produce broken, disjointed, unintelligible streams of words.

- On the other end of the spectrum, you find people saying that you should ignore grammar completely. It just gets in the way of learning to communicate quickly.

As is the case with most things in life, the truth lies somewhere in the middle. Ultimately, you can only internalize proper Japanese grammar through extensive input and active output, during which most of the heavy lifting is done by your brain at a subconscious level.

However, a little bit of grammar study *can* be of great help for adult learners if it is used in conjunction with the Anywhere Immersion activities detailed in this book. A quick peek at a grammar book or website once in a while can help you become more aware of the patterns you encounter in your input activities and answer some nagging questions you may have.

Just make sure that explicit grammar study does not replace what *really* makes the difference: spending enough time listening, speaking, reading, and writing in Japanese. If you do enough of these four activities—even with no formal grammar study—you will eventually internalize the essential structures you need to use and understand Japanese. As the polyglot Barry Farber argues in *How to Learn Any Language*:

"You do not have to *know* grammar to *obey* grammar."

Or as the Japanese language blogger Khatzumoto puts it:

"Learning grammar in order to use a language is like learning organic chemistry in order to make a sandwich."

One of the best ways to familiarize yourself with the basic grammar patterns used in Japanese is using Tim Ferriss' "Deconstruction Dozen" (see the next page). It's a great way to gather important grammatical insights without getting lost in minutiae or overwhelmed by excess. While twelve sentences obviously won't teach you everything you need to know about Japanese grammar to reach fluency, they do reveal plenty of useful high-yield patterns that you will need for everyday communication.

ENGLISH	JAPANESE
The apple is red.	*(sono) ringo-wa akai desu.* (その) りんごは赤いです。
It is John's apple.	*(sore-wa) jon-no ringo desu.* (それは) ジョン のリンゴです。
I give John the apple.	*jon-ni (sono) ringo-wo agemasu.* ジョンに (その) リンゴを上げます。
We give him the apple.	*watashitachi-wa kare-ni (sono) ringo-wo agemasu.* 私達は彼に (その) リンゴを上げます。
He gives it to John.	*kare-wa (sore-wo) jon-ni agemasu.* 彼は (それを) ジョンに上げます。
She gives it to him.	*kanojo-wa (sore-wo) kare-ni agemasu.* 彼女は (それを) 彼に上げます。
Is the apple red?	*(sono) ringo-wa akai desu ka?* (そのリ) リンゴは赤いですか？
The apples are red.	*(sono) ringo-wa akai desu.* (その) リンゴは赤いです。
I must give it to him.	*(watashi-wa sore-wo) kare-ni agenakereba narimasen.* (私はそれを) 彼に上げなければなりません。
I want to give it to her.	*kanojo-ni agetai desu.* 彼女に上げたいです。
I'm going to know tomorrow.	*ashita, shiru deshou.* 明日、知るでしょう。
I can't eat the apple.	*ringo-wo taberu-koto-ga dekimasen.* リンゴを食べることが出来ません。

Note the following fun facts you can gather from these twelve sentences:

- **You can see how verbs change (if at all) based on who is doing the action.** In the case of Japanese, the verb doesn't change form (woo hoo!) based on whether *I* complete the verb, *we* complete the verb, *you* complete the verb, or *he* or *she* completes the verb.

- **You can see how nouns change (if at all) based on case.** In many languages, the form of the noun might change based on gender or whether it's a direct or indirect object. As you can see, nouns have no grammatical gender in Japanese and keep the same form as direct and indirect objects. Hooray!

- **You can see the language's word order:** Reviewing these sentences, you will quickly see that Japanese word order is quite different from English. The verb comes *last* instead of in the middle (e.g. "Apple there is"), and there are *post*positions instead of *pre*positions (e.g. "him to" instead "to him").

Download a print-ready PDF version of the *Japanese Deconstruction Dozen* here: **bit.ly/mjdozen**

Master Your Self-Introduction

Another great way to acquire high-frequency words and structures is mastering your self-introduction. Not only will it prove extremely useful in your day-to-day life but it will also help put native Japanese speakers at ease. Some folks get quite nervous about the prospect of having to speak English with foreigners, so your flowing Japanese introduction will show them there's no need to panic.

Here's what to do:

1. Write out a brief bio discussing your family, job, background, interests, why you are learning the language, why you're visiting the country, etc.
2. Have this translated into Japanese by a native speaker, tutor, or teacher. Or for a good challenge, try translating yourself first and having your tutor add corrections and suggestions.

See my recommended tutoring sites and tools here:
Learn How to Learn > Work with a Tutor

---

3. Have your tutor record the script aloud. Make sure they read at a normal pace with natural intonation: you don't want your bio to sound like an over-enunciated

textbook dialogue.

4. Listen to the recording multiple times as you read the transcript, and then again a few times without reading.
5. Record yourself reading your bio, doing as much as you can from memory, glancing only at the transcript when necessary.

See *Learn How to Learn > Improve Your Speaking Skills > Record Yourself.*

6. Have your tutor go through your recording, noting any mistakes you may have made.
7. Rinse and repeat as many times as necessary until your tutor cannot identify any discernible mistakes and you know your bio frontwards and backwards.

Download the print-ready *Self-Intro Worksheet* PDF here: **bit.ly/mjselfintroduction**

Watch Japanese Shows & Movies With English Subtitles

Language learning "police" will tell you that it's "sink or swim" in a language, and that English subtitles are for sissies. Ignore them; they just have self-confidence issues they are playing out in the form of misguided language learning advice.

Enjoyment trumps all, and watching a Japanese movie with little to no Japanese ability is not a very enjoyable experience for most.

See *Choose Your Weapons > Japanese Videos* for my recommended shows, anime, movies, and more.

Master Hiragana & Katakana

If you want to learn to read and write Japanese, it all starts with *kana* (仮名, かな), the two Japanese "alphabet" systems (technically called *syllabaries* since they use syllables, not letters). There are two *kana* systems, which represent the same sounds but are used for different purposes:

- ***hiragana* (平仮名, ひらがな):** Used for verb and adjective endings, particles, words with rare *kanji* (ideophonetic characters borrowed from Chinese), and *kanji* pronunciations of Japanese origin in dictionaries.

- ***katakana* (片仮名, カタカナ):** Used to represent foreign loan words, foreign names, sound effects, and *kanji* readings of Chinese origin in dictionaries.

Even if you only want to understand and speak Japanese, it is still a good idea to learn *kana* since they will help familiarize you with the sounds of the language, and make it easier to look words up in a dictionary.

For tips and tools, see *Learn How to Learn > Improve Your Reading Skills > Learn to Read Kana.*

Start Learning "Common Use" Kanji

While governments sometimes do silly things when they try to regulate languages, the Japanese Ministry of Education did Japanese language learners a serious solid when they officially limited the number "common use" *kanji* required for basic literacy. Called *jouyou kanji* (常用漢字, じょうようかんじ), the official list constrains the tens of thousands of potential *kanji* down to a much more manageable set of 2,136 characters.

This is still a lot to learn, of course, but I assure you that it's not nearly as difficult as you might expect, especially if you go about learning *kanji* in the way detailed in this book.

Still, some may ask:

"Why should I start learning characters *now*? Someone on Reddit said I should wait until I'm fluent in spoken Japanese before I start learning *kanji*."

I agree that most of one's energy should be focused on mastering spoken Japanese first, but that doesn't mean you *need* to wait to start learning *kanji*. You can decide to wait if you wish, but here's why I suggest starting *kanji* right away:

- Contrary to popular belief, learning *kanji* (at least their meaning and writing) can actually be one of the easier and more logical parts of learning Japanese if you use adult brain-friendly memory techniques.

- The sooner you begin learning *kanji*, the sooner you will be able to read and enjoy authentic Japanese materials. This greatly expands your pool of potential learning tools and allows you to enjoy much more interesting content.

For tips and tools, see *Learn How to Learn > Improve Your Reading Skills > Learn to Read Kanji.*

INTERMEDIATE LEARNERS: SHARPEN YOUR SWORD

Once you have learned the basics covered in the last section and given your brain a significant amount of exposure to Japanese, it's time to sharpen your sword with more hands-on application, more authentic content, and lots of feedback on your speaking and writing.

Become Conversationally Fluent

As scary as it may seem, it's imperative that you spend as much time as you can speaking with native Japanese speakers or tutors. You can't get better at speaking unless you actually speak!

Find a tutor you like, make friends using social media, attend local meetups or conversation groups, or if you happen to live near native speakers, strike up conversations every chance you get.

In addition to furthering your motivation to keep learning, speaking also helps to "show you where your gaps are," as polyglot Steve Kaufmann puts it.

For my recommended tutoring sites and tools, see *Learn How to Learn > Work with a Tutor.*

Identify & Fix Mistakes Before They Become Fossilized

"The key to learning is feedback. It is nearly impossible to learn anything without it. Even with good feedback, it can take a while to learn. But without it, you don't stand a chance, you'll go on making the same mistakes forever." —Stephen Dubner, *Think Like a Freak*

One of the unique challenges of the intermediate stage is overcoming *fossilization*, a phenomenon related not to dinosaur bones but those pesky mistakes that have become entrenched habits. While such problems *can* be fixed with enough targeted practice and a whole lot of patience, it's far easier to nip them in the bud before they grow roots. To that end:

- **Always encourage correction of your mistakes.** In an effort to spare your feelings and preserve "face," most native Japanese speakers will politely ignore your mistakes. While they may resist, do everything you can to encourage Japanese friends, colleagues, tutors, and exchange partners to point out mistakes you make in pronunciation, word usage, and grammar. Most native speakers won't be able to explain *why* something is wrong (unless they have experience teaching the language), but any native speaker, even a child, can tell you *what* is wrong.

- **Have your tutor take detailed notes of your mistakes.** In tutoring sessions (especially those you've paid for), request that your tutor write down all your mistakes and then provide you a written report afterwards. Ideally, they will write down the actual mistake you made, followed by correct usage so you can see the difference. I used to do this for some of my business students in Taiwan and many found this style of correction to be far more valuable than their formal—and far more expensive!—classes.

For tips on getting corrections from your tutor, see *Learn How to Learn > Work with a Tutor > After Your Tutor Sessions.*

Continue Learning "Common Use" Kanji

By this stage, you have gotten the hang of learning new characters, though you probably still have quite a few to go. Don't let yourself get overwhelmed or discouraged! Just keep laying one brick at a time and before you know it, your "kanji castle" will be complete!

Learn the Most Frequent 3,000 Japanese Words

Once you've mastered the most frequent 1,000 words in Japanese, it's time to make the next jump to 3,000 known words. This will help you to understand over 85% of the language you are likely to encounter on a daily basis!

Watch Japanese Shows & Movies With Japanese Subtitles

It might still be a little difficult for you, but try to begin watching Japanese anime, TV shows, and movies with Japanese subtitles instead of English. This will accomplish three tasks at once:

- It will reinforce the words, *kanji*, and structures you have learned so far.
- It will help you to create a direct link between pronunciation and characters.
- It will help you start thinking *in Japanese* instead of constantly translating to and from English.

See *Choose Your Weapons > Japanese Videos* for my recommended shows, anime, movies, and more.

ADVANCED LEARNERS: GET YOUR BLACK BELT

In martial arts, a black belt means you can both apply *and* defend against all the basic techniques of that style and are now ready to move on to more advanced material. Contrary to popular belief, it does *not* mean you are now an "expert" who knows all there is to know. The advanced phase of your Japanese language journey is much the same. Once you've mastered the basics and sharpened your sword, it's time to fill in the holes, learn more advanced material, and continue refining what you've previously learned.

Listen to Podcasts Intended for Native Speakers

It's time to move past the learner-specific podcasts and begin listening to programs intended for native speakers of Japanese. At this level, the pool of potential listening content expands significantly, with programs available for nearly every possible interest.

See Choose Your Weapons > Japanese Podcasts > Japanese Podcast Directories & Apps.

Watch TV & Movies With Subtitles Turned Off

In the beginning stage, you watched anime, TV shows, and movies with English subtitles to build your understanding and create a clear context. In the intermediate phase, you switched to Japanese subtitles to build connections between the spoken and written language and reinforce your *kanji* knowledge. Now it's time to turn off subtitles altogether, so you can really test your understanding and focus on fluency. You can repeat programs you've already watched so that there is a clear context to stand on, or, if you're feeling adventurous, you can dive head first into new content and figure things out as you go!

See *Choose Your Weapons > Japanese Videos* for my recommended shows, anime, movies, and more.

Read Japanese Newspapers, Magazines & Novels

You have probably peeked at some authentic written material already in the beginning and intermediate stages, but now that you can recognize the vast majority of the characters and words without reaching for the dictionary every five seconds, it's time to jump into written Japanese with both feet. You can now begin enjoying reading for reading's sake and forget that you're learning Japanese.

See *Choose Your Weapons* for my recommended newspapers, magazines, and novels.

Change Your Device Display Languages to Japanese

With just a few clicks, you can change the display language on your smartphone, computer, and browser to Japanese. This creates a powerful form of immersion throughout your day and provides a meaningful, highly contextual source of authentic Japanese input.

See *Learn How to Learn > Improve Your Reading Skills > Change Your Device Display Language* for step-by-step instructions.

Begin Learning Upper-Level Characters

Once you've learned all 2,136 "common use" *kanji*, it's time to move on to upper-level characters which you will encounter if you study at a Japanese university, work for a Japanese company, or read any technical or industry-specific materials. Just as before, the key is to use fun, effective, adult-friendly memory approaches, not tedious, ineffective rote learning techniques like writing out a character hundreds of times. The best tool for this is *Remembering the Kanji 3: Writing and Reading Japanese Characters for Upper-*

Level Proficiency by James Heisig.

Available on Amazon here: **bit.ly/mjartk3**

FORMAT: PAPERBACK | PAGES: 368 | PUBLISHED: 2012 | GOODREADS: 4/5

Learn all Levels of Japanese Formality

"Moving parts in rubbing contact require lubrication to avoid excessive wear. Honorifics and formal politeness provide lubrication where people rub together." —Robert Heinlein, *Time Enough for Love*

Taking the trouble to master formal Japanese, known as *keigo* (敬語, けいご), will set you apart from nearly all foreign language learners, and even younger Japanese native speakers must often be trained in *keigo* by their employers. This does not mean, however, that *keigo* is "difficult" per se; it is just not used enough in daily speech to become familiar as quickly as less formal language.

See the *Japanese Honorifics* section in the *How Japanese Works* PDF: **bit.ly/howjapaneseworks**

MASTER YOUR DAY

"Start every day with the language to be learned as your first thought, your priority, your mission." —Mykel Hawke, *The Quick and Dirty Guide to Learning Languages Fast* [17]

Mastering *Japanese* starts with mastering your *day*. To that end, this chapter will show you:

- How to create useful goals and daily systems.
- How to optimize your time and timing.
- Why you should rely on *habits* instead of *willpower*.
- How to leverage the power of social and financial stakes.

Create Effective Goals & Systems

"If you aim at nothing, you will hit it every time." —Zig Ziglar

---

Before you set out on your language learning adventure, you need to know which way to point your compass. If you don't know where you want to go, how do you ever expect to get there? This is where goal setting comes in. But not just *any* goals will do...

MAKE YOUR GOALS "SMART"

Traditional goals are often unhelpful for two main reasons:

- **They're overly ambitious** and therefore difficult or impossible to achieve. When we fail to reach them, we blame *ourselves*, thinking that we are lazy failures.
- **They're poorly defined** and therefore difficult or impossible to measure. How can we achieve a goal if we don't even know whether we reach it or not?

To combat these common goal deficiencies, always remember the acronym "S.M.A.R.T." when creating your language learning goals: Specific, Measurable, Attainable, Relevant, and Time-Bound.

Specific

Exactly what do you wish to accomplish? Vague goals breed laziness. Precise goals breed action.

Measurable

As the great Peter Drucker said:

> "What gets measured gets improved."

If you can't measure your goals, you have no way of knowing if you're actually moving toward them or not.

Attainable

If your goals are beyond the reach of mere mortals, they will end up *demoralizing*—rather than *motivating*—you. Stretch yourself, yes, but don't reach so far and high that you snap along the way.

Relevant

To have the greatest impact, your goals should fit your personality, interests, obsessions, lifestyle, profession, etc.

Time-Bound

Perhaps the most important component of effective goals is urgency, which can easily be accomplished by adding a specific deadline or timeframe.

Here are two examples of ineffective goals and better, *smarter* alternatives:

INEFFECTIVE GOALS	SMART GOALS
"Get fluent in Japanese."	"Reach conversational fluency in 3 months."
"Master all Japanese *kanji*."	"Finish *Remembering the Kanji* by June 1."

 TAKE ACTION!

Set aside at least 15 minutes to think about what language learning goals you want to achieve.

1. Refer back to your personal WHY statement. Before you focus on *what* you want to achieve, it's always important to remind yourself *why* you want to achieve it in the first place.

2. Using the table on the next page or downloading the print-ready SMART Goals cheatsheet, write out 1 to 3 personal SMART goals for your Japanese journey. I don't recommend any more than 3 at one time as it will spread your focus too thin.

3. Make each goal hyper-specific, easy to measure, hard enough to *excite* but easy enough to *empower*, in line with your WHY, and bound by specific time constraints.

4. I recommend adding a mix of **immediate goals** (today, this week, this month), **mid-term goals** (3 to 6 months), and **long-term goals** (1 to 5 years).

GOAL	MEASURE	DEADLINE
YOUR SPECIFIC LEARNING OBJECTIVE	HOW YOU WILL MEASURE PROGRESS	WHEN YOU WILL ACHIEVE THE GOAL

Download the print-ready *SMART Goals & Daily Systems* worksheet here: **bit.ly/goalssystems**

THE LIMITATIONS OF GOALS

"Goals are good for *planning* your progress and systems are good for actually *making* progress." —James Clear

---

Although goals are a necessary *first* step to set your compass, goals alone won't get you very far. Why?

- Because we cannot control outcomes.
- Because focusing too much on goals prevents happiness.
- Because only long-term systems change our habits.

We Cannot Control Outcomes

"We have control of *effort*, not of *outcome*." —Aubrey Marcus

---

Assuming a linear theory of time, we cannot control what happens in the future or guarantee any specific outcome. Therefore, it's best to focus your energies on what we do today instead of worrying too much about what will or won't happen tomorrow, next week, or next year.

Excessive Focus on Goals Can Delay Happiness

When we focus too much on our goals and not enough on the present moment, we get stuck putting off fun and fulfillment to the future. We think to ourselves:

"Once I achieve my goal, *then* I will be happy!"

There are three big problems with this line of thinking:

- **Emotions can *only* be experienced *now*.** Human intellect is a beautiful tool, which allows us to envision a better future and then make plans to achieve it. But our species' forward-focus has a dark side: we tend to see the moment as a means to an end. We start defining happiness through future-bound "if/then" statements, not realizing that this forever locks away happiness, since it can only ever be experienced in the present moment.

"Happiness is not something you postpone for the future; it is something you design for the present." —Jim Rohn

---

- **We make success and failure binary.** When we look at the world only through the lens of future goals, it's easy to fall into a "pass/fail trap." When we hit our goals, we think, "Yes, I'm a success!" 😀 But when we miss our goals or haven't yet achieved them, we think "Darn, I'm a failure." ☹️ In reality, success and failure are not *absolutes*, but *trends*. What matters is whether, on average, we are moving *forward* or *backward*, *up* or *down*. The successful language learner sees *any* progress toward their goal as success.

- **Achieving goals leads to short-lived happiness.** We tend to assume that success will create a deep, lasting sense of happiness. But most people who manage to achieve a major milestone in their life—may it be reaching fluency in a language, earning a PhD, launching a successful business, or completing a full marathon—quickly realize that the expected happiness lasts far shorter than expected.

Achieving Goals Doesn't Change Your Behavior

Simply achieving a goal is a fleeting moment in time that will do little to affect our long-term growth. If, for example, you focus too much on simply finishing a certain book instead of developing a reading habit, you may find it difficult to start reading the *next* book. But if you leverage the power of goals and systems together, you can aim at the target while also building the habits and behaviors needed to continue progressing afterwards.

CONVERT YOUR GOALS INTO DAILY SYSTEMS

"The purpose of setting goals is to win the game. The purpose of building systems is to continue playing the game... It is about the cycle of endless refinement and continuous improvement. Ultimately, it is your commitment to the process that will determine your progress."
—James Clear, *Atomic Habits*[18]

We can solve all of these issues by focusing our attention on *daily systems* instead of just *goals*. This allows us to *work toward* future objects while simultaneously *enjoying* the journey and present moment.

So how do we convert our SMART goals into effective daily systems? The key is changing the focus from *results* to *processes*. "Fluency" (however you define it) is a *result*. The listening, speaking, reading, and writing practice you do every day to *reach* your fluency goals is the *process*. Let's now take the previous SMART goal examples and convert them to daily systems:

SMART GOALS	DAILY SYSTEMS
"Reach conversational fluency in 3 months."	Listen to Pimsleur every day from 7 to 8 am, and speak with a tutor from 12 to 12:30 pm.
"Finish *Remembering the Kanji* by June 1."	Study 10 new kanji before bed, and review previously studied kanji for 10 minutes every morning.

TAKE ACTION!

It's time now to convert your goals (i.e. desired results) into daily systems (i.e. effective processes).

1. Rewrite the SMART goals you created earlier in the left column.
2. In the right column, write down a few actions you can complete on a daily basis to work toward that objective.
3. A few questions to help you choose your systems:

   What will I enjoy doing in the moment?

   What will make the time and effort meaningful?

SMART GOAL	DAILY SYSTEM

Download the print-ready *SMART Goals & Daily Systems* worksheet here: **bit.ly/goalssystems**

Optimize Your Time

"The bad news is time flies. The good news is you're the pilot."
—Michael Altshuler

Time is our most valuable resource. We can always earn more money and we can get more energy by eating and sleeping. But time is non-renewable. And as the saying goes, time waits for nobody.

So how can we make the most of our precious time? How can we make the most progress in the shortest period? There are three keys:

- Follow a routine.
- Leverage "hidden moments" throughout your day.
- Maximize your efficiency *and* effectiveness by using the "80-20 rule," batching similar tasks, leveraging the power of "timeboxing," limiting distractions, and ignoring the "meaningless many."

FOLLOW A ROUTINE

"The word [routines] connotes ordinariness and even a lack of thought; to follow a routine is to be on autopilot. But one's daily routine is also a choice, or a whole series of choices. In the right hands, it can be a finely calibrated mechanism for taking advantage of a range of limited resources: time (the most limited resource of all) as well as willpower, self-discipline, optimism. A solid routine fosters a well-worn groove for one's mental energies and helps stave off the tyranny of moods."
—Mason Currey, *Daily Rituals: How Artists Work*[19]

Here is a sample routine employing many of the tips, methods, and tools detailed in the book, followed by a blank version to create your own. A few things to note:

- Which "chronotype" you are (an early bird, a night owl, or somewhere in between) will dictate the best time to do each of these things. *Chronotypes* will be discussed in detail later, but the following schedule is designed for the somewhere-in-between type, which accounts for about half the population. You can simply shift the tasks back or forward to better fit whether you're more of a morning person, or more of a night owl.

For more on optimizing study based on your chronotype, see *Learn How to Learn > Optimize Your Timing*

- This schedule represents a *best-case scenario* where you maximize immersion. I don't expect that a normal human being will do all these learning tasks every single day. Just try to do as *much* as you can *most* of the time.

TIME	ROUTINE
7:00 am: Wake Up	Remind yourself how excited you are to be learning Japanese, and how important learning the language is in your life. Spend 10 minutes reviewing new flashcards you learned last night (the intervening sleep will have helped solidify and consolidate the information).
7:15 am: Shower	Using the steamed-up shower door, write out as many hiragana as you can from memory. If the mood takes you, sing some lines from a Japanese children's song.
7:30 am: Get Ready	Play a JapanesePod101 lesson as you get ready.
8:00 am: Breakfast	Play an episode of your favorite Japanese anime with English subtitles turned on while cooking and eating breakfast.
8:30 am: Commute	As you contend with rush-hour traffic, listen to an episode of Pimsleur Japanese 1, making sure to speak aloud when prompted. If taking a bus or train, listen to a Japanese podcast or read manga instead.

TIME	ROUTINE
9:15 am: Morning Meeting	Yay, meetings! Everyone's favorite. Instead of checking email or just zoning out, if your full attention is not needed, use the opportunity to discreetly immerse yourself in some Japanese. Your colleagues will think you're looking at the same boring PowerPoint on your laptop that they are, when you are in fact going through flashcards!
12:00 pm: Lunch	Read 5 pages from a bilingual text, reading the Japanese side first, quickly highlighting—but not yet looking up—any unknown words or structures. Second, read the English side to increase comprehension. Third, go back and look up any unknown words in the Nihongo dictionary app.
12:45 pm: Tutor Session	Go back to your car, fire up the Skype app on your phone, and have a 15-minute chat with your Japanese tutor. Ask them questions about particular words, phrases, and constructions that came up during your listening and reading activities.
4:30 pm: Afternoon Meeting	Oh boy, more meetings! Since the afternoon meeting is probably even more worthless than its morning counterpart, discretely review any new words that came up during your lunch-time tutor session.
5:30 pm: Commute	Listen to the rest of the Pimsleur CD from this morning. Again, make sure to actually speak aloud when prompted as passive understanding is far less important than active recall.
6:00 pm: Gym	Re-listen to this morning's JapanesePod101 lesson as you stretch and warm up. Then switch to some high-octane Japanese rock as you hit the weights.

TIME	ROUTINE
7:00 pm: Dinner	Tap your toes to some Japanese tunes as you prepare dinner, or listen to a podcast if you have the energy.
7:30 pm: Nightly Entertainment	Stream a Japanese movie on Netflix. To help prevent the blue light from screwing with your circadian rhythm and making it hard to fall asleep later, don some orange glasses, dim the lights, turn the brightness on your device, and turn on Night Shift or F.lux.
9:30 pm: Before Bed	Listen to another JapanesePod101 lesson as you brush your teeth and get ready for bed.
9:45 pm: In Bed	Crack open your Japanese book, re-read the five pages you went through during lunch, and read another five for good measure.
10:30 pm: Lights Out	As you slumber, your hippocampus encodes new input and connects it with with previously learned information.

1. Using the blank schedule on the next two pages (or the print-ready PDF version here: **bit.ly/mjroutine**), create your own custom learning schedule.

2. Create a daily schedule you will *actually* enjoy completing. Don't overcommit or beat yourself up. That just leads to suffering, procrastination, and ultimately, wanting to quit. Instead, imagine that you are creating this schedule for someone you love.

3. Try to keep your chronotype in mind. If you are a morning person, schedule the most demanding language learning tasks earlier in the day. If you come alive later in the day, don't force yourself to study much in the morning.

4. Remember that this schedule works for *you*, not the other way around. Feel free to make changes and move things around after you experiment with what works best for your unique circumstances.

TIME	ROUTINE

TIME	ROUTINE

PDF Download the print-ready *Study Plan & Routine* PDF here: bit.ly/mjroutine

USE HIDDEN MOMENTS

"Harnessing your hidden moments, those otherwise meaningless scraps of time you'd never normally think of putting to practical use, and using them for language study—even if it's no more than fifteen, ten, or five seconds at a time—can turn you into a triumphant tortoise."
—Barry Farber, *How to Learn Any Language*[20]

Even the busiest person has small chunks of otherwise wasted time littered throughout the day that could be leveraged for language immersion:

- Waiting in line
- Waiting for the elevator
- Waiting for a call to connect
- Waiting on hold
- Waiting for meetings to start
- Commuting (especially if by bus, train, subway, etc.)
- Walking
- Shopping
- Doing household chores

Perhaps you use the time waiting in line for your morning cup of joe to quickly flip through a dozen flashcards in Anki. Then waiting for the elevator at the office, you finish three more cards. While on hold with customer service later in the day, you blast through another twenty cards. Such brief bursts may not seem like much at the time, but they can add up to quite a bit of time on-task by the end of the day.

MAXIMIZE YOUR EFFICIENCY & EFFECTIVENESS

Use the 80-20 Rule

The 80-20 Rule, also known as *The Pareto Principle*, posits that 80% of effects are caused by just 20% of causes. The principle is named after Italian economist Vilfredo Pareto, who noticed in the early 1900s that 80% of Italy's land was held by only 20% of its population, a notion he then took from real estate to the backyard, showing that 80% of the peas in his garden were produced by just 20% of the pea pods.

So what does this have to do with learning Japanese, you ask? Simple: the 80-20 Rule can be applied in our personal and professional lives to eliminate low-yield activities, prioritize high-yield activities, and free up significant time for learning Japanese:

1. Take out a sheet of paper and write down all the daily, weekly, and monthly tasks you can think of, including work, chores, play, exercise, and study. Nothing is sacred.

2. Next, scan the list and determine which tasks lead to the greatest, most perceivable pay-offs. These are the "big rocks" that you should prioritize.

3. Lastly, determine which tasks account for the least benefit or the greatest misery. Avoid these tasks like the plague. Not only are they making your life miserable, but they are also getting in the way of learning Japanese.

Batch Similar Tasks

> "There is an inescapable setup time for all tasks, large or minuscule in scale. It is often the same for one as it is for a hundred. There is a psychological switching of gears that can require up to 45 minutes to resume a major task that has been interrupted. More than a quarter of each 9–5 period (28%) is consumed by such interruptions."
> —Tim Ferriss, *The 4-Hour Workweek*

Once you've eliminated unproductive tasks from your life with a detailed 80-20 analysis, the next step is to group together any remaining "time vampires" that can't be avoided, lest you lose customers, your job, or your significant other.

The most likely offenders are email, social media, and phone calls, all of which can be powerful tools for communication if managed properly, or powerful weapons of mass distraction if handled carelessly. Checking your email, social media accounts, and voicemail incessantly throughout the day is not only a waste of time in and of itself, but also zaps your focus on *other* tasks. As Jonathan B. Spira and Joshua B. Feintuch argue in *The Cost of Not Paying Attention: How Interruptions Impact Knowledge Worker Productivity*:

"Interruptions now consume 28% of the knowledge worker's day . . . This translates into 28 billion lost man-hours per annum to companies in the United States alone. Assuming an average salary of $21/hour for a knowledge worker, the cost to business is $588 billion."[21]

The solution is to "batch" repetitive tasks together at specified times (e.g. checking your email **only** at 11 am and 4 pm). Instead of replying to each email as it comes, you instead go through a larger chunk all at once. This is far more efficient, takes less total time, and allows you to focus much more deeply on other high-impact tasks.

Leverage the Power of Timeboxing

Project managers and programmers have long known that limiting work sessions to short, pre-defined time limits helps boost focus and output, but the technique works just as well for language learners, too.

There are many different productivity techniques and tools based on short time limits, but my favorite is the *Pomodoro Technique*, a form of "timeboxing" developed by Francesco Cirillo.[22] The technique breaks down work or study into 25-minute intervals called "pomodoros" (the Italian word for "tomatoes"), followed by a 5-minute break. After every fourth pomodoro, you then take a longer 10-minute break.

CULTURE CORNER

Curious why Francesco named the technique after tomatoes? Simple: he happened to have a tomato-shaped kitchen timer on hand when he first began using the technique as a university student.

Studying in short bursts and taking frequent breaks offers many advantages:

- **It's less intimidating.** Knowing that you only have to do 25 minutes at a time is far less intimidating than longer stretches of time, meaning you are that much more likely to begin in the first place.

- **It helps you focus on execution.** This counter-intuitive fact is encapsulated in *Parkinson's Law*:

"Parkinson's Law dictates that a task will swell in (perceived) importance and complexity in relation to the time allotted for its completion. It is the magic of the imminent deadline. If I give you 24 hours to complete a project, the time pressure forces you to focus on execution, and you have no choice but to do only the bare essentials. If I give you a week to complete the same task, it's six days of making a mountain out of a molehill. If I give you two months, God forbid, it becomes a mental monster. The end product of the shorter deadline is almost inevitably of equal or higher quality due to greater focus."
—Tim Ferriss, *The 4-Hour Workweek*

- **It increases mental agility and stamina.** Taking frequent breaks (e.g. every 25 minutes if you're using the Pomodoro Technique) improves your focus on the task at hand, and if you walk around or do some quick exercises during the break, you can increase the oxygen flow to your brain, thus boosting your performance during the following study session.

To get the most out of timeboxing, make sure to:

- **Set one specific goal or learning objective per session.** Don't just set a time limit and work until the buzzer. Make sure you know exactly what you want to accomplish within the allotted time. This is actually one of the hidden purposes of timeboxing: breaking work up into short time limits forces you to break the work itself up into smaller, more specific chunks.

- **Use a pomodoro app.** The only basic tool you need for timeboxing is a clock or watch. But there are a number of excellent pomodoro apps available that make the technique much easier to follow.

My favorite pomodoro app is *Forest*: **bit.ly/mjforest**

PRICE: FREE | **PLATFORMS:** iOS & ANDROID

- **Keep the timer visible.** Some may argue that this is distracting, but by keeping the countdown clock within view, you keep that sense of urgency that helps give timeboxing its power.

- **Take your breaks.** After every session, make sure you actually take your break. Get up out of your chair, walk around, listen to some music, do some breathing exercises, knock out some pushups, whatever you prefer. But for the love of all that's holy, do not continue working along: this will quickly undermine both your productivity and attitude.

Limit Distractions

Many of us think that we are good multitaskers, but it turns out that we are neurologically incapable of doing more than one thing at a time. When we think we are "multitasking," we are in fact just quickly switching back and forth between multiple tasks. Doing so is extremely taxing to our brains, and leads us to do all the tasks less well than if they had been completed in isolation.

To get the most out of your Japanese study time, therefore, make sure to eliminate all distractions and focus on only one single learning task at a time.

- **Prevent *webrocrastination*:** The most insidious distractions of the modern world are aimless web surfing, Netflix, Hulu, email, and social media. To help ensure that none of these can pull you away from your Japanese studies, make sure to turn off new message notifications and install software on your devices that automatically blocks access to specific sites (e.g. Netflix, Facebook, Instagram, Gmail, etc.) or all internet access for a predefined period of time.

My favorite blocker is *Freedom*: **bit.ly/mjfreedomapp**

PRICE: $2.42/MONTH | **PLATFORMS:** MAC, WINDOWS, iOS, ANDROID

- **Close the door:** If there is a door to your learning area, close it. Put up a sign if need be telling your children, spouse, significant other, friends, roommates, or evil stepmother that you are busy plotting world domination and wish not to be disturbed.

- **Turn off your phone:** Completely powering off is best, but if you put it on silent, make sure to place it out of your field of vision so the blinking light of incoming calls or texts cannot distract you. While you're at it, turn off your email program or at least disable new message notifications.

- **No TV:** Seriously, turn off the damn television! That means Netflix and Hulu, too. The only exception to this rule is if you will be watching Japanese programs as part of your learning.

- **No music with words:** Any language input will automatically grab your brain's attention and eat up "cognitive bandwidth." The exception to this rule is if you are specifically studying the lyrics of a Japanese song.

Ignore the "Meaningless Many"

It is all too easy to convince ourselves that *everything* is important. We see every task on our to-do list as mission critical, so we get nothing done. We see every email in our inbox as urgent and worthy of a response, so we spend our whole day replying to email instead of doing work that really matters. We see every belonging as precious and refuse to throw things out even if we never use them, so we end up with overwhelming clutter. Learning to separate the "vital few" from "trivial many" takes practice, presence, and patience, but it is the single most important thing you can do if you want to live a life of purposeful meaning.

As Greg McKeown explains in *Essentialism: The Disciplined Pursuit of Less*:

> "The way of the Essentialist means living by design, not by default. Instead of making choices reactively, the Essentialist deliberately distinguishes the vital few from the trivial many, eliminates the non-essentials, and then removes obstacles so the essential things have a clear, smooth passage. In other words, Essentialism is a disciplined, systematic approach for determining where our highest point of contribution lies, then making execution of those things almost effortless."[23]

Or as Tim Ferriss puts it in *The 4-Hour Workweek*:

> "Slow down and remember this: Most things make no difference. Being busy is a form of laziness—lazy thinking and indiscriminate action. Being overwhelmed is often as unproductive as doing nothing, and is far more unpleasant. Being selective—doing less—is the path of the productive. Focus on the important few and ignore the rest."

Optimize Your Timing

When you learn can be just as important as *how much*. Here are a few tips to help you optimize the timing of your Japanese immersion activities for maximum retention.

RESPECT YOUR CHRONOTYPE

"'When' is the ultimate life hack. It's the foundation of success, the key that unlocks a faster, smarter, better, and stronger you. Knowing 'when' enables you to perform 'what' and 'how' to your maximum potential. If you didn't change a thing about what you do and how you do it, and only made micro-adjustments to when you do it, you'd be healthier, happier, and more productive, starting... right now."
—Dr. Michael Breus, *The Power of When*[24]

In his book *The Power of When*, Michael Breus, Ph.D. (a.k.a. "The Sleep Doctor") explains that humans fall into one of four basic chronotypes, which he nicknames after animals with similar characteristics:

- Lions
- Bears
- Wolves
- Dolphins

To find out your chronotype, take the free *Power of When Quiz* here: **bit.ly/mjwhen**

Are You a Lion?

Lions are classic go-getter "morning people" who hit the ground running, but start running out of steam in the afternoon. They account for 15-20% of the population.

Are You a Bear?

Bears are fun-loving, easygoing folks who follow the sun and are at their best from 9 to 5. This is the largest group, representing about half the population.

Are You a Wolf?

Wolves are classic "night owls" who are groggy in the morning and at their best in the evening. They make up 15 to 20% of the population.

Are You a Dolphin?

Dolphins are insomniacs and light sleepers, so named because actual dolphins "sleep" with half their brain still awake. About 10% of people fall into this category.

Why Your Chronotype Matters

Why is it so important to honor one's chronotype and the circadian rhythm they follow? Because our natural biological clocks affect every single body system, including our ability to learn, consolidate, and remember. We can force ourselves into unnatural schedules for a short period of time, but it comes at a steep cost:

- Less efficiency.
- Less efficacy.
- Less happiness.
- Less health.

It's time to stop attaching *morality* to *biology* and begin honoring our natural *chronobiologies*. Though our culture attaches virtue to waking early, there is nothing morally superior about rising at the crack of dawn. Likewise, there is nothing inherently lazy about staying up late and sleeping in. What matters is whether we get *enough* sleep and what we *do* with our waking hours, whenever they happen to occur.

"Early birds get the worm, but the second mouse gets the cheese."
—Stephen Wright

LEARN NEW INFORMATION BEFORE SLEEP

We all know that sleep is good for our health, but it turns out that it's good for our *Japanese*, too! A study published in the journal *Psychological Science* showed that sleeping between two learning sessions cut the required practice time in half and greatly increased long-term retention.[25] Another study showed that improvements in memory were greatest when sleep occurred immediately after learning,[26] so I recommend learning new words, phrases, *kanji*, etc. right before you hit the hay, whether for a full night's sleep or just a quick afternoon snooze.

For more on the connection between sleep and learning, see *Learn How to Learn > Optimize Brain Health*.

REVIEW INFORMATION UPON WAKING

While it's ideal to *learn* new information *before* sleep, it's ideal to *review* the same information *after* sleep to cement memories and improve long-term recall.

For more about memory formation and recall, see *Learn How to Learn > Optimize Your Memory*.

Make Japanese a Habit

"There's nothing you can't do if you get the habits right."
—Charles Duhigg, *The Power of Habit*[27]

You now have SMART goals to align your compass, effective daily systems to move you toward your objectives, and a routine to "defend from chaos and whim." Now comes the hard part: actually putting one foot in front of the other, day in and day out. So how can we make sure that we show up every day and continue to make consistent progress?

There are seven keys:

- Not relying on willpower.
- Creating robust habit loops.
- Maintaining the "habit of the habit."
- Leveraging convenience and inconvenience.
- Leveraging existing habits.
- Leveraging your natural response to internal and external expectations.
- Not breaking the chain.

DON'T RELY ON WILLPOWER

A war is always raging inside of our brains between our rational mind and our emotional impulses. In his book *The Happiness Hypothesis*,[28] the psychologist Jonathan Haidt illustrates this tension using the analogy of a tiny rider perched on a massive elephant. Though the rider holds the reigns and *seems* to be in control, his influence is tentative, precarious, and unpredictable. At any given time, the elephant can easily overpower the rider and disregard his or her instructions. And this, of course, is precisely what *does* happen when the two are at odds too often or for too long. As Haidt explains:

> "Modern theories about rational choice and information processing don't adequately explain weakness of the will. The older metaphors about controlling animals works beautifully. The image that I came up with for myself, as I marveled at my weakness, was that I was a rider on the back of an elephant. I'm holding the reins in my hands, and by pulling one way or the other I can tell the elephant to turn, to stop, or to go. I can direct things, but only when the elephant doesn't have desires of his own. When the elephant really wants to do something, I'm no match for him."

When we continually rely on willpower (the "rider") to study Japanese or avoid other activities, our elephant gets annoyed and will eventually mutiny no matter how much the rider shouts or cajoles.

So what can we do? There are four non-violent tools at our disposal for training our unruly elephants:

- Realize that willpower is a muscle. It can get stronger, but it also gets tired if overused.
- We can preserve our willpower in the first place by minimizing and eliminating choices.
- We can create a learning schedule so we don't have to constantly to decide *if* or *when* to learn.
- We can make Japanese a habit so we don't have to decide at all.

Realize That Willpower Is a Muscle

"Willpower isn't just a skill. It's a muscle, like the muscles in your arms or legs, and it gets tired as it works harder, so there's less power left over for other things." —Mark Muraven, Professor of Psychology, University at Albany

---

Every decision you make taps your precious willpower reserves, a phenomenon that psychologists call *decision fatigue* or *ego depletion*.[29] The more self-control required to make a decision—deciding to stick your hand into a bag of *carrots*, for example, instead of a bag of *cookies*—the more willpower that choice will cost you and the more unruly your elephant will become. But even seemingly insignificant choices (e.g. which brand of dish soap to buy) can lead to ego depletion, especially if you pile up a whole bunch of tiny choices in a short period of time. Ever wonder why you feel so exhausted after shopping for groceries? You guessed it: ego depletion caused by making hundreds of tiny, back-to-back purchase decisions.

When we present ourselves with too many choices throughout the day (big or small), we will likely end up with:

- An empty willpower tank.
- A mouth full of chocolate chip cookies.
- Zero motivation to study Japanese.

The theory of *ego depletion* has become somewhat controversial in the field of psychology since past studies on the topic have struggled to withstand the rigors of scientific replicability. Regardless, I have certainly found ego depletion to be true in my own life and that of many people I know. I am quite aware that the plural of "anecdote" is not "data" or "evidence," but that doesn't mean that personal experience is not useful. On the contrary! The most relevant information often comes from so-called "N=1 experiments" in which *you* are the single study participant.

Minimize & Eliminate Choices

To prevent an empty willpower tank and the rampaging elephant that could ensue, do everything you can to minimize or eliminate choices in your daily life. Here are a few suggestions on where to start:

- **Make Japanese the default:** Instead of constantly choosing between Japanese and English input, design your environment so that Japanese is the default. For example, change the interface language of your devices and online tools to Japanese. Stock your home with Japanese media and add Japanese programs to your "Watch Later" lists in Netflix, YouTube, etc.

See the *Choose Your Weapons* chapter for detailed resource recommendations.

- **Create a detailed learning schedule:** You should never have to decide *when* or *whether* to learn. Schedule your weekly learning schedule right on the calendar, defining exactly *when* you will learn, *where* you will learn, and for *how long*. Instead of, "I wonder when I am going to study my Japanese SRS flashcards today," you know that you already made a commitment to yourself to have your butt in your chair at exactly 9 AM no matter what.

See *Master Your Day > Optimize Your Time > Follow a Routine* for detailed tips and a sample immersion schedule.

- **Minimize your food choices:** Instead of constantly having to decide what to eat each day, create a meal plan for the week and then batch cook once a week. Instead of deciding what groceries to buy, have a CSA (Community Supported Agriculture) box delivered right to your doorstep instead. Or, employ intermittent fasting, skipping breakfast altogether so you only have to worry about cooking and cleaning up for 2 meals per day.

- **Minimize your clothing choices:** Donate any clothing that you never wear, that no longer fits, or that "doesn't spark joy" as KONDOU Marie (近藤麻理恵, こんどうまりえ) puts it in *The Life-Changing Magic of Tidying Up: The Japanese Art of Decluttering and Organizing.*[30] Create a capsule wardrobe that includes a small collection of timeless, practical pieces that match one another and don't go out of fashion. Or pull a Steve Jobs and wear the exact same outfit every single day!

Read Inc. Magazine's article *Why Successful People Wear the Same Thing Every Day* for more: **bit.ly/mjclothes**

- **Stop shopping in stores.** Use *Amazon Subscribe & Save* to have household essentials automatically delivered at set intervals. This lets you save willpower, time, *and* money!

Sign up for *Amazon Subscribe & Save* at **bit.ly/mjasave** to save up to 15% and receive free shipping.

CREATE ROBUST "HABIT LOOPS"

An even better strategy is to avoid choice and willpower altogether by creating what psychologists call *habit loops*. These automatic psychological programs include four main parts:

- **A *cue* that triggers the habit.** This can be a certain *time* (e.g. late evening), *location* (e.g. arriving at your office), *event* (e.g. attending a meeting), emotion (e.g. boredom), or *group of people* (e.g. seeing your family).

- **The *habit* itself:** This is referred to as a *routine*, and is the behavior or set of behaviors that are triggered by the cue.

- **A *reward*:** The routine leads to a physical or neurophysiological reward, may it be good feelings, a buzz, a temporary distraction, etc.

- **A *craving*:** The reward, in turn, triggers the hypothalamus to release a small amount of *dopamine*, a neurotransmitter and hormone involved in motivation, habit formation, and addiction. It creates cravings that keep "the elephant" coming back for more, even when our conscious brain ("the rider") know we shouldn't...

Each of us has dozens or even hundreds of habit loops that spin away each day, often without our conscious awareness.

For example, most of us check email and social media updates dozens of times throughout the day. Without thinking, we reach for our phone or click over to Gmail, Facebook, etc. If we were to peer inside our brain, the habit loop behind the behavior might look something like this:

- **Cue:** We hear an alert, feel a vibration in our pocket, see a new message notification on the screen screen, or notice the little red icon indicating new messages.

- **Routine:** We stop what we're doing to check email, text messages, or social media.

- **Reward:** We receive a break from demanding work and an increased sense of self-importance, validation, or belonging.

- **Craving:** Once a given routine is tied to a reward, we start to crave more of it the next time we experience the same cue. We start anticipating how new messages, updates, likes, etc. will make us feel and will have a hard time resisting the temptation, even when our conscious minds know we have more important things to do.

Or here's another example of habit loops at work, this time with everyone's favorite workplace treat: donuts!

- **Cue:** Seeing, smelling, or even just thinking about donuts.
- **Routine:** Stuffing bear claws into our face-hole.
- **Reward:** A happy tongue and temporary energy boost.
- **Craving:** Anticipation of the sweet goodness and the subsequent sugar high.

Okay, so all that makes sense for emails and donuts, but how can we apply habit loops to learning Japanese?

First, you will need to determine what specific behavior you want to transform into a habit. Let's use the example of learning the meaning and writing of all common use *kanji* in three months. Your habit loop may look something like this:

- **Cue:** Seeing a stack of flashcards placed on the nightstand.
- **Routine:** Study 10 new cards and review any cards you had trouble with yesterday.
- **Reward:** The buzz from now knowing some *kanji* that

were challenging or completely unknown yesterday.

- **Craving:** Anticipation for feeling good when you master new information.

1. Review the daily systems you created earlier.

____

____

____

2. For each system, define a clear cue, routine, reward, and craving.

____

____

____

3. Don't skimp on the rewards! To make your habit loops keep spinning round and round, you need to choose rewards that genuinely make you feel good and trigger *actual* cravings.

MAINTAIN THE "HABIT OF THE HABIT"

"The habit of the habit is even more important than the habit itself."
— Gretchen Rubin, *Better Than Before: Mastering the Habits of Our Everyday Lives*[31]

Daily routines and habit loops are powerful ways to build consistency and make progress toward your Japanese goals, but they are superseded by an even more crucial commitment: **maintaining the "habit of the habit."**

Completing the habit *itself* is of course important, but it's even *more* important to solidify your identity as a person who shows up every day and does what they say they will do—to prove to yourself that you are the kind of person who does what is *meaningful* instead of what is *expedient*.

Here are three strategies to solidify the habit of the habit:

- Commit to a small set of "minimum effective habits" you complete every day no matter how busy, stressed, or depressed you might be.
- Leverage "keystone habits" that create momentum to complete your daily language learning habits.
- Leverage the power of convenience and inconvenience.

Commit to "Minimum Effective Habits"

You can often spot a new language learner by the scale of their language learning goals and daily habits. When we first start out in a new language, the excitement makes it easy to commit to big, hairy, audacious language learning goals and herculean daily routines. Perhaps we commit to listening to three hours of foreign language audio a day, reading one foreign language novel a week, or speaking with a language tutor for an hour every single day. We might keep this up for a few days or weeks, but eventually, our motivation will run out and we'll fall off the pace. For example:

- We have a bad day at work and cancel our tutor session.
- We have a fight with our spouse and don't feel like studying any flashcards.
- We get sick and opt to binge watch *Narcos* instead of listening to language podcasts.

One missed day turns into *two*, and then *three*, and then weeks or months of zero language study. Most people—especially those of us that are perfectionists—then think to ourselves:

"Well, since I can't do it *all*, I guess I will do *nothing*."

Fortunately, we can avoid this all-or-nothing-perfectionist trap by committing instead to a **minimum effective dose** (MED) of daily language study. Tim Ferriss outlines the MED concept well in his book *The 4-Hour Body*:

"The minimum effective dose (MED) is the smallest dose that will produce a desired outcome. To boil water, the MED is 212° F (100° C) at standard air pressure. Boiled is boiled. Higher temperatures will not make it 'more boiled.' Higher temperatures just consume more resources that could be used for something else more productive."[32]

For language learning, the MED is the minimum amount of time you can spend each day listening, speaking, reading, or writing to continue making progress in the language. Everyone has their own unique MED depending on their personal language learning goals (remember: one size *never* fits all!), but whatever you choose, I recommend committing to much, *much* smaller habits than you think you are capable of. Your MED can literally be as tiny as:

- "Study one Japanese flashcard."
- "Listen to one minute of a Japanese podcast."
- "Read one paragraph of a Japanese graded reader."

You can do more of course if you have the time and motivation, but set the barrier to entry low enough that you can still get over it when you are busy, stressed, or depressed. *These* are the days that end up making the difference between *wanting* to learn a foreign language and *reaching* fluency.

Your daily systems and habits should not be the *biggest* tasks you could *possibly* achieve, but rather the *smallest* tasks you will *actually* achieve no matter what.

"Progress is progress. Stop making up fake hard rules. Make easy rules. Make easy games. Winnable games. Less heroics. More consistency. More sustainability. You need a pace you can keep. That means, yes, don't have standards. Instead, have wide standards. That means standards you can sustain. I don't care how many kanji you do per day and neither should you. What matters is how many days you keep coming back to the kanji. High standards say: 'Do 100 kanji per day.' Wide standards say: 'Do kanji, no matter how little, for 100 days straight.'" —Khatzumoto, AJATT.com

---

Leverage Keystone Habits

There are certain magical habits that have the power to change our entire day, for better or worse. Once toppled, these lead dominoes trigger a cascade of positive or negative effects. For me, it's meditating, eating right, and weightlifting. If I do these three things throughout the week, all my other target habits fall into place on their own.

- I diligently study my target languages every day.

- I spend my money more mindfully.
- I read instead of watch TV.

But if just one "bad domino" falls—failing to meditate, eating things I know I shouldn't, or skipping a workout—all hell breaks loose. Not only do I end up missing even *more* meditations, eating even *more* junk, skipping even *more* workouts, but I *also*:

- Fail to put in my daily foreign language MED.
- Spend more money and make more impulse purchases.
- Watch TV instead of read.

Charles Duhigg noted the same pattern in *The Power of Habit*:

> "Typically, people who exercise start eating better and becoming more productive at work. They smoke less and show more patience with colleagues and family. They use their credit cards less frequently and say they feel less stressed. It's not completely clear why. But for many people, exercise is a keystone habit that triggers widespread change."

Once we identify our own keystone habits, we can then do everything in our power to maximize the positive lead dominoes and minimize the negative lead dominoes.

TAKE ACTION!

Spend some time in deep, honest self-reflection and ask yourself:

- What 3 positive behaviors tend to have the biggest effect on your overall productivity and happiness? How can you maximize these?

- What 3 negative behaviors tend to push you off the path? How can you avoid these?

Use the Strategies of Convenience & Inconvenience

"Convenience shapes everything we do. When it's convenient to spend, we spend. That's why merchants constantly dream up new ways to make spending more convenient, with impulse items arrayed next to the checkout line, offers of easy credit, and websites that store information to make pushing the 'buy' button an easy, one-click habit. Hotels stock handy in-room minibars with overpriced items, and nowadays some hotels even place the items in plain sight, right on the tabletop, to make it even easier to rip open that four-dollar bag of chocolate-covered peanuts." —Gretchen Rubin, *Better Than Before*

The *Strategy of Convenience* is another powerful strategy from Gretchen Rubin's book *Better than Before.* As the name implies, it helps you adopt desirable habits by making positive choices the *easiest* and *fastest* option, removing as many obstacles as possible between us and the habit.

For example:

- Fill your devices with Japanese music, podcasts, and videos so Japanese input is always one tap away.
- Stock Japanese *manga*, magazines, and books in the bathroom.
- Stack Japanese DVDs next to the TV or save Japanese shows and movies to your watchlist in Netflix, Hulu, etc.

Similarly, we can use its inverse—the *Strategy of Inconvenience*—for habits we're trying to minimize or quit. In this case, we make negative choices the most *difficult* and *time consuming* option, adding as many obstacles as possible between us the habit.

For example:

- Put English language DVDs, books, magazines, etc. in a closet where you won't see them.
- Remove all English language movies and TV series from your watchlist.
- Remove all bookmarks to English language websites.

LEVERAGE EXISTING HABITS

Leverage the Strategy of Pairing

Instead of trying to create completely new habits from scratch, you can instead *pair* them with firmly entrenched habits you *already* do without significant effort or thinking. Gretchen Rubin calls this the "Strategy of Pairing," and it can be a very effective way to add in new language learning habits with minimal effort.

The key is creating what psychologists call *implementation intentions*, "if-then" statements that link a given action you already perform on autopilot with a *new* desired behavior. For example:

- "I will study 10 Japanese flashcards in Tinycards every time I get into or out of bed."
- "I will listen to a JapanesePod101 podcast when I brush my teeth."
- "When I drive to work in the morning, I will complete my day's Glossika reps."

TAKE ACTION!

1. Review your MED list of habits.
2. Consider how you can tie each to an existing habit in your life.
3. Write out your *implementation intentions* below:

____

____

____

Repurpose Existing "Bad" Habits

"The difference between an amateur and a professional is in their habits. An amateur has amateur habits. A professional has professional habits. We can never free ourselves from habit. But we *can* replace bad habits with good ones." —Steven Pressfield, *Turning Pro*[33]

Do you spend hours playing video games, checking social media, or watching Netflix each day? Do you reach for your phone every few minutes out of habit?

The bad news is that these are signs of addictive behavior. Wait, *addiction*? Isn't that a word reserved for alcoholics and drug addicts? The truth is that video games, smartphones, and social media can activate the same basic neural pathways and reward systems that get us hooked on alcohol and drugs. Just like we saw with tangible treats earlier (i.e. donuts), these intangible digital products can *also* form powerful habit loops:

- **Cue.** Feeling bored or stressed. Seeing our phone, TV, or game console. Hearing a notification or feeling a vibration in our pocket. Noticing new message notifications or unread badge counts.
- **Routine.** Play a game, watch a show, or check email, text messages, or social media for new content, likes, etc.

- **Reward.** Distraction. Escape. A shot of dopamine, the feel-good hormone that keeps our habit loops spinning round and round.

- **Craving.** Anticipation of distraction. Wanting to escape stress or anxiety.

Once formed, these habit loops are extremely hard to break. Savvy tech companies are quite aware of this, and spend lots of time and money designing their products to be as addictive as possible. Moreover, they know that they can save marketing dollars and increase adoption by linking their product to *existing* habit loops we already have.

> "Instead of relying on expensive marketing, habit-forming companies link their services to the users' daily routines and emotions."
> —Nir Eyal, *Hooked: How to Build Habit-Forming Products*[34]

The good news is that we can *hijack* these tech habit loops and use them to learn Japanese instead. How? We can keep the cue and reward the same, but simply insert a new, more productive routine. For example:

- Each time you are tempted to check email or social media, open a language or flashcard app instead.

- When you have a craving to play a video game or watch a show, just make sure that the content is *in* Japanese.

TAKE ACTION!

1. Identify existing habit loops that don't serve you.

   ____

   ____

   ____

2. Identify the cues which trigger them (e.g. certain times of the day, locations, preceding events, emotions, or people).

   ____

   ____

   ____

3. When the habit loop is triggered, decide which new routine you will follow instead. To make this decision more effective, write out *implementation intentions.*

   ____

   ____

   ____

LEVERAGE YOUR TENDENCY

Okay, one final Gretchen Rubin tip to help you better stick to your habits: **leverage your natural response to expectations**.

Gretchen has long been fascinated by human nature, and wanted to know why some people *easily* adopt new habits while others *really struggle* to change. After years of investigation, she realized these differences could be explained (and better managed) by identifying how a person responds to expectation: both ***inner* expectations**, like New Year's resolutions or personal goals, and ***outer* expectations**, like a work deadline or request from family or friends.

The personality framework she developed—detailed in her book *The Four Tendencies: The Indispensable Personality Profiles That Reveal How to Make Your Life Better*[35]—divides people into one of four basic personality groups depending on how they respond to both types of expectation:

- Upholders
- Questioners
- Obligers
- Rebels

As Gretchen puts it:

"Our Tendency shapes every aspect of our behavior, so using this framework allows us to make better decisions, meet deadlines, suffer less stress, and engage more effectively."

The framework is an extremely useful tool for language learning: once you figure out your Tendency, you can choose the methods and resources that best fit *your* personality.

Take the *Four Tendencies Quiz* for free here:
bit.ly/mj4tend

Are You an Upholder?

Upholders readily meet both inner expectations they place upon themselves *and* outer expectations placed upon them by others. They love planning for the future, creating to-do lists, following detailed schedules, and upholding defined rules and guidelines. A favorite saying of many Upholders is:

"Poor planning on *your* part doesn't constitute an emergency for *me*."

In language learning, Upholders tend to do best with more structure (e.g. textbooks, classes, or courses), clear deadlines for finishing specific resources, and a detailed daily study schedule.

Learn more about creating a personalized study schedule here: *Master Your Day > Optimize Your Time > Follow a Routine.*

Are You a Questioner?

Questioners question *everything*. And they will only commit to an expectation if it makes sense to *them*.

Essentially, to meet an *external* expectation, Questioners must first transform it into an *internal* one.

You will often hear Questioners ask the following:

"Why are we doing things this way?! It doesn't make *any* sense!"

And if someone responds, *Because that's the way it's always been done*, you will see what an angry Questioner looks like. It's critical for Questioners to have a clearly defined WHY for learning a language in the first place, as well as every resource and method they use along the way.

See the *Prerequisites for Success* section for tips on defining your personal WHY.

Are You an Obliger?

Those with the Obliger tendency have a much easier time meeting outer expectations (especially those of friends, family, and colleagues they respect), but have a tough time sticking to self-made commitments no matter how important they may be.

Gretchen Rubin gives Obligers the following motto:

"You can count on me, and I'm counting on *you* to count on me."

In language learning, Obligers will do much better if they:

- **Choose a study buddy:** Having someone to learn with (and *for*) significantly helps motivate Obligers.

See *Master Your Day > Create Public Accountability* for tips on working with a study buddy.

- **Get a language tutor:** Though Obligers will benefit from learning alongside friends, getting a private language tutor is another powerful motivator.

See my recommended tutoring sites and tools here: *Learn How to Learn > Work with a Tutor*

- **Attend Japanese meetups:** Many areas have local Japanese language and culture meetups that are perfect places for Obligers to, well, *oblige.*

Find a language and culture meetup near you: **bit.ly/mjmeetup**

- **Make friendly wagers with friends:** For more competitive Obligers, wagers and bets with friends can be another powerful motivator to learn more Japanese.

See my tips for friendly competition here: *Master Your Day > Put Your Money & Reputation on the Line*

Are You a Rebel?

Rebels resist *all* expectations, including those put upon them by others and even those they try to put upon themselves. As Gretchen Rubin puts it, their motto is:

"*You* can't make me, and neither can *I*!"

This may seem like a paradox for Rebels wanting to learn a language, but many successful language learners are actually Rebels. How can this be? It's because Rebels can do whatever they *want* to do if the following conditions are met:

- **Learning the language fits their identity:** The strongest driving force in a Rebel's psyche is personal identity. Rebels can accomplish truly amazing feats of discipline *if* their actions inform and solidify who they are. In fact, it's not uncommon to find Rebels in the military and organized religions. This may seem counter-intuitive on the surface, but it's actually consistent with the Rebel tendency: they will do *anything* they want to do if fits their personal identity, even if it requires following rules and meeting outer expectations.

- **They learn the language for their own reasons:** Rebels tend to resist actions labelled "should" or "have to." So instead of making a Japanese ***to**-do* list, a Rebel may prefer making a ***could**-do* list instead.

- **They greatly enjoy the learning process:** Rebels want to do what they *feel* like doing. The more they associate fun (and dopamine!) with language learning, they more likely they will put in the time.

- **They can freely choose what, when, and how to learn:** To succeed in language learning, a Rebel needs to have the freedom to choose their resources, when they use them, and how they use them. Because of this, Rebels are much better suited to the *Anywhere Immersion* approach detailed in this book than traditional classroom based learning. They love being able to wake up and ask themselves, "What do I feel like learning today? How?"

NOTE!

Most people have a primary and a secondary Tendency. As you can see in the Venn diagram, each Tendency has slight overlap with the two others adjacent to it. For example, I'm a Questioner that tips toward Rebel, while my wife is a Rebel that tips toward Questioner. But certain Tendencies don't overlap, so a Questioner won't tip toward Obliger, or vice versa, just as an Upholder won't tip toward Rebel, or the other way around.

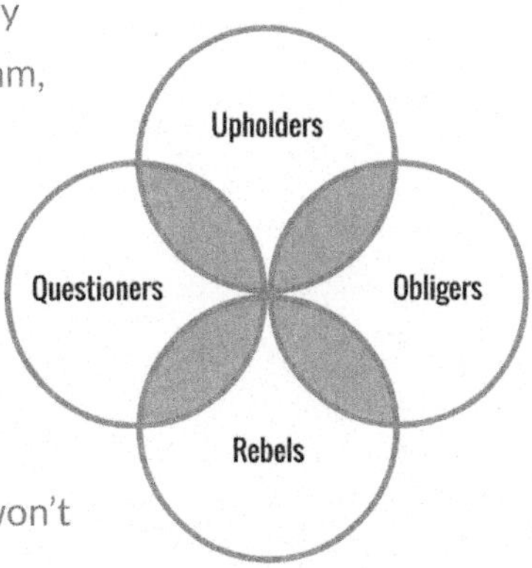

TAKE ACTION!

1. If you haven't already, take the *Four Tendencies Quiz* here: bit.ly/mj4tend
2. Read or reread the sections in the book that are especially congruent with your tendency.
3. Select the resources and tools that fit your tendency from the *Choose Your Weapons* chapter.
4. Never apologize for who you are. No tendency is "good" or "bad," and each has advantages and disadvantages when it comes to language learning. What matters is how you play the hand you've been dealt.

DON'T BREAK THE CHAIN

Every so often, we have chance encounters with true masters that change our lives forever. For Brad Isaac—a software developer trying to learn the ropes of standup comedy—his pivotal encounter occurred backstage at a comedy club when he happened to meet the one and only Jerry Seinfeld. He asked him if he had any advice for getting better at comedy, and his response is a simple but profound recipe for learning *any* skill, including Japanese:

> "The way to be a better comic is to create better jokes and the way to create better jokes is to write every day. . . After a few days you'll have a chain. Just keep at it and the chain will grow longer every day. You'll like seeing that chain, especially when you get a few weeks under your belt. Your only job is to not break the chain." —Jerry Seinfeld

---

Interestingly, this phenomenon is actually the *sunk cost fallacy* in reverse. Normally sunk costs lead people to continue negative, unhealthy behaviors:

- People often keep investing in failed businesses because they've *already* put in so much money.
- People often stay in an unhealthy relationship because they've *already* been together so long.

But in the case of adopting a new habit or skill, this

psychological tendency can be used to our advantage. The longer our study chain gets, the less likely we are to break it. We think to ourselves:

"I've come this far. I can't stop now and throw away my perfect streak!"

To be clear, I am advocating *consistency* here, **not** *perfectionism*. Give yourself an "X" on the calendar for any day that you "show up" and accomplish your "MED" habits.

For this technique to be as effective as possible, you need to use a **physical calendar** placed somewhere you will see it everyday. Calendar apps are great for some things, but they are *not* very effective for habit formation. Why?

- **Too Much Potential Distraction:** When you go to access your calendar on your phone or computer, it is very easy to get distracted by notifications, other apps, etc. You start out wanting to simply add a digital "X" to a day and end up wasting 30 minutes on Facebook.

- **Insufficient Cues:** As discussed above, a new habit requires an effective cue. Since you use your phone and computer for so many other tasks, it alone won't be a sufficiently strong cue to remind you to mark the calendar each day (or hit your daily learning goal so you *can* mark off the day).

On the other hand, a prominently placed physical calendar:

- **Prevents distraction.** You can dedicate your calendar completely to your Japanese mission instead of using it to track other events and responsibilities.
- **Increases emotional impact.** We tend to value things more when they are tactile and tangible.
- **Provides an effective cue.** A large calendar provides a highly visual cue that you won't miss.

TAKE ACTION!

1. Get a big wall calendar and large permanent marker.
2. Hang it somewhere you will see it every day.
3. Write a large X on the calendar each day that you complete your pre-defined daily learning goals.

Use a Habit Tracking App

While I think a *physical* calendar is ideal given its greater emotional impact, some may prefer the convenience and portability of a habit tracking app. Go with whichever option you will actually *stick to* every day.

For iOS, I recommend the *Streaks* app: **bit.ly/mjstreaks**

PRICE: $4.99 | PLATFORMS: IOS

For Android, I recommend *HabitShare*: **bit.ly/mjhabitshare**

PRICE: FREE | PLATFORMS: ANDROID

Never Miss Twice

> "If I skip practice for one day, I notice.
> If I skip practice for two days, my wife notices.
> If I skip for three days, the world notices."
> —Vladimir Horowitz

Though the "chain" method above can be a powerful motivator, don't beat yourself up too much if you happen to miss a day. We've all been there. We get a good habit streak going and are so excited to see a long string of red Xs in a row on our calendar.

We think:

"I am a habit BOSS! Nothing can stop me!"

Then life happens.

Stress, illness, depression, or major life events override our best intentions to stick to our study habits "no matter what" and we end up missing a day. We awake the next day to find our beautiful "Seinfeld Chain" broken.

Given the *negativity bias* (our tendency to focus on the few things that go wrong instead of the myriad things that go right), we dwell on the empty box in our calendar instead of celebrating the proud string of Xs that precede it.

When a break in our chain inevitably occurs, we must resist the temptation to beat ourselves up or succumb to the "What the Hell Phenomenon" (more colorfully know as the "F*ck It Phenomenon") in which we tell ourselves:

"What the hell, I broke my diet by eating *one* donut, so I might as well eat the *whole box*!"

Applied to language learning, we might think:

"What the hell, I broke my chain *this* week, so I might as well wait until *next* week to start over."

Of course, "next week" often becomes "never." Every additional day you miss makes it all the harder to restart the habit. To prevent this from happening, follow habit expert James Clear's tip to "never miss twice."

"Never miss twice. If I miss one day, I try to get back into it as quickly as possible. Missing one workout happens, but I'm not going to miss two in a row. Maybe I'll eat an entire pizza, but I'll follow it up with a healthy meal. I can't be perfect, but I can avoid a second lapse. As soon as one streak ends, I get started on the next one. The first mistake is never the one that ruins you. It is the spiral of repeated mistakes that follows. Missing once is an accident. Missing twice is the start of a new habit."

One of the keys to developing long-term habits is never letting a *little* stumble become a *fatal* fall. Success and failure are not binary and missing one day will not make a difference in the long run. But letting one day become two, then three, then a week, then a month, most certainly *will*.

Put Your Money & Reputation on the Line

Here's another extremely effective way to make new habits stick: **put your money and reputation on the line.**

SET FINANCIAL STAKES

"People who put stakes—either their money or their reputation—on the table are far more likely to actually achieve a goal they set for themselves." —stickK

There are two main ways to set financial stakes for your language learning habits:

- Use an online service like *stickK* or *Beeminder.*
- Set wagers directly with friends.

stickK

Developed by Yale economists, *stickK* uses the power of "commitment contracts" to help you form new habits. The process is simple but highly effective:

1. You set a goal and specific stakes (e.g. how much money you must pay—and to whom—if you fail).

2. You designate a referee (the person who will confirm your success or failure).

3. You make the goal and stakes public or keep them between just you and the referee.

I especially like their use of "anti-charities." Here's how they explain it:

> "Are you a proponent of gun control? Then make the *National Rifle Association Foundation* your recipient, and know that your failure is serving to defend the right to bear arms! The less you believe in the cause, the harder you'll work to succeed at your goal! In this case, you know exactly to which cause your money went."

Sign up for a free account at **bit.ly/mjstickk** and make sure to download their free apps on iOS and Android.

Beeminder

If you are the tech-savvy type who wants more detailed goal tracking stats, *Beeminder* is a good alternative with the same "stick and carrot" benefits of *stickK*. The primary feature of Beeminder is the "Yellow Brick Road," a colorful graph that shows your progress over time. If your progress dots stay happily on the road, *Beeminder* remains free, and you continue making progress toward your goals. But if you veer off the road, financial consequences ensue! As they put it:

> "Beeminder is Quantified Self plus Commitment contracts. Keep all your datapoints on a Yellow Brick Road to your goal or we take your money. The combination is powerful. We call it flexible self-control."

Sign up for a free account at **bit.ly/mjbeeminder** and make sure to download their free apps on iOS and Android.

Friendly Wagers

For a simple, low-tech solution, you can simply use the power of greed and competition to increase your motivation:

- Gather a group of friends also learning a language and set the rules of the game (e.g. who can spend the most hours this month speaking with a tutor).
- Have each competitor pitch in a set amount of money (e.g. $10), ideally physical money that can be stored in a jar you can all see on a regular basis.
- At the end of the competition, the winner (as agreed upon by the group) gets the jar and the bragging rights that go with it.

CREATE PUBLIC ACCOUNTABILITY

Another powerful way to ensure consistency is leveraging the power of social stakes and public accountability:

- Schedule daily progress check-ins with a study buddy.
- Leverage leaderboards.
- Start a language progress blog.
- Record and post monthly progress videos.

Schedule Daily Progress Check-Ins

Get a study buddy, loved one, friend, or colleague you trust to check in with you at a specific time each day (preferably at the same time so the clock can act as a "cue" for the habit). Given them a list of your "minimum effective daily habits" and have them inquire about the status of each one by one.

Q: "Did you listen to a Japanese podcast for 10 minutes today?"
A: "Yes."

Q: "Did you read one Japanese article today?
A: "Not yet."

That's it! There should be no judgement or criticism. The power of this technique rests not on the fear of negative feedback but the joy of connecting with others.

Leverage Leaderboards

Many language learning apps include leaderboards which rank users based on activity, points, known words, etc. For more competitive individuals, these rankings can be a powerful extrinsic motivator for showing up and getting in some language reps each day. Duolingo does an especially good job of this with their League system. Each week, you are randomly assigned to a group of 50 people. At the end of each 7-day period, the top ten users are promoted to the next level up, while the bottom ten are demoted. You can also compete directly with friends by comparing your total XP (experience points) to date:

1. Navigate to the "Profile" page (tap the face icon at the bottom of app).

2. Tap the "Friends tab on the right.

3. Tap "Add" to invite friends to Duolingo or find existing users via search or Facebook.

Download Duolingo here: **bit.ly/mjduolingo**

PRICE: FREE W/ IN-APP UPGRADES | **PLATFORMS:** IOS & ANDROID

Start a Language Progress Blog

Blogs are a great way to keep track of your progress, share small wins, vent frustrations, and pose questions to other learners who are further along in their Japanese journey. Commit to posting something at least once a week. Knowing that you will have to share what you've accomplished that day, you will be that much more motivated to do something worth sharing.

Create a free WordPress blog here:
bit.ly/mjwordpress

Record Monthly Progress Videos

Perhaps the most powerful form of public accountability is sharing monthly progress videos on social media or your language blog. Knowing you will be on camera every 30 days provides ample daily motivation to practice, and also provides a useful way to track your progress over time.

On macOS, use the built-in *QuickTime* app to record video:
bit.ly/mjquicktime

On iOS, use the free *Clips* app to record video:
bit.ly/mjclips

On Windows, use the free *Camera* app:
bit.ly/mjmscamera

On Android, use the free built-in *Google Camera* app:
bit.ly/mjgoogcam

MASTER YOUR MIND

"As you think, so shall you become." —Bruce Lee

To master a language, you must *first* master your own mind. If this were a video game, winning the language learning game means defeating the following four bosses:

- Busting common myths and limiting beliefs.
- Facing your fears.
- Increasing and sustaining motivation.
- Developing diamond-tough discipline.

Bust the Myths

Your beliefs about the Japanese language—and your ability to learn it—can ultimately make the difference between success and failure. Unfortunately, many Japanese language learners fail before they even begin because they believe:

- They aren't good at languages.
- They are too old to learn.
- They have a bad memory.
- They don't have enough time to learn.
- They don't have enough money to learn.
- They have to attend classes.
- They have to move abroad.
- That Japanese is difficult, vague, and illogical.
- That learning Japanese will take decades.

The good news is that we can slay *all* of these psychological dragons with the right attitude. But before we banish these limiting beliefs, me must first clearly define and detail each.

MYTH: "I'M NOT GOOD AT LANGUAGES"

"If you think about a young child trying to learn to walk, that child will fall down and hurt itself hundreds of times. But at no point does that child ever stop and think, 'Oh, I guess walking just isn't for me. I'm not good at it.'" —Mark Manson, *The Subtle Art of Not Giving a F*ck* [36]

Stop me if you've heard this one...

Q: *What do you call someone who can speak 2 languages?*

A: *Bilingual.*

Q: *What do you call someone who can speak 3 languages?*

A: *Trilingual.*

Q: *What do you call someone who can speak 4 languages?*

A: *Quadrilingual.*

Q: *What do you call someone who can speak 1 language?*

A: *American!*

Ha, ha, ha! My sides! My sides!

It *is* true that most adults fail to learn foreign languages well despite years of study in high school and university, but this failure is a product of bad mindsets, bad materials, and bad methods, *not* a lack of innate ability. If you spend enough time with the language, your brain *will* eventually make sense of it. All you have to do is show up and put in the effort on a consistent basis. It's a matter of *time* and *effort*, not *intellect* and *genius*.

Say the following quotes aloud and post them somewhere you will see them every day:

- "In language learning, it is *attitude*, not *aptitude*, that determines success." —Steve Kaufmann
- "Persistence matters more than talent. The student with straight As is irrelevant if the student sitting next to him with Bs has more passion." —Andrew Ross Sorkin
- "Continuous effort—not strength or intelligence—is the key to unlocking our potential." —Winston Churchill
- "Tenacity matters more than talent." —Bear Grylls
- "Greatness isn't born. It's grown." —Daniel Coyle, *The Talent Code*
- "...success is less about brains and more about hard work and perseverance. —Hashi, *Tofugu*

MYTH: "I HAVE A BAD MEMORY"

One of the most common reasons people cite for struggling with languages is possession of a supposedly "bad memory." While some of us certainly do have an easier time encoding and recalling memories than others, almost *everyone*—other than those with severe neurodegenerative diseases—has a sufficiently "good" memory to acquire a foreign language.

The problem is usually a matter of *method*, not *memory*. For example:

- An inexperienced language learner may stare at a flashcard for a few seconds, flip it over, and then beat themselves up when they are unable to produce the correct word, character, phrase, definition, etc.

- A partygoer may meet a new person and then forget their name seconds later.

Do these people have "bad memory"? Of course not! It's just that our brains are designed to let go of information that isn't considered urgent and/or important. Unless we use special mnemonic techniques (more on this later), it takes dozens and dozens of meaningful exposures to a new piece of information before it sticks. This is how our brains evolved to process what would otherwise be an overwhelming deluge of sensory input. We remember what matters (at least from our *brain's* biological perspective), and one of the easiest ways to prove to our brain that something is worth remembering is seeing or hearing it again and again.

There *are* some powerful mnemonic techniques that can significantly reduce the number of repetitions it takes to memorize and recall new information, but these are but icing on the proverbial cake. The bulk of your Japanese memories will be formed automatically when you get sufficient exposure and practice.

See the *Optimize Your Memory* section for tips on how to better remember new Japanese words, phrases, kanji, etc.

So when someone says, "I just can't remember new Japanese vocabulary," what this *really* means is that:

- They haven't yet had enough exposure to those words in meaningful contexts.
- They are studying boring content, which inadvertently tells the brain that the words aren't worth remembering.

If they instead immerse themselves in tons and tons of interesting, meaningful content, the words will stick all on their own.

MYTH: "I DON'T HAVE TIME TO LEARN JAPANESE"

Many people claim that they would *like* to learn a language but just don't have the time. With work, family, bills, etc., almost every minute of the week seems to get used up, leaving us with little to no time left for language learning. Inevitably, we get "bogged down in the thick of thin things" as Stephen R. Covey puts it, going days, weeks, or even months without making any progress in the language.

The reality is that there *is* time in our schedules for what matters most, but we have to make time for the important tasks *first*. If you are waiting for big, convenient swaths of time to open up for Japanese in your life, you are going to be waiting a long time indeed...

Covey drives the point home in his famous "big rock" demonstration. He first reveals a large glass container, a metaphor for one's life. He then pulls out a big bag of little pebbles and fills up the container nearly to the top:

"This is analogous to all the small things that fill up our lives. Little by little they just accumulate."

Next to the bucket, he has laid out a number of big rocks, each labelled with important elements that create a happy, healthy, productive life. He then asks a volunteer to try and add in as many of the rocks as possible into the nearly full container. The first rock she shoves in is titled "Planning, Preparation, Prevention & Empowerment." She then works in a rock that says "Relationships & Family." She manages to push in "Employment & Major Projects" by moving the gravel around. She struggles to fit in "Service, Community & Church," even rolling up the sleeves on her suit jacket as she moves around the other rocks in a futile attempt to make more space. She picks up "Sharpen the Saw" but immediately puts it back on the table as there is obviously no room left for any more rocks. Covey quips:

"She just put down 'Sharpen the Saw.' How many frequently do that? 'I just don't have time today to sharpen the saw.' You ever been too busy driving to take time to get gas?"

Covey then takes survey of all the rocks still on the table. "Urgent & Important" and "Vacation" are among the many that don't make it into the "Life Bucket." He then gets down to the point of the whole exercise:

"I'll tell you what you can do if you want to. You can work out of a different paradigm altogether."

The volunteer is then shown a second glass container, but this one is empty. This time, she is encouraged to put in the big rocks *first*. Every last one fits in with room to spare. What's more, she manages to pour in the entire amount of small pebbles, too!

The lesson is clear:

Focus on the most important tasks *first* lest they get crowded out by less important tasks.

Or to put it another way:

Don't *find* the time to learn Japanese. *Make* the time for it.

"Schedule specific blocks of time in advance for your rocks so you don't have to think about them. Don't rely on wishful thinking (e.g. 'I'll get that workout in when I have some downtime.'); if you can't see your rocks on your calendar, they might as well not exist." —Drew Houston, CEO & co-founder of Dropbox (excerpt from *Tribe of Mentors*)

See the *Optimize Your Time* section for tips on using your precious minutes, hours, and days as efficiently as possible.

Download my study schedule template here:
bit.ly/mjroutine

MYTH: "I CAN'T AFFORD TO LEARN JAPANESE"

Much like the "I don't have time" excuse above, the "I don't have enough money" excuse is a matter of shifting beliefs and priorities, not happening upon a pile of cash. Does it help to have more money to throw at Japanese learning? Of course! But the good news is that you can get everything you need for free:

- You can access more free online Japanese resources and media than you can consume in a lifetime.

See the *Choose Your Weapons* section for hundreds of resource recommendations, many of which are free.

- You can connect with language exchange partners for free online.

- You can check out books, DVDs, and audio programs from your local library for free, and many have licenses for language learning programs and courses, too.

And if learning Japanese is truly a priority, you can likely free up at least a little bit of cash by cutting out expenses that don't bring value or joy into your life.

MYTH: "I HAVE TO ATTEND JAPANESE CLASSES"

Another common myth is the belief that one has to attend formal classes to learn Japanese well. This often goes hand-in-hand with the time and money excuses above, making it all too easy for one to put off learning due to exorbitant tuition fees and the difficulty of committing to pre-defined hours week in and week out.

Fortunately, you do not need a classroom, or even a teacher, to learn Japanese.

Now don't get me wrong: having spent many years in language classrooms as both learner *and* teacher, I know first hand how important a teacher can be:

- They can help motivate students to learn by creating a cultural context for the language.
- They can scour the web for useful materials that fit one's unique needs and interests (something a native speaker can do far faster than a language learner).
- They can point out your mistakes in speech and writing and let you know if something sounds natural or not.

But the fact is that none of these benefits *require* a teacher or school:

- You can motivate yourself (and create a cultural context to boot) by learning more about Japan through film, food, etc.
- A Japanese tutor or friend can help suggest materials that fit your interests and needs.
- Any Japanese native speaker, even a child, can tell you if your word usage or structures sound right or wrong even if they don't know *why*. In language learning, the *whys* are perhaps interesting, but they're irrelevant to learning the *whats* of fluent speech.

See my recommended tutoring sites and tools here: *Learn How to Learn > Work with a Tutor*

MYTH: "I'M TOO OLD TO LEARN JAPANESE"

Contrary to popular belief, children do not necessarily learn languages more quickly or easily than adults. The wee little ones actually struggle quite a bit with their first languages, and spend years actively listening to the input around them before uttering a single word. And when they *do* start speaking, children make many of the same mistakes in grammar and pronunciation as non-native adult learners.

For example:

"I ***ated*** the cake." [sic]

As babies, we simply don't yet have the language to put our linguistic frustrations into words. And by the time we *do* have the requisite words and syntax at our disposal, we have long since forgotten how much time, effort, and trial-and-error it took us to reach fluency.

It's certainly true that few ever reach the same level of fluency in second languages as in their first, but so what? We can get pretty darn close with enough time and effort, and more importantly, we can reach conversational fluency far more quickly than children if we capitalize on the adult learner's myriad advantages:

Adults Already Have Massive Vocabularies

As an adult, you already know what tricky conceptual words like "metaphor" mean. All you have to do is learn their equivalents in Japanese.

---

hiyu (比喩, ひゆ, "metaphor")

Good luck explaining such a concept to a four-year-old in Japanese *or* English!

Adult Learners Can Seek Out Materials and Contexts

Unlike infants who are dependent on the listening input they happen to hear around them from their parents, peers, TV, etc., the adult learner has the means to seek out Japanese input via the internet, Japanese tutors, and international travel.

Adults Know How To Learn

You have already learned how to drive, operate the printer at work, program the clock on your microwave, and fix that toilet that keeps running for some reason. You learned all of these things more quickly than any child ever could because you have already learned so many *other* things. Every task you learn helps you pick up the next, just as every language you delve into makes acquiring another that much easier.

Adult Learners Have a Choice

Having the choice of *whether* to learn Japanese is a highly under-appreciated advantage. The freedom to choose significantly increases motivation and enjoyment, which in turn improves retention. As I observed in East Asia, many people develop a hatred for English learning largely because it is a *mandatory* subject. If it were made an optional course, I am confident that more people would enjoy learning the language, and their skill levels would surely rise.

Our Brains Retain Their Plasticity Long Into Old Age

Scientists now believe that the human brain remains "plastic" (that is, able to change, grow, and rewire itself) long into old age. For most people, "I'm too old to learn" is a *psycho*logical—not *physio*logical—limitation. A great real life example is Steve Kaufmann, the founder of LingQ.com, who speaks more than 15 languages, most of which he has learned in his 50s and 60s! And he continues to learn more languages in his 70s.

How plastic your brain remains depends on how you treat it, however, so it's essential to support optimal brain function through nutrition, movement, and sleep.

See the *Optimize Brain Health* section for tips on maintaining brain function through diet, rest, and exercise.

MYTH: "I HAVE TO MOVE TO JAPAN"

"...where you are isn't what decides whether or not you'll be successful. Attitude beats latitude (and longitude) every time. It's more about creating an immersion environment, exposing yourself to native speakers, and doing everything you can in that language."
—Benny Lewis, *Fluent in 3 Months*[37]

Is it ideal to learn Japanese *in* Japan? **Yes.**

Is it a *mandatory* condition? **Absolutely not.**

Let me be clear: living abroad was one of the most amazing experiences in my life, and I go back to visit Japan as often as possible. While living overseas can certainly provide Japanese learners many advantages, it's critical to understand that it's not a requirement for success. In today's world, "I can't learn Japanese because I live in rural Kansas" is an emotional *excuse*, not an objective *reality*. With internet access, a little creativity, and a lot of hard work, you really can learn any language, anywhere.

On the flip side, living abroad is no guarantee that you will pick up the language. While immersion is essential, language acquisition depends on *active learning*, not *passive osmosis*. Consider the ridiculously high number of Western expats who spend years in Japan and never reach even a moderate level of fluency in Japanese.

Or take the case of English speakers learning French in New Brunswick, Canada: despite being surrounded by French both in and outside of the classroom for 12 years, a government report showed that only 0.68 percent reached even an intermediate level in the language![38]

No, my friends, *mere exposure* is not enough. You have to be hungry to learn and do everything you can to **actively** assimilate the language.

MYTH: "IT WILL TAKE ME DECADES TO LEARN JAPANESE"

On the one extreme, overzealous marketers bombard us with ridiculous claims like "Learn a Language in 10 Days." If we exercise common sense, we know that these are marketing lies, not pedagogical promises.

On the other extreme, you can find many blogs and forums bellyaching about how difficult languages are, especially Japanese. Some hardcore linguistic naysayers claim that Japanese is "the one true hardest language in the world," vehemently asserting that it takes decades to reach fluency and that you must take formal classes lest you forever speak like Tarzan.

Fortunately, these pedantic pessimists are just as wrong as the marketing liars. The road to fluency *can* be long and windy, but the smart traveler uses the right tools, methods, and framing to speed their progress, lighten their load, and have a hell of a lot more fun along the way!

Yes, it is going to take you quite a bit of time to learn Japanese, or any foreign language for that matter. But by "quite a bit," I mean thousands of hours, not decades. That said, if you only study Japanese in a traditional classroom setting, live in an English-speaking bubble even within Japan, and believe that Japanese is a "difficult" language, it may very well take you ten years to learn the language, if not many decades more!

MYTH: "JAPANESE IS DIFFICULT"

"This is no such thing as a 'hard' language; any idiot can speak whatever language his parents spoke when he was a child. The real challenge lies in finding a path that conforms to the demands of a busy life."
—Gabriel Wyner, *Fluent Forever*[39]

The US Foreign Service Institute asserts that the more different a language is from English, the longer it will take you to reach fluency. And Japanese is indeed *very* different from English. But "different" and "time-consuming" needn't be synonymous with "difficult." Yes, learning Japanese, like any language, will pose unique challenges. And yes, it will probably take you longer to reach fluency in Japanese than French or Spanish. But so what?

What matters is interest. If you really want to learn Japanese, who cares if it takes you a few more months of effort to reach the same level you would studying a language more similar to English?

Believing that "Japanese is a really difficult language" is a self-fulfilling prophecy that will only slow your progress. What you believe about the language directly affects your ability to learn it, so focus on maximizing the positives and mitigating the negatives. Instead of dwelling on the empty half of the Japanese glass, why not focus more on the many ways in which Japanese is actually quite easy for native speakers of English? There are many:

Japanese Has a Massive Number of English Loan Words

If you grew up speaking English, congratulations! You won the Linguistic Lottery! From day one in Japanese, you will have a massive pre-existing vocabulary to draw on, thanks to the thousands and thousands of English words borrowed into the Japanese language to date. As Bill Bryson puts it in *The Mother Tongue: English and How it Got that Way*:

"The most relentless borrowers of English words have been the Japanese. The number of English words current in Japanese has been estimated to be as high as 20,000. It has been said, not altogether wryly, that if the Japanese were required to pay a license fee for every word they have used, their trade surplus would vanish." [40]

These "foreign loan words," or *gairaigo* (外来語, がいらいご), offer native speakers of English a massive head start, allowing you to understand and communicate a great deal of information even with shaky Japanese grammar and zero *kanji* knowledge.

Here is but a small taste of English loan words in common use today:

ENGLISH	LOAN WORD	PRONUNCIATION
beer	ビール	*biiru*
calendar	カレンダー	*karendaa*
camera	カメラ	*kamera*
hotel	ホテル	*hoteru*

ENGLISH	LOAN WORD	PRONUNCIATION
mic	マイク	*maiku*
supermarket	スーパー	*suupaa*
television	テレビ	*terebi*

You will of course need to learn the "Japanified" pronunciation of English loan words, but the phonetic patterns are highly predictable and consistent. All you need to do is learn *katakana* (something you can do over a weekend), and then familiarize yourself with how English sounds are transferred into Japanese.

See *Learn How to Learn* > *Improve Your Reading Skills* > *Learn to Read Kana* for *katakana* tips and tools.

Once you have the phonetic patterns down, a powerful language hack is at your disposal: When in doubt about how to say a given word in Japanese, just can try saying the English word you know using Japanese syllables. More times than not, you will be understood.

Even if a given English loan word is *not* actually used in Japanese, chances are good that people will have "learned" (i.e. memorized but not really acquired) the English word in high school or university. Since most Japanese learners of English add little *katakana* reading guides above English words to approximate their pronunciation, they will better recognize English words when wrapped in Japanese pronunciation. Or even more so when written out on paper. This habit may be bad for *their* English, but is at least good for *your* ability to communicate.

Lastly, I should point out that there are occasional differences in meaning between English loan words and their Japanese derivations. But radical semantic changes are few, and even when there *are* significant gaps, the comedic effect is usually enough to make the words stick on their own.

CULTURE CORNER

My favorite example of this: I loved telling my American friends back home that I lived in a "mansion" while in Japan. And it was the truth! What they *didn't* know is that the loan word *manshon* (マンション, まんしょん) actually refers to an *apartment*, not a *palatial residence*.

English Already Has Some Japanese Words, Too

The borrowing has gone the *other* way, too, though certainly not to the same extent. Here is a handful of Japanese words that you already know in alphabetical order:

ENGLISH	JAPANESE	MEANING / ORIGIN
emoji	*emoji* 絵文字, えもじ	"picture character"
futon	*futon* 布団, ふとん	Originally from Chinese *pútuán* (蒲團, "meditation cushion")
haiku	*haiku* 俳句, はいく	lit. "actor phrase"
(head) honcho	*hanchou* 班長, はんちょう	"squad leader"
karaoke	*karaoke* カラオケ, からおけ	"open orchestra" (from 空 + オーケストラ)
kimono	*kimono* 着物, きもの	lit. "wear thing"
koi	*koi* 鯉, こい	"carp"
manga	*manga* 漫画, まんが	lit. "cartoon picture"

ENGLISH	JAPANESE	MEANING / ORIGIN
ninja	*ninja* 忍者, にんじゃ	lit. "sneak person"
origami	*origami* 折り紙, おりがみ	lit. "fold paper"
otaku	*otaku* お宅, おたく	lit. "house" (i.e. someone who spends a lot of time inside)
ramen	*raamen* ラーメン, らあめん	lit. "pulled noodles" (from Chinese *lāmiàn* 拉麵)
sake	*sake* 酒, さけ	"alcohol"
samurai	*samurai* 侍, さむらい	lit. "servant" or "retainer"
senpai	*senpai* 先輩, せんぱい	lit. "ahead comrade" (i.e. an older student, colleague, etc.)
sensei	*sensei* 先生, せんせい	lit. "ahead born" (i.e. a teacher is usually older than you)
shiatsu	*shiatsu* 指圧, しあつ	lit. "finger pressure"
sushi	*sushi* 寿司, すし	From 酸し, an archaic word for "sour rice"
tatami	*tatami* 畳, たたみ	From *tatamu* (畳む) meaning "to fold"

ENGLISH	JAPANESE	MEANING / ORIGIN
teriyaki	*teriyaki* 照り焼き, てりやき	"shiny grill" (referring to the shiny glaze)
tofu	*toufu* 豆腐, とうふ	lit. "fermented beans"
tsunami	*tsunami* 津波, つなみ	lit. "harbor wave"
typhoon	*taifuu* 台風, たいふう	lit. "table wind" (likely from Chinese 大風, meaning "big wind")
wasabi	*wasabi* 山葵, わさび	This is an *ateji* (当て字) with *kanji* used for sound only
zen	*zen* 禅, ぜん	lit. "absorption" (from Chinese 禪 and Sanskrit ध्यान)

Japanese Verbs Don't Have To "Agree" With Subjects

Unlike many languages that have different verb forms to match different pronouns (e.g. "I am...," "You/We/They are...," and "He/She/It is..."), in Japanese, you use the *same* form of the verb no matter who is doing it.

Take the verb "to eat," for example. *En español*, you have to learn six different verb forms for just the present tense (one for each pronoun group), plus all the myriad tense variations.

In Japanese, you only need to learn *one* single verb form for each tense. No matter who does the eating, the verb *taberu* (食べる, たべる, "eat") stays exactly the same!

ENGLISH	SPANISH	JAPANESE
I eat.	Yo como.	Taberu.
You eat.	Tú comes.	Taberu.
He / She eats.	Él/Ella come.	Taberu.
We eat.	Nosotros comemos.	Taberu.
You (pl., fam.) eat.	Vosotros coméis.	Taberu.
You (pl.) / They eat.	Uds./Ellos comen.	Taberu.

You *do* have to learn different verb tenses in Japanese, and there are different levels of formality to consider, but hey, at least matching pronouns and verbs is one less thing to worry about when you're starting out. Don't look a gift linguistic horse in the mouth!

There Aren't "Masculine" or "Feminine" Nouns

Japanese lacks grammatical gender (i.e. pesky "masculine" and "feminine" nouns), which should come as a relief to learners of Romance languages that require you to change adjective forms to match the noun they are hanging out with. Buddha be praised! In Japan, you can just order your dark beer instead of trying to remember whether the noun "beer" is feminine or masculine as you would have to in Spanish:

"Let's see… I really want a dark beer. *Cerveza* is feminine I think… Or is it masculine? It seems masculine. Just think of all the dudes with beer bellies. But it ends with an 'a' so I think it should be a feminine noun. Okay, assuming it is indeed feminine, I need to use the feminine form of the adjective for "dark"… Hmm… I think it's *oscura*…"

Meanwhile, the waiter has come and gone and you are left to wait in thirsty frustration. Halfway around the world, the Japanese learner is already on his or her second round of gender-free *kuro biiru* (黒ビール, くろびいる, "dark beer," lit. "black beer").

Japanese Kana Have One-To-One Pronunciations

Japanese is a syllabic language, made up of 45 basic syllables. While the number 45 may sound more intimidating than the 26 letters found in English, keep in mind that each Japanese syllable can be pronounced only ***one*** way. This is in stark contrast to English, which despite having *fewer* letters actually contains far *more* sounds. Depending on the word (and where in the word it lies), most English letters can be pronounced myriad different ways.

Take the letter E for example. It can be pronounced as:

- A "short" E like in "empty" (IPA: /ɛ/)
- A "long" E like in "key" (IPA: /i/)
- A "long" A like in "résumé" (IPA: /ei/)
- A "schwa" like in "taken" (IPA: /ə/)
- A "silent" E like in "axe"

Complex stuff!

Pick any Japanese *kana*, on the other hand, and no matter where it's used, it will be pronounced one—and only one—way.

The Japanese *e* sound for example (written え in hiragana) is always pronounced as a "short e" (ĕ or /ɛ/). It doesn't change if the syllable comes at the beginning, middle, or end of a word.

There are two important exceptions to this rule. When used as grammatical particles, the following *kana* take on special pronunciations:

- は is pronounced ***wa*** not *ha* when used as a topic particle.
- へ is pronounced ***e*** not *he* when used as a direction particle.

Japanese "Recycles" Lots of Kana

As any good citizen knows, we should do our best to reduce, reuse, and recycle. To fulfill its civic duty, Japanese greatly reduces the number of potential kana you need to learn by recycling a small set of basic symbols to represent a much larger number of sounds. The key to this linguistic efficiency is the use of little double slash marks called *dakuten* (濁点, だくてん, "voiced marks"). As the name implies, these diacritic marks transform each of the "voiceless" sounds in Japanese into their "voiced" counterparts.

Here are a few examples. Note that these are each what linguists call "minimal pairs," sounds that are produced in exactly the same part of the mouth (i.e. they have the same basic "manner of articulation"), but have a single difference that creates a distinction in meaning.

In this case, the *only* difference in pronunciation is voicing, and the only difference in writing is the *dakuten* in the upper-right corner:

- *ka* = か → *ga* = が
- *sa* = さ → *za* = ざ
- *ta* = た → *da* = だ

There are many more such pairs in Japanese, meaning that these two tiny marks save you from having to learn dozens of additional symbols. Thank you, *dakuten*!

See *Japanese Pronunciation* in the *How Japanese Works* PDF for more info: **bit.ly/howjapaneseworks**

Japanese Has Few New Sounds for English Speakers

The vast majority of Japanese sounds have direct (or at least very similar) equivalents in English. This is great news for the English speaking learner of Japanese, but tough times for Japanese learners of English. Consider yourself lucky! You've already mastered English's notorious L and R distinctions, for example, and will never have to endure the embarrassment of saying "erection" when you meant "election"!

There are only two Japanese sounds you will likely struggle with in the beginning:

- **The Japanese R sounds: *ra* (ら), *ri* (り), *ru* (る), *re* (れ), and *ro* (ろ).** To English speaking ears, they sound somewhere between an R, L, and D, and are pronounced with a quick flip of the tongue somewhat like the tapped R and trilled R in Spanish. You can find a similar sound in American English buried in the middle of the word "water." When sandwiched between vowels, we Yanks turn the poor little T into what's called a "flap," which is precisely what the Japanese R sound is, too. The Japanese R is denoted as /ɾ/ in the International Phonetic Alphabet (IPA).

- **The Japanese TSU sound (つ).** We actually have a similar sound in English (the *ts* in words like "rats"), but the difference is that we never pronounce such a sound at the *beginning* of syllables in English as they do in Japanese. The sound is simply denoted as /ts/ in the IPA.

But worry not! Your ears and mouth will eventually get the hang of these sounds with enough listening and speaking practice. Just do your best to imitate native speakers, and make sure to record yourself to better gauge your pronunciation and monitor your progress over time.

For tips on recording yourself, see the following section:
Master Your Mind > How to Track Your Language Progress

Japanese Is Not a Tonal Language

Unlike Mandarin, Cantonese, Vietnamese, Thai, etc., Japanese is *not* a tonal language, where meaning changes based on tone. Hooray! (As a rough example of this in English, consider the difference in meaning between "*Okay!*" and "*Okay...?*")

The Japanese language *does* sometimes differentiate meaning using a high-low distinction called "pitch accent," or *koutei akusento* (高低アクセント, こうていあくせんと), but the good news is that you do not need to learn a specific tone for each and every syllable like you do in languages like Chinese.

See *Japanese Pronunciation* in the *How Japanese Works* PDF for more info about pitch accent: **bit.ly/howjapaneseworks**

And in the fairly infrequent cases when pitch *is* used to distinguish meaning, the context will almost always do the heavy lifting for you. For example: Even though the word *hashi* can mean "chopsticks" (箸), "bridge" (橋), or "edge" (端) depending on the pitch accent (in this case, high-low, low-high, and flat), you will know that somebody wants you to pass the "chopsticks" when at a restaurant, not a "bridge," or the "edge" of the table.

You Can Often Guess the Meaning of New Words

Once you know the meaning of individual kanji, you can often guess the meaning of compound words they combine to create. To do the same thing in English requires extensive knowledge of Latin, Greek, Germanic, and so on.

My favorite example of this is the English word "homonym." Unless you know the Greek etymology of this term (homo = "one and the same," -ōnym = "named"), it is all but impossible to dig out its meaning without the help of a dictionary.

The Japanese equivalent, *dou-on-igi-go* (同音異義語, どうおんいぎご, "same sound different meaning word"), on the other hand, can be easily guessed at by anyone with basic literacy in Japanese.

You Can Often Guess the Pronunciation of New Kanji

Contrary to popular belief, most *kanji* are not pictographs. The vast majority are in fact "pictophonetic" compounds comprised of two chunks:

- A "phonetic indicator" that points to the character's *pronunciation.*
- A "semantic indicator" that points to the character's *meaning.*

This may sound complex, but it's actually very good news for language learners! Familiarizing yourself with the most common phonetic and semantic chunks (or "radicals") enables you to then make educated guesses about the pronunciation and meaning of *new* characters when you don't have a dictionary on hand.

For example, all of the following kanji share the same phonetic chunk, 工 ("craft"), which is pronounced *kou* (こう). Lo and behold, each of the following *kanji* it contains are *also* pronounced *kou*, at least when using their *on-yomi* (音読み, おんよみ, "*kanji* readings of Chinese origin"):

- 紅 ("crimson")
- 虹 ("rainbow")
- 江 ("creek")
- 攻 ("aggression")
- 功 ("achievement")
- 巧 ("clever")

Chances are good that if you come across a new *kanji* that includes the 工 phonetic chunk, it *too* will be pronounced *kou*.

MYTH: "JAPANESE IS VAGUE"

We can thank the Japanese themselves for the myth that "Japanese is a vague language." This misconception is well exemplified in an NPR interview with a member of the Tokyo String Quartet who claimed that English allowed him and other Japanese members of the ensemble to communicate more effectively than in Japanese (they began speaking in English once a non-Japanese member joined the group).

As Dr. Jay Rubin points out in Making Sense of Japanese, the perceived difference in communication ease is a matter of *culture*, not *linguistics*:

> "While he no doubt believes this, he is wrong. The Japanese language can express anything it needs to, but Japanese social norms often require people to express themselves indirectly or incompletely."
> —Jay Rubin, *Making Sense of Japanese*[41]

Directness in communication is usually frowned upon in Japanese culture, while it is often the primary goal in most English-speaking countries (except among politicians, who famously love to dance around a question without actually answering it). Anyone who has lived in Japan or done business with a Japanese company knows that this difference in communication style can be a major source of frustration and cross-cultural miscommunication. As things go, it's usually the cultural—not linguistic—barriers that cause tempers to flair, negotiations to break down, and relationships to fail.

So as you learn to speak, read, and write Japanese, make sure to give just as much attention to the "language" left *out of* the conversation and *off* the page. Realize that few Japanese people will ever say "No" outright, opting instead for statements like "It's under consideration..." or "I'll give it some thought..."

Also be aware that when someone says "*Chotto...*" (ちょっと, "a little") and then breathes in through their teeth with a slight grimace as they rub the back of their head, that they are expressing apprehension or disapproval but are culturally forbidden to say what exactly they are "a little" (or likely, "very") unsure about...

CULTURE CORNER

I had mentioned this use of "Chotto..." to my now father-in-law many months before I proposed to his daughter. When I summoned the courage to ask her parents' blessing to propose, he didn't miss a beat. He paused, put on a look of concern, and rubbed the back of his head while breathing in through his teeth! We all burst out laughing given the perfect comedic timing and the patience to wait for this ultimate "Dad joke" moment. After the laughs, both parents said they'd be honored if I asked their daughter for her hand. And even more fortunately, the daughter said yes and is now Mrs. Fotheringham!

MYTH: "JAPANESE IS ILLOGICAL"

This statement makes the false assumption that English is somehow more intuitive or well-structured by comparison. The truth is that *no* natural languages are purely "logical." As they evolve organically over great expanses of time, languages inevitably take on illogical quirks and inconsistent patterns. English is no exception, as Richard Lederer comically illustrates in *Crazy English*:

> "There is no egg in eggplant, and you will find neither pine nor apple in a pineapple. Hamburgers are not made from ham, English muffins were not invented in England, and French Fries were not invented in France. Sweetmeats are confectionery, while sweetbreads, which are not sweet, are meat. And why is it that a writer writes, but fingers do not fing, humdingers do not hum, and hammers don't ham. If the plural of tooth is teeth, shouldn't the plural of booth be beeth?" [42]

While it is perfectly natural to compare and contrast Japanese with English, it's best to avoid making value judgements about the two languages. Human languages are the way they are. *Why* they are that way is an interesting question for historical and comparative linguists, but has little to do with language learning.

To summarize, here are some of the most common limiting beliefs and empowering truths to replace them:

MYTH	TRUTH
"I'm just not good at languages."	"I learned my first language, so I can learn another."
"I don't have time to learn Japanese."	"I can make time to learn by making Japanese my top priority."
"I can't afford to learn Japanese."	"I can learn using free online resources."
"I have to attend Japanese classes."	"I can learn by immersing myself and working with a tutor."
"I'm too old to learn Japanese."	"Adults are actually better language learners in many ways."
"I can't learn Japanese well because I can't move to Japan."	"I can create an immersion environment anywhere in the world."
"It will take me decades to learn Japanese."	"I can learn enough in a few months to have simple conversations."
"Japanese is a really difficult language."	"Japanese is just *different*, not difficult."
"Japanese is a really vague language."	"Japanese culture often requires vagueness, but the language itself isn't vague."
"Japanese is such an illogical language."	"All language have illogical elements because they evolve organically."

Conquer Your Fears

"The cave you fear to enter holds the treasure you seek."
—Joseph Campbell

One of the most important—yet most often overlooked—components of effective language acquisition is overcoming one's fears. We *all* have them. For some of us, our language-learning fears are but mild anxiety about looking foolish if we make mistakes. For others, fear can lead to debilitating anxiety that completely blocks growth.

Whatever your fears, it's important to realize that having them is completely normal. They are the product of *human evolution*, not *personal failing*. That said, just because we are hard-wired to fear certain stimuli does not mean that we don't have the power to overcome them. We do. There is a *simple*—though certainly not *easy*—process we can use conquer any fear:

- **Step 1:** Define your fears.
- **Step 2:** Break them down into manageable pieces.
- **Step 3:** Build courage and competence.

STEP 1: DEFINE YOUR FEARS

"Named must your fear be before banish it you can." —Yoda

Before we can *conquer* our fears, we must first *define* what they are. We can't fight something if we don't even know *what it is* or *where it lives.*

So what scares *you* about learning and practicing Japanese? We are all unique bioindividuals, and what scares *me* might not intimidate *you* in the slightest, and vice-versa. That said, there *are* some common language-related scenarios that induce anxiety in many people. Do any of these fears sound familiar?

- The fear of not understanding or not being understood *by* native speakers.
- The fear of not being able to express one's feelings.
- The fear of making mistakes, looking foolish, or committing a linguistic or cultural gaffe.
- The fear of making a bad first impression or offending someone.
- The fear of ordering the wrong food, getting on the wrong train or bus, etc.

- The fear of wasting money or being swindled.
- The fear of doing poorly on a placement test critical to one's academic or professional career.
- The fear of not landing a Japanese-related job or losing a business deal.

1. Take a moment now to identify what aspects of learning Japanese scare *you* most.

   ____

   ____

   ____

2. Whatever the source of your fears, be as honest and specific as possible.

   ____

   ____

   ____

Miraculously, the simple act of writing down our fears often takes away much of their power. Our fears feed off of uncertainty, ambiguity, and nebulousness, so putting pen to paper can shine the light of certainty, clarity, and specificity, which are all toxic to fear.

But even after writing them down, some fears will still remain sufficiently strong to block action and progress. For these, we need to proceed to the next step: breaking them down into bite-size chunks we can more easily "eat" away.

STEP 2: TAKE BABY STEPS

The Fine Line Between "Hormesis" and "Trauma"

In his book *Antifragile: Things That Gain from Disorder*, Nassim Nicholas Taleb argues that:

> "Some things benefit from shocks; they thrive and grow when exposed to volatility, randomness, disorder, and stressors and love adventure, risk, and uncertainty."

What kind of things benefit from such shocks? Most natural systems—including the human body and mind—get stronger when we're exposed to a certain quantity of stress or discomfort. When we lift weights, our muscles get temporarily damaged but come out bigger and stronger with a few days of rest. Likewise, each time we face our fears, our courage gets a little stronger, and we find bravery to step ever further into the unknown.

This is in stark contrast to fragile artificial systems and manmade objects that are damaged or destroyed by even small stressors.

To describe this difference in fragility properly, Taleb realized that he had to invent a new word: *antifragility*. Why? Because the opposite of "fragile" is not "robust," as you may first think. *Robustness* simply implies that something *resists* damage from a stressor, not that it's *improved* by it. Human beings aren't just robust: we're antifragile. Up to a certain point, stress makes us *stronger*, not weaker. We not only *survive* shocks, we can *thrive* because of them.

One of the main challenges in conquering our fears is finding the balance point between *not enough* and *too much* discomfort. There is a fine line between *hormesis* (stressors that make us stronger) and *trauma* (stressors that make us weaker).

So what should we do? The answer is to gradually push past our current level of courage and competence, instead of jumping directly into the deep end of the pool. We can't get better at swimming if we can't even keep our head above the water.

Take Baby Steps Into Discomfort

Instead of giant leaps, we should take "baby steps" like Bill Murray's affable character Bob in *What About Bob?*

"Baby step to the elevator. I'm in the elevator. AHHHHH!!!"
"Baby step on the bus... Baby step on the bus..."
"Baby step to 4 o'clock... Baby step to 4 o'clock..."

The movie took the baby steps concept to the extreme for comedic effect, but this shouldn't discount the life-changing power of incremental change.

Breaking our fears down into tiny, manageable chunks allows us to gradually build the confidence and competence we'll need to face even greater fears. Each micro-exposure to fear and challenge makes us that much stronger, that much more antifragile.

The key is to choose a small enough step that you can easily manage it *today*. If it's too big of a jump, you will find an excuse to put it off. But if the step is *just* outside the ring of your current comfort zone, it will be easier to take action and build the confidence you'll need to take a slightly bigger step tomorrow. And then an even bigger step the next day.

Before you know it, you will have strengthened your change muscles to the point where you can easily "lift" extremely uncomfortable and unfamiliar experiences without breaking a sweat. While others are panicking, you will be calm, collected, and enjoying the moment.

If, for example, you are terrified of communicating with native Japanese speakers, you could try the following baby steps to build up your confidence:

1. **Speak to yourself in Japanese.** This is the lowest stakes way to start getting used to speaking. Throughout your day, try speaking Japanese words and phrases aloud (or under your breath if the situation demands).

2. **Speak in Japanese in the mirror.** We will now up the ante a little, and speak in the mirror. It's still only you, but having a reflection can *feel* like having another person there. Set a time 1-minute and try to keep going the entire 60 seconds even if you repeat yourself a few times.

3. **Speak in Japanese with someone you trust.** Now we're going to bring someone else into the mix, but we're still keeping the stress and stakes as low as possible. You can choose your partner or spouse, a trusted friend, etc. It doesn't matter if they understand what you're saying. In fact, it's probably better if they *don't*. The key is to get you used to producing Japanese—however choppy—in front of other human beings. Again, set a timer for 1 minute and try to keep going.

4. **Schedule a short language exchange.** We will now take the next baby step to communicating with a native Japanese speaker. Since *they* are learning English, it helps balance out the potential stress of *you* having to speak Japanese. You will both be extremely patient and empathetic about the other's efforts and mistakes.

5. **Schedule a conversation with a Japanese tutor.** Once you have a few language exchanges under your belt, hire a Japanese language tutor. Start with short sessions (e.g. 15 minutes) and work your way up to 30 minutes or an hour. Be picky. If a tutor makes you feel uncomfortable, choose another. The key at this stage is building confidence and getting used to speaking with others, so you don't want any extra stress caused by personality mismatches.

See my recommended tutoring sites and tools here:
Learn How to Learn > Work with a Tutor

---

6. **Communicate with real native speakers:** Finally, graduate to speaking with native Japanese speakers who are not experienced language tutors. They will probably have less experience communicating with non-native speakers, meaning that you will have to up your game to understand and be understood.

7. **Call someone on the phone in Japanese.** The final challenge is calling someone in Japanese on the phone. Removing the visual context makes communication that much more difficult, which is why this is saved for last. Find the phone number for a store or business in Japan, think of a question to ask, and dial away!

1. Break down each fear you identified in Step 1 into as many tiny steps as possible.

2. Now look at the coming days or weeks and decide which days you will complete each baby step. Consider each step an important commitment that you will not miss, no matter what.

STEP 3: BUILD COURAGE & COMPETENCE

Once you've identified your fears and broken them down into manageable baby steps, the final step is building your confidence and competence through sufficient practice.

Confidence Comes From *Acting*, Not *Thinking*

"You do not *think* your way into confidence.
You *act* your way into confidence."
—Tim Ferriss

The human capacity for conscious thought is one of the most impressive products of evolution. Our ability to think, weigh options, and plan for the future has literally changed the world. But for all the attention and prestige afforded to *thought*, we must remember that thinking alone won't get us very far. We have to *act*. But taking action can be scary, especially when we face the uncertainty, ambiguity, and risk of social awkwardness that learning a foreign language entails.

So we rationalize. We deliberate. We procrastinate.

The hard truth is that no amount of thinking will *ever* produce confidence. Somewhat paradoxically, we can only attain confidence *after* taking the very actions we wish we had the confidence to take in the first place. In other words, we get the courage to jump once we've *already* jumped!

Get Comfortable With Discomfort

"There's nothing comfortable about being courageous." —Brené Brown

---

Facing fears is far from comfortable. It goes against every evolutionary instinct to avoid dangers, minimize conflict, and prevent social ostracism. But it's an essential step if you want to master Japanese. The more time you spend outside your comfort zone, the better your language skills will become. The better *you* will become.

Learn To Act Despite Your Fear

As you face your fears, you may notice an interesting phenomenon. You still feel fear with each baby step you take. The difference now is that the fear doesn't *control* you as it did before. It no longer stops you from taking action.

The reality is that fear never fully goes away. What happens instead is that we get braver and braver, learning to act *despite* our fears.

As the clinical psychologist Jordan Peterson puts it:

> "[When people face their fears] they don't get less afraid, they get braver. The best you can hope for is courage, not cessation of fear."

Though our fears never fully fade away, they *can* at least diminish with sufficient exposure. Every time we face a given fear, *it* becomes a little less scary and *we* become a little braver. Moreover, the courage we build facing *one* fear can then be applied to *all others*. For example, if you learn to face your fear of speaking in Japanese with native speakers, you might find that you feel a little less anxiety next time you fly in an airplane, have a difficult conversation with your spouse, or ask for a raise.

Take Improv Classes

Taking improvisational ("improv") classes will arm you with a set of powerful psychological skills you can use to conquer fears and become a better communicator in *any* language:

- The confidence to handle whatever comes.
- Full engagement with the present moment.
- Focusing on what's being said by *others* instead of what *you* are going to say next.

- Performing in front of others.

Few of us realize it, but we are *all* actors playing out scripts. Improv teaches us to throw the script in the trash, and instead react honestly and spontaneously in the moment. This takes lots of practice (and so does speaking in Japanese, of course), but the time is well worth the confidence and competence it bestows.

To find an improv class near you, simply search for "improv classes" on Yelp or Google.

Remember That You Are on a Hero's Journey

The last tip for facing and overcoming your language learning fears is to remember that you are a hero on a hero's journey. Yes, *you* are Luke Skywalker. And because you are a hero, you have the courage, competence, and power to face your "Darth Vader." All of these heroes felt fear, too, but they acted *despite* it. That is precisely what makes them heroes. And it's what will make *you* a hero, too. As Cus D'Amato—Mike Tyson's former manager and trainer—said:

> "The hero and the coward both feel the same thing, but the hero uses his fear, projects it onto his opponent, while the coward runs. It's the same thing, fear, but it's what you *do* with it that matters."

Master Your Motivation

In this section, we will walk through how to spark your motivation, fan the flames, and build a roaring inferno with both *internal* and *external* fuel.

GET MOTIVATED FROM THE INSIDE

Realize Motivation Is a Choice

When we see people working with all their might toward a lofty goal—may it be becoming fluent in a language or losing 100 pounds—many assume they are simply "blessed" with deep reserves of willpower and motivation. We think, "Gosh, I wish I had *that* kind of drive!" The reality is that all of us *can* tap into the same fuel. But we have to choose—again and again and again. Every time we are tempted with a lesser, easier path, we have to again choose to pursue what we want *most* over what we want *now*. As Brendon Burchard puts it in *The Motivation Manifesto*:

> "Purpose does not strike as a lucky lightning bolt of inspiration. Motivation and purpose are choices. The only thing needed to spark motivation is a decision to heighten your ambition and expectancy—to sit down, think about what you desire, and believe you can go get it. To keep that motivation, you must give constant attention and effort."

Clarify Your Motives

If you struggle to build and sustain your motivation to learn Japanese, the first step is going back and reviewing your reasons and goals for learning the language in the first place. Why? Because the root of "motivation" is *motive.*

- What excites you about understanding, speaking, reading, or writing Japanese?
- What do you want to accomplish with the language?
- How will Japanese skills improve your life?

Review your WHY (see *Prerequisites for Success*) and SMART Goals (see *Make Your Goals "SMART"*).

Keep Your Eyes on the Prize

"Eyes on the prize, Violet, eyes on the prize." — Mrs. Beauregarde, *Charlie and the Chocolate Factory*

Once you've clarified your motives and goals, the next steps is keeping them top of mind on a daily basis. There are three keys ways to accomplish this:

- **Review first thing every morning:** Before the distractions of the world and the stresses of the day rob you of your focus, review your personal WHY statement and list of SMART Goals.

- **Journal each day before bed.** Lastly, journalling about the day's language learning journey is a great way to increase motivation by highlighting successes and identifying what you'll do differently tomorrow.

- **Meditate daily:** Meditation not only reduces stress, but it can help eliminate mental distractions and increase your focus. You can use a guided meditation app (see my recommendation below) or simply focus on your breath.

There are many great meditation apps available today, but my favorite is Headspace: **bit.ly/mjheadspace**

NOTE!

The goal of mediation is not to *eliminate* thoughts, but to simply *acknowledge* the thoughts that come, and then let them go without chasing them. Instead of being controlled by the incessant impulses of our "monkey mind," we can create some quiet space to better assess and act toward what matters most.

Expect Success

"Whether you think you can or you think you can't, you're right."
—Henry Ford

Far too many learners create a self-fulfilling prophecy of failure. Deep down, they don't believe they will every reach their fluency goals, and sure enough, they don't. But those who truly believe in their ability to succeed, *do*. Or at least they get a heck of a lot closer to success.

Yes, luck is a factor. Some have to overcome more challenges than others. But regardless of what is happening *out in the world*, the most important factor is what's happening *in your head*.

Do not *hope* for motivation. Choose it.

Do not *hope* for success. Expect it.

Choose To Follow Your Curiosity

"I have no special talents. I am only passionately curious."
—Albert Einstein

Motivation thrives on curiosity. The human compulsion to explore and understand the world has led to our species' greatest technological and cultural advances. And the same basic drive can provide the fuel, motivation, and discipline needed to master Japanese. Don't waste time learning what you *think* you should be learning; instead, learn what piques *your* curiosity and fits *your* unique interests.

- Fall down rabbit holes.
- Get lost in Japanese Wikipedia.
- Max out your library loans.

You never know where the path will lead you or what other unexpected adventures will arise.

But there is *one* you *can* be certain of: your Japanese will get much better along the way!

Choose To Act Even When Unmotivated

"Action isn't just the *effect* of motivation; it's also the *cause* of it."
—Mark Manson, *The Subtle Art of Not Giving a F*ck*

If you only study Japanese when you feel motivated, you won't get very far in the language. Waiting for motivation to act is like waiting for a lawnmower to start on its own. It's not gonna happen, dude. *We* have to pull the starter rope first. And probably more than once if the engine is really cold or the machine hasn't been used in a long time. But once the engine gets started, it hums along with no further outside help.

We have to do the same thing with language learning sometimes. On those days we don't feel like studying or are tempted to cancel a tutoring session, we have to muster the motivation to pull the rope and get our learning engines started.

Leverage the Zeigarnik Effect

If we manage to get started despite a lack of motivation, a curious effect often happens. We find that we don't want to stop! Just moments ago, we wanted to do anything *but* begin the task at hand, and now we feel highly motivated to finish.

Psychologists call this the *Zeigarnik Effect*, named after the Soviet psychologist and psychiatrist Bluma Wulfovna Zeigarnik (1901-1988). In her research, she observed that once an individual begins a task, they are much more likely to carry on until it is complete. The human brain, apparently, doesn't like the tension created by unfinished tasks.

We can leverage this effect to our advantage in language learning. We just have to muster the tiny bit of motivation it takes to *get started.*

So on low-energy or low-motivation days, don't think about completing your ideal set of daily language learning habits. Instead, pick just one tiny task. Or set a timer for five minutes, and tell yourself:

"It's just five minutes. If I hate this, I can stop when the timer goes off."

My wife and I will often do this with cleaning the kitchen after cooking dinner. With a full belly and a full day's work behind us, the *last* thing we want to do is work through the mountain of dishes. So, we set a timer for just five minutes and agree that if we *want* to, we can stop cleaning when the time is up. More often than not, we get into the swing of it, and end up happily cleaning for 30 minutes or more.

When you find yourself unmotivated to do *any* language learning, try committing to studying just a single flashcard, listening to just 1 minute of a podcast, or reading just one paragraph of a Japanese book.

You may get to the end of the card, minute, or paragraph, and call it quits. And that's totally fine! A *little* Japanese is better than *no* Japanese. But chances are good that you will keep going, and end up spending many more minutes on task once you get some "motivational momentum."

GET MOTIVATED FROM THE OUTSIDE

While developing *internal* motivation is a critical piece of long-term success in language learning, there are some powerful *external* tools we can use to help jumpstart our engines when we're feeling unmotivated.

Follow Polyglots

Polyglots—those who can speak multiple languages—can be a great motivator for those trying to learn their first foreign language. Most polyglots are just ordinary folks who achieve extraordinary results thanks to *effective methods*, not *outlier intellects*, and when you hear them tell their stories, you realize can do the same if you follow their example. Here are a few names to Google to get you started (arranged in alphabetical order by last name):

- Mike Campbell
- Sara Maria Hasbun
- Steve Kaufmann
- Luca Lampariello
- Benny Lewis
- Lýdia Machová

- Olly Richards
- Richard Simcott
- Gabriel Wyner
- Lindsay Williams

You can hear interviews with the above polyglots (and many more) on *The Language Mastery Show*: **bit.ly/LMSHOW**

Get Inspired by Other Language Learners

"We're the most social creature on the planet. Everything depends on collective effort and cooperation. When we get a cue that we ought to connect our identity with a group, it's like a hair trigger, like turning on a light switch. The ability to achieve is already there, but the energy put into that ability goes through the roof." —Dr. Geoff Cohen

It's often said that we are the average of the five people we spend the most time with. So if we want to achieve great *things*, we need to hang out with great *people*. If you want to master a language, it's far easier (and far more likely!) if you spend lots of time with other learners. They don't even need to be learning the same language as you, though that can certainly be a plus. What matters is that they have similar goals and values. In aggregate, these friends will help normalize language learning and make it feel like the "cool" thing to do, not a weird hobby. So where can you find fellow language lovers? Here are three places I recommend:

- **Join the *Language Mastery Insiders* Facebook Group:** If you're on Facebook, click below to join my private group where you can get encouraged and ask questions.

Request to join the Facebook Group here:
bit.ly/lmfbgroup

- **Attend language meetups.** Most cities have regular language and culture meetups dedicated to popular world languages. If not, you can always take initiative and start one yourself!

Visit **bit.ly/mjmeetup** to browse language and culture meetups near you or create your own group.

- **Attend polyglot conferences and gatherings:** There are now dozens of polyglot events each year all over the globe, with more and more popping up every year. Some of the best include *LangFest*, *The Polyglot Conference*, and

The Polyglot Gathering. Despite their name, these events are open to anyone interested in languages (regardless of ability level or fluency), not just those who speak many foreign tongues.

See my post *5 Reasons to Attend a Polyglot Event Even if You Don't Consider Yourself a Polyglot*: **bit.ly/LMBpolyglot**

Make a Motivation Playlist

There's a reason that every movie has a soundtrack and almost everyone at the gym is wearing headphones: **music motivates**. We all have certain songs that always amp us up even on days when we're feeling lazy and unmotivated. Go through your music library and create a playlist you can use to spark the flame and get you going. Here are few suggestions of where to start:

Check out Akira the Don's "Meaningwave" music: inspiring talks set to catchy "lofi" beats on YouTube. **bit.ly/mjakira**

Check out this "pump up" Spotify playlist crowdsourced by former coworkers (some lyrics are NSFW). **bit.ly/mjamped**

Read & Listen to High Achievers

Most motivational speakers are cheesy and clichéd, but there *are* a few rare souls out there who walk their talk and speak with the power of honesty, integrity, and experience. When I am feeling lazy and unmotivated, here are a few of the inspiring folks that shake me out of my funk and get me back on the path. Perhaps they can do the same for you…

- **Jocko Willink** is a former Navy SEAL commander and author of *Discipline Equals Freedom* [43] and *Extreme Ownership*.[44] He wakes up at 4:30 am every single morning, exercises every single day, and no matter what comes, makes sure to "Get after it!"

Check out Akira the Don's mix of Jocko Willink on why "discipline equals freedom": **bit.ly/mjjocko**

- **David Goggins** is another former Navy SEAL, an ultra-distance runner and cyclist, and the former world record holder in the most pull-ups completed in 24 hours (4,030!). His physical feats are truly impressive, but what's even *more* inspiring is that he used to be 100 pounds overweight, working a job he hated (exterminating cockroaches), and generally living a miserable existence. Through sheer will and self-discipline, he turned his life around and achieved his greatest dreams.

Get David Goggins' book *Can't Hurt Me*: **bit.ly/mjbchm**

OVERCOME OVERWHELM

The last key to building and preserving motivation is managing overwhelm. No matter your level in the language, you will inevitably encounter days when the sheer enormity of the task ahead causes anxiety and even depression. You find yourself plodding along in the language, but suddenly pause to look up at the lofty heights of Japanese Mountain. Despite having made significant progress, you find yourself dwelling on all the words and *kanji* you *don't* yet know. All the mistakes you *still* make. All the structures and utterances that *continue* to cause you trouble.

These are all perfectly normal feelings and there is nothing wrong with feeling them.

But you needn't let these feelings overwhelm your mind and sabotage your progress. You can take active steps to reframe and refocus:

- Instead of thinking about the *entire* journey, you can choose to ratchet down your focus to the smallest, most immediate chunks possible.
- Instead of focusing on the distance between where you are *now* and where you want to get *eventually*, aim your mind at only the very next step.

I have two favorite examples of this reframing approach in practice:

- Taking it "bird by bird."
- Taking it "brick by brick."

Take It Bird by Bird

In her book *Bird by Bird*, author Anne Lamott recounts how her father once helped her older brother overcome overwhelm with one simple strategy:

> "Thirty years ago my older brother, who was ten years old at the time, was trying to get a report written on birds that he'd had three months to write, which was due the next day. We were out at our family cabin in Bolinas, and he was at the kitchen table close to tears, surrounded by binder paper and pencils and unopened books about birds, immobilized by the hugeness of the task ahead. Then my father sat down beside him put his arm around my brother's shoulder, and said, 'Bird by bird, buddy. Just take it bird by bird.'" [45]

Take It Brick by Brick

Similarly, the actor Will Smith shared on *The Charlie Rose Show* how his dad once helped him reframe a seemly insurmountable task (building a brick wall with his brother) into something much more manageable:

"You don't set out to build a wall. You don't say 'I'm going to build the biggest, baddest, greatest wall that's ever been built.' You don't start there. You say, 'I'm going to lay this brick as perfectly as a brick can be laid. You do that every single day. And soon you have a wall." [46]

Track Your Progress

WHY YOU SHOULD TRACK

"The human mind loves to receive feedback. One of the most motivating things we can experience is evidence of our progress. This is why measurement is so critical for effective goal setting. By measuring your results, you get insight on whether or not you are making progress." —James Clear

---

Effective tracking is crucial for the success of your Japanese learning mission:

- It increases motivation.
- It helps you identify what's working (and what's not).
- It shows you which methods and resources have the highest ROI (return on investment).

Tracking Increases Motivation

Perceived progress is one of the greatest motivators in language learning. As the polyglot Barry Farber puts it:

"Expertise is a narcotic."

But it can be hard to tell on a day-to-day basis if you are actually improving or not. Like all complex skills, language acquisition is a slow, incremental process that is difficult to perceive on an intuitive, personal level. Tracking takes out the guesswork and makes progress (or lack of it) crystal clear.

Tracking Helps Identify What's Working

"If you can't measure it, you can't improve it." —Peter Drucker

---

When you first start out in language learning, you have to throw a lot at the wall and see what sticks. Not every technique or resource will work for you, but you won't be able to separate the proverbial wheat from the chaff unless you track.

Tracking Helps Increase Your ROI

Not only will tracking show you what works, it will show you *how well* it is working. You can then decide which investments of time, energy, and money produce the largest "dividends" of progress and skill acquisition. You can then redirect your investments to the few activities, methods, and resources that produce the highest ROI and enjoyment.

HOW TO TRACK LANGUAGE PROGRESS

Measure What Matters

> "Knowing what to measure, and how to measure it, can make a complicated world less so." —Steven Levitt & Stephen Dubner, *Think Like a Freak*

Modern technology makes it easier than ever to track a dizzying array of metrics. But just because you *can* track something, doesn't mean you should. Moreover, many of the *easiest* things to track are actually the *least* important.

There are a lot of "vanity metrics" you can track in language learning (e.g. the number of vocabulary words you've memorized or your score on a standardized test) that might *seem* important on the surface, but actually have very little to do with the ultimate goal: **communicating with human beings**.

Instead of measuring the meaningless, you can instead track your progress in listening, speaking, reading, and writing (what truly matters) using the following free, at-home assessments.

Track Your Listening Progress

1. Get out a journal or open a new note on your device. Write down the date.
2. Choose a specific Japanese podcast or audiobook.
3. Choose a specific 1-minute section of the audio file and note the start and end timestamps.
4. Without looking at the transcript or companion text (if there is one), note how many words you *don't* know or easily understand. Write them down.
5. Set a calendar reminder for 3 months into the future.

6. When that day comes, repeat steps 1 through 4, and then compare the list of unknown words. If you have been diligently practicing the language everyday, the list should gradually get smaller.

7. Set another calendar reminder for 3 months into the future, and then rinse and repeat as many times as you find useful.

For more on how to practice listening, see *Learn How to Learn > Improve Your Listening Skills.*

Track Your Speaking Progress

Tracking your speaking skills is more of an art than a science, but here's a simply way to track your growth while also reinforcing a critical skill: *self-introductions*.

1. Record yourself giving your self-introduction (you can read a script if necessary, but you'll get a better baseline if you speak off the cuff).

2. Have your tutor review the recording and note any mistakes (e.g. word use, grammar, pronunciation, etc.)

3. Like above, set a calendar reminder for 3 months into the future.

4. When that day comes, repeat steps 1 and 2.

5. If you have been consistently practicing, you should see a decrease in the quantity of mistakes, and an increase in the quality of your speaking between the two recordings.

6. Set another calendar reminder for 3 months into the future, and then repeat the same process.

For more on how to practice speaking, see *Learn How to Learn > Improve Your Speaking Skills.*

Track Your Reading Progress

Tracking your progress in reading is arguably the easiest of the four language skills:

1. Find a book at or just above your current level that you enjoy and will be willing to reread a few times.

2. Pick a specific page in the book that is all or mostly text. Write down the page number somewhere you won't lose it.

3. Time how long it takes to read the single page and write down the time in minutes and seconds. For extra credit, also note how many words you don't know on the page.

4. Set a calendar reminder for 3 months into the future.

5. When that day comes, repeat steps 1 through 4, and compare your numbers. If you get enough reading practice, you should gradually get faster and faster, and encounter fewer and fewer unknown words.

6. Set another calendar reminder for 3 months into the future, and then repeat the same process.

For more on how to practice reading, see *Learn How to Learn > Improve Your Reading Skills.*

Track Your Writing Progress

One of the best ways to track your progress in writing is keeping a daily journal in Japanese and then submitting it to your tutor or Lang-8 for correction. This helps you fix mistakes before they become bad habits, while also showing you how far you've come when you look back at past entries.

See *Learn How to Learn > Improve Your Writing Skills > Get Your Writing Corrected.*

Develop Your Discipline

The final—and arguably most important—aspect of mastering your mind is developing the strength of character and commitment you need keep going no matter what. This is where the dreaded d-word comes in: *discipline.*

Conquering your fears is a crucial first step. And stoking the flames of motivation can help propel us forward. But without discipline, few of us will stick with Japanese long enough to reach our goals. We'll be fair-weather learners who quit when the first storm clouds roll in. We'll turn back when the path up Japanese Mountain gets a little too steep. We'll choose what we want *now* over what we want *most*.

But if we develop sufficient discipline, we will have the fortitude to resist the siren calls of procrastination and quitting. And if we combined discipline with courage and motivation, we become an unstoppable language learning juggernaut!

Just like a muscle, our discipline gets *stronger* the more we use it and weaker the *less* we use it. Every time you choose to study Japanese instead of watch TV in English, your discipline muscle grows. Each time you open your flashcard app instead of Instagram, your discipline gets that much more shredded. Like with weightlifting, our muscles grow faster when we lift heavier weights. The harder the decision or habit (i.e. the more discipline it takes to accomplish), the stronger and more disciplined you become. But also like weights, you have to work your way up slowly. If you're inexperienced, throwing 500 pounds on your barbell will cause *injury*, not *growth*.

Start with a small daily learning habit and commit to hitting it **NO MATTER WHAT**! Once you've hit every day for two weeks, then expand the habit and go two more weeks. Then expand again. Rinse and repeat until discipline has become a robust habit. Until discipline has become part of who you are.

See the *Make Japanese a Habit* section for more on habit formation and "minimum effective habits."

Say the following *Mindset Mantra* aloud and post it somewhere you will see it every day:

- I have faith in my ability to learn Japanese.
- I choose motivation because I choose my motives.
- I have the discipline to persist no matter what.

LEARN HOW TO LEARN

"Learning how to learn is life's most important skill." —Tony Buzan

Despite having spent about 25,000 hours in school by the time we graduate from college, most of us never learn *how to actually learn*. While it's tempting to throw blame at the modern industrial education system (whose weaknesses are not hard to find), we must remember one of the prerequisites for mastering Japanese: **having an *internal***

locus of control. School may have done a crappy job of teaching us how to learn, but that's the past. All that matters is what we do *now*.

In this chapter, you will learn how to supercharge your language learning machine by:

- Maximizing your exposure to Japanese through *Anywhere Immersion*.
- Learning Japanese through fun activities instead of boring textbooks.
- Improving all four language skills: listening, speaking, reading, and writing.
- Maximizing "myelin" (our neural insulation that drives skill acquisition) through deep, deliberate practice.
- Optimizing memory through mnemonics, spaced repetition, and effective note taking.
- Optimizing your brain health through nutrition, sleep, and movement.

Learn Through Immersion

"Make sure that Japanese is visible and audible in your life. Perpetually, prominently, repeatedly, more-often-than-not, visible and audible. Ask yourself: 'What am I seeing? What am I hearing?'" —Khatzumoto

---

WHY IMMERSION?

It doesn't take a randomized, double-blind, placebo-controlled study to show that immersion is an effective way to learn languages. All you need to do is think back on how *you*, dear reader, learned your first language. Yup, good old fashioned immersion! As an infant, you were surrounded by your native tongue twenty-four hours a day, seven days a week. Thanks to this all-you-can-listen-and-speak buffet, you went from linguistic zero to linguistic hero in just a few years.

So why do so many adults fail to reach fluency in a foreign language despite years or even decades of study? Because most adult learners only spend a few hours a week with the target language. If you spent the same number of hours immersed in a foreign language as a child learning their first tongue, you too would reach fluency just as quickly, if not even faster since adults tend to acquire new skills more quickly than children.

See *Myth: "I'm Too Old to Learn Japanese"* for more about the many learning advantages of adults.

So how can you immerse yourself in Japanese much like you were immersed in your first language as a child? The answer is what I call *Anywhere Immersion*, a fun, effective, adult-friendly approach that only requires a little creativity, a decent dose of discipline, and an internet connection.

- Instead of having to move abroad, you will create a Japanese immersion environment right at home, work, and in your car.
- Instead of forcing yourself through boring textbooks, you will learn through engaging podcasts, anime, videos, TV shows, movies, manga, magazines, blogs, and books, all of *your* choice.
- Instead of paying for expensive, location-dependent classes, you will work with a free language exchange partner or low-cost tutor online.

See my recommended tutoring sites and tools here:
Learn How to Learn > Work with a Tutor

In short, you will learn:

- *Whatever* you want.
- *Whenever* you want.
- *Wherever* you want.

Anywhere Immersion vs. Traditional Academic Language Learning

The *Anywhere Immersion* approach represents some important differences from the traditional ways languages have been taught in formal academic settings:

- ***Anywhere Immersion* is more fun.** You can choose engaging materials and activities that you love. You're not stuck with the topics, materials, and activities chosen by your teacher or school.
- ***Anywhere Immersion* is more convenient.** You to learn anytime, anywhere. You don't need to move abroad or even travel to a classroom.
- ***Anywhere Immersion* is less expensive.** Language classes and textbooks can be extremely expensive. This approach lets you choose modern resources that are extremely affordable, if not free!
- ***Anywhere Immersion* is automatic.** When you properly

design your environment, you get highly contextual exposure to Japanese throughout your day as you engage in activities you would do anyway.

- ***Anywhere Immersion* is more natural.** Humans have learned languages through immersion for hundreds of thousands of years. It's how our brains are wired.

- ***Anywhere Immersion* is personalized.** This approach allows you to tailor the learning process to *your* unique interests, needs, learning style, and schedule.

ACADEMIC APPROACH	ANYWHERE IMMERSION
The curriculum is chosen by the teacher, school, or government	The curriculum is chosen by the individual learner
Content tends to be too easy or too difficult for a given learner	Individuals can choose content that better fits their current level
The class goes as fast as the slowest learner	Learners can progress as quickly or slowly as they want
Materials center around generic, mainstream topics	Learners can choose topics that fit their unique interests, career, etc.
You have to pay expensive tuition fees	Many resources are free online or from local libraries, or at least very low cost compared with classes
You have to travel to a classroom in a specific place at a specific time	You can learn anytime, anywhere (pants optional)

HOW TO OPTIMIZE IMMERSION

Stick to an Immersion Schedule

"A schedule defends from chaos and whim." —Annie Dillard

A major benefit of *Anywhere Immersion* is that it helps make Japanese exposure the default in your life, instead of something you have to constantly choose. That said, unless you are living in Japan, your native language will inevitably seep into your day and rob precious time that could be spent acquiring Japanese. To ensure that you get a consistent chunk of immersion each and every day, it's essential to create and follow an immersion schedule.

See *Master Your Day > Optimize Your Time > Follow a Routine* for detailed tips and a sample immersion schedule.

Actively Engage With the Language

For immersion to work, it has to be *active*. Languages are not learned through osmosis, as proven by the large number of expats who have lived in Japan for years or even decades and can't even order a *nama biiru* (生ビール, なまびいる, "draft beer") at the bar without help from a Japanese speaking friend or significant other.

For example, listening to a Japanese podcast as you cook or do chores is better than *no* exposure, but you will get the most benefit if you actively engage with the content:

- Give the audio your entire focus.
- Pause to repeat phrases and mimic native pronunciation.
- Pause to look up new words and then add create new flashcards to review them.

Be Unreasonable

"The reasonable man adapts himself to the world; the unreasonable one persists in trying to adapt the world to himself. Therefore all progress depends on the unreasonable man." —George Bernard Shaw

---

Creating an effective *Anywhere Immersion* environment will not always be easy, automatic, or comfortable. It may entail some awkward conversations with your family and friends as you alter familiar routines and habits. It may sometimes require pushing back against accepted social norms as you prioritize learning over comfort.

Learn Through Action

"Action may not always bring happiness, but there is no happiness without action." —Benjamin Disraeli

---

Learning Japanese through action is not only more *fun*, but it's also a heck of a lot more *effective*:

- It forces you out of your head and into your body.
- It requires two-way communication with other people.
- It helps build strong procedural memories.

LEARN A JAPANESE MARTIAL ART

"There is no losing in jiu jitsu. You either win or you learn." —Carlson Gracie, Brazilian jiu-jitsu expert

---

Training in martial arts has been one of the most rewarding, meaningful pursuits of my life, and I highly encourage you to give one a try if you've yet to don a *dougi* (道着, "training uniform") or hit the *tatami* (畳, "straw mats"). Martial arts training has numerous benefits:

- Increased focus, discipline, and self-control.
- Improved strength, flexibility, agility, and bodily awareness.
- A better chance of defending oneself from bullies, criminals, assailants, etc.

But learning a martial arts offers *another* potential advantage that few people talk about: **highly contextual Japanese immersion!**

If you live in Japan or happen to be near a Japanese-speaking *Sensei* (先生, "teacher") or *Shihan* (師範, "master instructor"), learning *bujutsu* (武術, "martial arts") can be a phenomenal way to learn Japanese:

- **It's extremely context-rich:** Practicing in a *doujou* (道場, "a hall used for martial arts training") and seeing *waza* (技, "techniques") demonstrated in real-time provide a clear, tangible context for the language being used and make it easier to understand and internalize new vocabulary, phrases, and structures.
- **It gets you out of your head and into your body:** One common problem that beginner and intermediate language learners face is getting stuck in one's head, overthinking usage, and second-guessing oneself. The immediacy of martial arts gets you out of your own way into the moment.

- **It's fun and addictive:** Learning a martial art can be challenging, but it's also a hell of a lot of fun. You will make new friends, push yourself to new limits, and develop a new appreciation for what the body and mind are capable of. And as you start to notice your progress (in both the art and the language), your brain will trigger little doses of dopamine, a neurotransmitter involved in habit formation that will keep you coming back for more.

Even if you don't live in Japan or near a Japanese speaking instructor, you can still learn a fair amount of Japanese through martial arts books, manga, videos, etc.

Here now are some of the most popular Japanese martial arts, arranged in alphabetical order.

Aikido

Formalized by martial arts legend *UESHIBA Morihei* (植芝盛平, うえしばもりへい) in the aftermath of World War II, *aikidou* (合気道, あいきどう, "The Way of Unifying Life Energy") was created as a self-defense system to foster peace and minimize injury to both the practitioner and attacker.

Learn more about Aikido on Wikipedia:
bit.ly/mjaikido

Judo

Literally meaning "The Gentle Way," *juudou* (柔道, じゅうどう), involves the skilled use of throws and takedowns. While it still retains some of its martial efficacy, it is practiced now (at least by most) as a sport, not a martial art.

Learn more about Judo on Wikipedia:
bit.ly/mjwikjudo

Jujutsu

Despite using the characters for "gentle art," *juujustu* (柔術, じゅうじゅつ) is anything but "soft." The core techniques of the martial art were developed by samurai for use when they lost their weapon on the battlefield and had to face an armed opponent with nothing but their wits and martial skills. Note that the "jiu-jitsu" spelling refers to the Brazilian form of the art, popularized by the Gracie family.

Learn more about Jujutsu on Wikipedia:
bit.ly/mjjujutsu

Karate

Karate (空手, からて, lit. "empty hand") originated in *Okinawa* (沖縄, おきなわ), though the martial art is heavily influenced by Chinese fighting arts from across the sea, which is why the word was originally written with the characters 唐手, meaning "Chinese Hand."

Learn more about Karate on Wikipedia:
bit.ly/mjkarate

Kendo

Originally designed as a non-lethal way to practice sword-fighting, *kendou* (剣道, けんどう, "The Way of the Sword"), is now a full-fledged martial art with ranks and competitions. The beauty of Kendo—like many other Japanese martial arts—is that *skill* beats *size*. Case in point: when I worked at a high school in rural Japan, I was regularly schooled by kendo students half my size but with many times my ability.

Learn more about Kendo on Wikipedia:
bit.ly/mjkendo

Sumo

Considered by many to be the "national sport" of Japan, *sumou* (相撲, すもう) is one of the nation's most iconic traditions. The objective of the sport is simple: either force the opposing *rikishi* (力士, りきし, "wrestler") to leave the circular ring called the *do-hyou* (土俵, どひょう), or force them to touch the ground with any part of their body other than their feet.

Learn more about Sumo on Wikipedia:
bit.ly/mjwiksumo

LEARN A JAPANESE ART FORM

"We're all born artists. The challenge is to stay one as you grow up."
—Pablo Picasso

May it be pottery or samurai swords, Japanese artists bring an element of the divine into even the most mundane—or deadly!—objects.

Here are but a few of the many world-renowned Japanese art forms in alphabetical order.

Japanese Animation

Japanese animation, called *anime* (アニメ, あにめ), represents one of the most expressive and varied forms of animation in the world.

The art form is highly interrelated to its print counterpart, *manga* (漫画, まんが), with many anime series having their start as comic books.

For specific anime recommendations, see *Choose Your Weapons > Japanese Videos > Recommended Anime Series.*

Japanese Calligraphy

In Japan, *shodou* (書道, しょどう, "calligraphy") is considered a fine art on par with painting. Learning Japanese calligraphy is an excellent way to reinforce your knowledge of Chinese characters (especially for those with strong bodily-kinesthetic intelligence).

See photos and learn more in this Wikipedia article: bit.ly/mjwikcalligraphy

---

Japanese Cuisine

While most wouldn't consider food to be an art form, if you have ever been to a formal *enkai* (宴会, えんかい, "Japanese banquet"), you'll know why it's on the list. Perhaps most worthy of "art" status among Japanese cuisine is *kaiseki ryouri* (懐石料理, かいせきりょうり), a traditional form of multi-course eating with dozens of ornate dishes, delectable flavors, and myriad textures and colors.

See photos and learn more in this Wikipedia article:
bit.ly/mjkaiseki

Japanese Flower Arranging

Flower arranging may not be on your bucket list, but don't write off *ikebana* (生け花, いけばな) just yet. The Japanese art form, also known as *kadou* (華道, かどう), can actually be a very cathartic practice and provides a simple, low-cost way to beautify your home.

See photos and learn more in this Wikipedia article:
bit.ly/mjwikikebana

Japanese Gardening & Landscaping

Represented best by the quintessential Japanese rock garden, called *karesansui* (枯山水, かれさんすい), Japanese landscaping tends to be very simple and austere, and that is just the point: to represent the "formless, infinite, and unspeakable" with finite gravel, stones, and shrubs.

See photos and learn more in this Wikipedia article: bit.ly/mjwikgardens

Japanese Literature

Japan has produced some of the world's most respected authors, including greats like *NATSUME Souseki* (夏目漱石, なつめそうせき) and *MURAKAMI Haruki* (村上春樹, むらかみはるき). Reading Japanese literature is a wonderful way to improve your reading skills, expand your vocabulary, and gain a deeper understanding of Japanese culture and thinking.

See *Choose Your Weapons > Japanese Books* for my recommended authors and novels.

Japanese Manga

Japanese comics, called *manga* (漫画, まんが), are one of the reasons many Westerners get into Japanese learning in the first place. But even if you are not yet a *manga* fan, I highly recommend giving comics a try given their vivid visuals, gripping storylines, high-frequency vocabulary, and extensive use of *furigana* (振り仮名, ふりがな, "*hiragana* pronunciation guides next to *kanji*").

See *Choose Your Weapons > Japanese Comics* for my recommended series.

Japanese Music

From traditional instruments like the *koto* (琴, こと) and *shamisen* (三味線, しゃみせん), to modern J-Pop (ジェイポップ, じぇいぽっぷ), Japan is home to a wonderfully eclectic mix of music types, most of which you can happily belt out at one of Japan's ubiquitous *karaoke bokkusu* establishments (カラオケボックス, からおけぼっくす, individual rooms that can be rented out with your friends or colleagues).

For recommendations, see *Choose Your Weapons > Japanese Music > Recommended Artists & Bands.*

Japanese Origami

Literally meaning "folded paper," *origami* (折り紙, おりがみ) is one of Japan's most iconic art forms. Most people are familiar with *origami* cranes, and may have even folded a few in lieu of paying attention in class. But the creativity of *origami* goes far beyond simply animals: thanks to complex mathematical models, origami masters can now create highly complex 3-D creations.

See photos and learn more in this Wikipedia article:
bit.ly/mjwikorigami

Japanese Painting

Kaiga (絵画, かいが, "painting") is one of Japan's most prestigious art forms. Not only are Japanese paintings beautiful spectacles to behold in their own right, but they also represent a microcosm of Japanese culture and history. Much like the culture of Japan, *kaiga* integrate a mix of native Japanese ideas with techniques, philosophies, and influences from foreign lands (e.g. China, Europe, etc.).

See photos and learn more in this Wikipedia article:
bit.ly/mjwikaiga

Japanese Poetry

We've all heard of *haiku* (俳句, はいく), Japan's unique 3-line poem style created with five syllables, seven syllables, and five syllables (technically, they're based on phonological units called *mora*, not syllables, but the distinction is something linguists argue about after a few too many glasses of wine and is probably not something you need to worry about). In addition to *haiku*, there are many other Japanese poetry types worth investigating, including *tanka* (短歌, たんか) and *kanshi* (漢詩, かんし). A good place to start your Japanese poetry journey is with the poet *MATSUO Bashou* (松尾 芭蕉, まつおばしょう), considered by many to be the greatest Japanese of poet of all time.

Learn more in this Wikipedia article:
bit.ly/mjwikpoetry

Japanese Pottery, Porcelain & Lacquerware

Japanese *toujiki* (陶磁器, とうじき, "pottery and porcelain") and *shikki* (漆器, しっき, "lacquerware") are adored all over the world. Styles and specific techniques vary from region to region in Japan, which can make for great fun as you travel around the archipelago. But one thing remains constant throughout Japan: unparalleled craftsmanship and quality.

See photos and learn more in this Wikipedia article:
bit.ly/mjwikpottery

NOTE!

The sap used in Japanese lacquerware is poisonous to the touch until it has completely dried.

Japanese Rakugo

Combining comedy and the painful *seiza* (正座, せいざ) position, *rakugo* (落語, らくご) is perhaps the most "Japanese" of all Japanese art forms. Being able to understand the complex, highly nuanced monologues of *rakugo*—and laughing right along with your fellow audience members—should be considered a major milestone in your Japanese studies.

Learn more about rakugo on Wikipedia:
bit.ly/mjwikrakugo

Watch an example on YouTube here:
bit.ly/mjrakugo

Japanese Swordsmithing

Toukou (刀工, とうこう, "swordsmithing") is a sacred art in Japan, complete with a variety of *Shintou* (神道, しんとう, "Way of the Gods") rituals, fiercely guarded craft secrets, and long apprenticeships. A *katana* (刀, かたな, "single-edged sword") can take weeks to construct, with myriad complex steps that must be completed perfectly to ensure the high level of craftsmanship, strength, and sharpness the swords are known for. In addition to unmatched craftsmanship, one of the keys to Japanese blades is their use of *tamahagane* (玉鋼, たまはがね), a special steel made from pure iron sand.

See photos and learn more in this Wikipedia article:
bit.ly/mjwiksword

Japanese Tea Ceremony

Experiencing a Japanese tea ceremony firsthand is a must for any true Japanophile. And no, getting a matcha latte at Starbucks doesn't count! Called *chadou* (茶道, ちゃどう, "The Way of Tea") or *cha no yu* (茶の湯, ちゃのゆ, lit. "hot water for tea"), the highly refined ceremony involves the ceremonial preparation and presentation of *matcha* (抹茶, まっちゃ, "powdered green tea"). The tea is usually accompanied with *wagashi* (和菓子, わがし), extremely sweet

Japanese confections that complement the bitterness of the tea.

See photos and learn more in this Wikipedia article:
bit.ly/mjwiktea

Japanese Theater

There are two major styles of Japanese theater: *nou* (能, のう) and *kabuki* (歌舞伎, かぶき). There is a lot of overlap between the two (especially to the untrained eye and ear), but *noh* is technically considered "music drama" while *kabuki* is considered "dance drama." A third type of theater worth mentioning is *bunraku* (文楽, ぶんらく), a.k.a. *ningyou jouruti* (人形浄瑠璃, にんぎょうじょうるり), which includes the various forms of Japanese puppetry.

See photos and learn more in this Wikipedia article:
bit.ly/mjwiktheater

TRAVEL AROUND JAPAN

"We travel, initially, to lose ourselves; and we travel, next to find ourselves. We travel to open our hearts and eyes and learn more about the world than our newspapers will accommodate. We travel to bring what little we can, in our ignorance and knowledge, to those parts of the globe whose riches are differently dispersed. And we travel, in essence, to become young fools again—to slow time down and get taken in, and fall in love once more." —Pico Iyer

---

Travel is one of the most effective and enjoyable ways to improve your understanding of both the Japanese culture and language. And contrary to popular belief, travel needn't be a prohibitively expensive undertaking, even in relatively high-cost countries like Japan. With enough creativity and compromise, you can travel on even the most meager budget.

Read *Vagabonding* by Rolf Potts

For those wanting to travel long-term and get off the beaten path, I highly recommend *Vagabonding* by Rolf Potts. In his essential guide to long-term, low-cost, self-guided travel, he encapsulates in words what I have long felt but struggled to express to friends who have never lived abroad or traveled for extended periods of time.

Here is a good quote to sum up Rolf's travel philosophy:

"Vagabonding is about using the prosperity and possibility of the information age to increase your personal options instead of your personal possessions. Vagabonding is about looking for adventure in normal life, and normal life within adventure. Vagabonding is an attitude—a friendly interest in people, places, and things that makes a person an explorer in the truest, most vivid sense of the word. Vagabonding is not a lifestyle, nor is it a trend. It's just an uncommon way of looking at life—a value adjustment from which action naturally follows. And, as much as anything, vagabonding is about time—our only real commodity—and how we choose to use it."[47]

Get Lonely Planet's Travel Guide & Phrasebook

There are dozens and dozens of travel guides, books, and sites available today, but Lonely Planet is my favorite. They offer just enough information to be useful, but not so much to take the adventure out of travel. I especially like that they include *kanji* in their Japan guidebook and Japanese phrasebooks (most competing guides use only *roumaji*).

The *Lonely Planet Japan Travel Guide* is available on Amazon here: **bit.ly/mjlpguide**

The *Lonely Planet Japanese Phrasebook & Dictionary* is available on Amazon here: **bit.ly/mjlpphrase**

Try Couchsurfing

Boasting 14 million members in 120,000 cities around the world, the Couchsurfing "hospitality exchange network" offers cash-strapped travelers an affordable way to see the world, while also enabling them to give back to the community by hosting travelers in their *own* homes.

To help build your own reputation on the site and ensure a wider pool of available lodging in Japan, I suggest offering up your own couch to community members while still in your home country. Incidentally, this in itself can be a great way to practice languages right in your home country. In exchange for offering up your guest bedroom, couch, or cot, you open up chances to speak with native Japanese speakers visiting your town. Time permitting, you can even act as their local tour guide, a highly effective, rewarding, context-rich form of language immersion.

Learn more about Couchsurfing, connect with hosts, and up for a free account here: **bit.ly/mjcouch**

NOTE!

Like any social network of its size, there are bound to be some bad apples, but their rating system does a pretty good job of weeding them out and highlighting the best hosts.

Try Housesitting

Housesitting is the perfect win-win: those with pets can find someone to watch their animals and house while they're away, and the housesitter can stay in a nice home without paying for accommodation. Sits can be short (just a few days) to long-term (up to six months). My wife and I actually used this strategy in the final phase of paying off debt: not only did we save a lot of money not paying rent, but we got to make new friends, travel the world for free, and spend time with amazing animals.

The best way to find sits is using TrustedHousesitters. Use this link to get 25% off membership: **bit.ly/mjsits**

Try WWOOFING

For you budding gardeners out there, *World Wide Opportunities on Organic Farms* (or "WWOOF" for short) is a great way to travel the world on the cheap while also learning how to grow sustainable, organic crops, and making friends with other environmentally-conscious travelers.

Learn more about WWOOFING Japan and complete a membership application here: **bit.ly/mjwwoof**

WORK IN JAPAN

Teach English

Teaching English is one of the easiest ways for native English speakers to obtain the income and legal status they need to live in Japan long-term. In addition to the financial incentives, teaching in Japan also provides:

- A valuable window into how languages work. You never truly understand something until you teach it to others.

- An easy way to make friends. Many of my friendships in Japan and Taiwan originated in the classroom. For this (and the next) reason, I recommend that you apply for positions teaching adults, not children.

- A path to better job opportunities. If you excel in your role as teacher, there is a chance that you will receive job offers from your students. These may take the form of lucrative private teaching gigs or even non-teaching positions in multinational corporations!

The only basic requirement to teach in Japan is a Bachelor's degree (in *any* subject) from an accredited institution. A TESOL (Teaching English to Speakers of Other Languages) certificate will likely increase your employment options and improve both the quality and quantity of your classes, but it's certainly not required.

Apply for the JET Programme

JET (short for the "Japan Exchange and Teaching Programme") is the route I chose to get to Japan after graduating from college. There are very diverse opinions about JET, but I personally think it is well worth applying:

- The salary is more than fair, and higher than what most college grads will get back home.
- Work loads are generally quite low (so you have plenty of time to study and practice Japanese).
- You get access to a good support network.

The JET Programme offers two job types, which pay the same but entail significantly different types (and volumes!) of work:

- **ALTs:** *Assistant Language Teachers* are placed in public junior and senior high schools around Japan. Their duties include helping the primary English teacher in the classroom, preparing materials and activities, and participating in school events. One downside is that you may at times feel like you are little more than a human tape-recorder, but you will probably have a fairly light workload, meaning more time to learn Japanese and enjoy Japan.

- **CIRs:** Coordinators of International Relations, called *Kokusai-Kouryuu-In* (国際交流員, こくさいこうりゅういん) in Japanese, are placed in prefectural government offices around Japan. Their duties include interpretation, translation, "native checks" (checking the English translations of professional Japanese translators), and advising ALTs in one's prefecture as a so-called "Peer Advisor."

NOTE!

You can apply to be a CIR directly, or start out as an ALT and then apply to be a CIR if an opening arises. I took the latter route, first teaching English at a rural high school my first year and then working at a prefectural government office my second year. There are pros and cons to each position, but I highly recommend experiencing *both* worlds if possible.

Learn more about the JET Programme, eligibility requirements, and application process here: **bit.ly/mjjet**

Find a Non-Teaching Job in Japan

Although teaching is usually the default route for Westerners wanting to work in Japan, there's no need to limit your search to language related jobs if you have the requisite experience, skills, Japanese ability, and most importantly, connections:

- If you currently work for a multinational company, check and see if they have a branch office in Japan or offer international placements.
- If your Japanese reading comprehension skills are up to the task, you can consider becoming a translator in Japan. Written translation is far easier than spoken interpretation since you have time to look things up.
- Consider starting out in as a Business English teacher, and then leverage relationships you build with executives or business owners to find non-teaching job openings down the road.

For more tips, see Tofugu's post *Tired of Teaching English: A Guide to Your New Career in Japan.* **bit.ly/mjtofugujobs**

WORK FOR A JAPANESE COMPANY AT HOME

If moving to Japan is not an option for you, perhaps you can find work at a Japanese company in your home country "Gung Ho" style.

If you haven't watched the 1986 Michael Keaton classic *Gung Ho*, you can rent it here: **bit.ly/mjgungho**

CULTURE CORNER

The term *gung-ho*, which tends to mean "enthusiastic" in modern English, was borrowed from the Chinese word *gōng hé* (工合), which in turn is an abbreviation of *gōngyè hézuòshè* (工業合作社, "Chinese Industrial Cooperatives"). It was first brought into English via the U.S. Marine Corps during WWII. Why a movie about Japanese car manufacturing uses a Chinese word is beyond me...

Having Japanese colleagues means forty plus hours a week of potential Japanese language practice, and having strong Japanese language and cultural skills will greatly improve your chances of promotion.

Here is a Wikipedia list of Japanese companies with overseas operations: **bit.ly/mjcompanies**

Improve Your Listening Skills

"Spam your brain with listening input." — Sara Maria Hasbun (a.k.a. Miss Linguistic), a linguist, polyglot, and entrepreneur

---

Many people—especially those who have only studied languages in a traditional classroom setting—think that listening is a "difficult" language skill. The truth is that it only *seems* difficult because they haven't practiced listening as much as reading. Whatever we practice, we improve. So if you want to develop strong Japanese listening skills, you have to listen. A lot. Fortunately, there are more ways than ever to do exactly that. Here are seven suggestions.

LISTEN AS YOU DO OTHER ACTIVITIES

The beauty of listening input is that you can improve your Japanese as you do *other* activities you would do anyway:

- Doing chores around the house
- Commuting
- Exercising
- Walking

Just throw in a pair headphones or connect to a Bluetooth speaker, hit play on your device, and "spam" your brain with Japanese as you do the dishes or drive to work.

TIP!

I find listening while walking to be a particularly positive combo. It's good for your language goals *and* your health. Try it everyday for a few months and you will be amazed how *far* you get, both in terms of Japanese progress *and* miles walked!

USE AN AUDIO-BASED LANGUAGE COURSE

Most traditional language courses spend too much time on reading and grammar, with little attention spent to listening and pronunciation. However, there *are* a few good audio-based language courses that focus on developing listening skills and accurate pronunciation instead.

See *Choose Your Weapons > Japanese Audio Courses* for my recommended audio-based Japanese courses.

LISTEN TO JAPANESE PODCASTS

Podcasts are my go-to source of Japanese input. They're free, plentiful, and cover a wide range of interesting topics. I recommend using learner podcasts to get a feel for the ins and outs of the language, but then moving onto podcasts intended for native speakers as soon as possible.

See *Choose Your Weapons > Japanese Podcasts* for recommended podcast apps and shows.

LISTEN TO JAPANESE MUSIC

Music is a wonderful way to immerse yourself in the Japanese language. Not only are the melodies and rhythms pleasurable to the ear, but they also help phrases and patterns stick in our long-term memory.

See *Choose Your Weapons > Japanese Music* for where to find Japanese music and to see my recommended artists.

WATCH JAPANESE VIDEOS

Video is one of the most powerful sources of listening input. The visual component increases context and comprehension, and the compelling storylines keep you coming back for more. From *anime*, to TV dramas, to movies, to online videos, Japanese learners can choose from thousands and thousands of titles.

See *Choose Your Weapons > Japanese Videos* for my recommended anime series, TV shows, movies, and more.

LISTEN TO JAPANESE AUDIOBOOKS

Audiobooks are another great source of listening input. Like with podcasts, they allow you to get valuable listening input in Japanese as you go about other tasks and chores. Though audiobooks might be out of reach for less advanced learners, you can always get the e-book version of the same book to act as a "transcript" and help increase comprehension.

See *Choose Your Weapons > Japanese Books* for recommended audiobook titles and where to find them.

GET DRIVING DIRECTIONS IN JAPANESE

If you change your smartphone display language, you unlock a cool bonus: turn-by-turn directions in Japanese when using Apple Maps or Google Maps.

See *Learn How to Learn > Improve Your Reading Skills > Change Your Device Display Language* for step-by-step instructions.

Improve Your Speaking Skills

"Mazu-wa, oto dashite. Oto dasanakya, ongaku hajimaranai no yo!"
「先ずは、音出して。音出さなきゃ、音楽始まらないのよ！」
("Make noise first. You have to make noise before you can make music.")
—KANEKO Sharon (金子シャロン), *Space Brothers*

In this section, you will learn how to improve your Japanese speaking skills in two key ways:

- Developing more native-like pronunciation.
- Speaking with native speakers as much as possible.

MASTER PRONUNCIATION FIRST

"Half of a good accent is simply a matter of timing. Singers learn pronunciation first, and as a result, we don't have to fight years of bad habits. We learn to parrot words accurately before we have an idea of what they mean, so that we can get onto a stage without embarrassing ourselves. You should do the same. If you wait until later to work on your accent, you will have butchered every word in your vocabulary hundreds (or thousands) of times." —Gabriel Wyner, *Fluent Forever*

One of the most common language learning mistakes I've seen (especially in Japan) is spending lots of time practicing reading, but rarely practicing listening and speaking. This leads to a predictable—but highly unfortunate—outcome: highly literate learners who can read novels but can't understand or participate in even basic conversations. And when they *do* try to speak, their thick accent is extremely difficult to understand.

Do your best to avoid this mistake by focusing on pronunciation from the very beginning, and spending much more time on listening and speaking than reading, especially in the early stages of your journey.

LEARN THE IPA FOR JAPANESE

"We're looking for a way to see what we're hearing and, equally important, what we're *not* hearing. Our eyes are a powerful source of input. If we aren't careful, they can trick our ears into a state of inattention, and inattention can prevent us from learning the patterns we need." — Gabriel Wyner, *Fluent Forever*

I'd like to talk about one of the most underappreciated tools for improving your Japanese pronunciation: **IPA**. No, I'm not talking about India Pale Ale, though slight inebriation certainly can help some overcome the fear of conversing in Japanese. The IPA I am referring to here is the *International Phonetic Alphabet*. I first learned about this powerful phonetic transcription system while studying Linguistics in university, and it has been an indispensable part of my language-learning toolkit ever since. Why is learning IPA helpful?

The IPA Makes Us More Aware of How Words Are *Really* Pronounced

Ideally, we should learn how to speak a language well before we learn how to read and write it. We can then more easily attach spellings and writing conventions to words we already understand and know how to pronounce. In practice, however, we will inevitably get a mix of spoken and written input alongside each other (especially as adult learners). While reading can be a wonderful way to immerse ourselves in our target language, it comes with a potentially problematic side effect: we can pick up bad pronunciation habits when we *think* a word is pronounced one way but it's actually pronounced *another*.

For example, I thought that word "hyperbole" was pronounced "**high**-per-bowl" for YEARS until the proper pronunciation was brought to my attention by a teacher. (Unfortunately for my fragile teenage self-esteem, the error was revealed in front of the entire class!) Almost everyone has a few embarrassing pronunciation mistakes like this, created when we've only encountered a word with our *eyes* and never our *ears*.

But our eyes *can* be our allies when we learn the International Phonetic Alphabet. This is because each IPA symbol can only be pronounced *one*—and *only* one—way. Always.

The IPA Provides Detailed Pronunciation Instructions

Each letter in the IPA is more than a mere symbol. It's actually a mini instruction manual on exactly how to position your tongue, teeth, and lips, and whether your vocal cords should be vibrating or not (think about the difference between “B” and “P”). When you learn the IPA, you realize, for example, that S and Z, K and G, T and D, etc. are all “minimal pairs”: they are all produced in exactly the same “manner of articulation” (the same tongue, lip, and palate positions), and differ only in their “voicing” (vibration of the vocal cords). Cool, right?!

So as you learn the IPA symbols for your target language, you also learn the exact ways you should position your tongue, lips, and teeth to sound more like a native speaker. To that end, I highly recommend watching videos that demonstrate proper mouth positions.

See the *IPA Tools* section for my recommended IPA demonstration videos.

The IPA Helps You Master New Sounds More Quickly

Learning the IPA for your target language will take a bit of time and effort up front, but it will actually *save* you a significant amount of time and effort in the long run. Instead of having to unlearn bad pronunciation habits, the IPA helps you develop accurate pronunciation from the beginning. Instead of guessing or risking false assumptions, you will know exactly how to pronounce any given word you encounter. Moreover, the extra layer of information provided by the IPA improves your awareness and memory (it may seem counterintuitive, but adding complexity and challenge actually *improves* our memory).

IPA Tools

Here are some recommended tools for learning the IPA:

- **International Phonetic Alphabet chart:** The Wikipedia page listed below includes interactive charts to see and hear all of the standard IPA symbols, as well as a downloadable PDF of the revised 2018 chart.

Access the *International Phonetic Alphabet chart* entry on Wikipedia here: **bit.ly/mjwikipa**

- **Handbook of the International Phonetic Association:** This comprehensive guide introduces all IPA symbols, how they're used in various world languages, the alphabet's history, and much more.

Available on Amazon here: **bit.ly/ipahandbook**

FORMATS: KINDLE, PAPERBACK & HARDCOVER | **PAGES:** 216 | **PUBLISHED:** 1999

- **Japanese IPA chart:** The *Japanese Phonology* article on Wikipedia includes detailed, interactive tables for all the sounds used in Japanese. Click any sound to see how it's produced and hear it pronounced aloud.

Access the *Japanese Phonology* article on Wikipedia here: **bit.ly/mjwikphono**

- **Glossika:** The Glossika web app—which is one of the best ways to build fluency—includes IPA transcriptions for all example sentences.

Register for Glossika here: **bit.ly/mjglossika**

PRICE: $30/MO | PLATFORMS: WEB

- **Fluent Forever (YouTube):** Gabriel Wyner is a former opera singer, polyglot, and now the founder of the most crowdfunded app in history: *Fluent Forever*. He has created a useful set of videos on the basic sounds of Japanese as well as the IPA symbols that represent them.

Watch the 4-part series on YouTube here: **bit.ly/mjffipa**

- **Wiktionary:** Dubbed "The Free Dictionary," this open source Wikimedia resource includes detailed definitions and IPA transcriptions for many world languages.

Access the Wiktionary here: **bit.ly/mjwiktionary**

PRICE: FREE | PLATFORM: WEB

RECORD YOURSELF

Much like listening to your voicemail message, recording yourself speaking Japanese may cause some "cringey" moments at first:

"What?! I sound like *that?!*"

But the long-term benefits are well worth the temporary discomfort:

- You can better identify and fix pronunciation mistakes.
- You can share your recordings with tutors for feedback.
- You can better track your progress over time.

Use a Voice Memo App

Here are two ways to record yourself quickly, easily, and for free:

- **Use a voice memo app on your smartphone:** On iOS, you can use the built-in *Voice Memos* app, while on Android, you can install the free *Easy Voice Recorder* app.

Learn more about the iOS *Voice Memos* app: **bit.ly/mjiosvm**
Install the *Easy Voice Recorder* app: **bit.ly/mjandroidvr**

- **Use an audio recorder on your desktop:** On macOS, you use the built-in *Voice Memos* app. On Windows, you can install the free Voice Recorder app.

Learn more *Voice Memos* on macOS: **bit.ly/mjmacvm**
Install the free *Voice Recorder* Windows app: **bit.ly/mjmsvr**

TIP!

To improve audio quality, record somewhere without too much background noise and make sure to use headphones to prevent echoing.

Get Your Pronunciation Corrected

Once you have recorded a Japanese sample, you can then have your Japanese tutor review it for mistakes or areas where you can improve. I recommend using one of the following two tools:

- **SoundCloud Timeline Comments:** Many people use SoundCloud to stream indie music and podcasts, but did you know that it's also one of the most underappreciated pronunciation tools? Using their nifty *Timeline Comments* feature, your Japanese tutor can leave comments and make suggestions at specific seconds of the recording.

Learn more about SoundCloud Timeline Comments here: **bit.ly/mjscc**

- **Dropbox Timestamp Comments:** Dropbox has a similar feature called *Timestamp Comments*, but to use it, the file will need to be hosted in a Dropbox Professional, Business Advanced, Enterprise, or Education account.

Learn more about timestamp comments: **bit.ly/mjdbt**
Sign up for Dropbox here: **bit.ly/mjdropbox**

DON'T WAIT UNTIL YOU FEEL "READY"

"If you wait until you don't make any mistakes you will probably never speak." —Benny Lewis

---

Though I encourage you to generally follow the above order of operations, I encourage you to start practicing your speaking and writing skills before you feel fully "ready." Many adult language learners spend years in an input-only bubble (listening and reading) and never practice output (speaking and writing). They say to themselves, "I just need to learn a *bit* more first, and *then* I will feel comfortable communicating with native speakers."

Sadly, for most, this day never comes. Fear and perfectionism keep them on the sidelines and they never get the practice they need to activate their passive knowledge. Don't let the same happen to you. You cannot learn how to speak unless you *actually* speak. Yes, what you learn from listening and reading can *support* your speaking skills, but it's no substitute for the messy, high-speed, two-way interaction that speaking entails. I know it can be scary at first, but be brave and know that the discomfort is worth the growth it provides.

See my recommended tutoring sites and tools here:
Learn How to Learn > Work with a Tutor

IDENTIFY YOUR GAPS

> "Speaking is a great way to notice the gaps in our language knowledge, and to trigger meaningful input, input with high resonance which improves our language skills." —Steve Kaufmann

Human beings crave and feed off social interaction, and being able to communicate an idea, feeling, or request in Japanese (no matter how few words you happen to know), can be extremely gratifying. This creates a positive feedback loop that pushes you to keep learning more and more of the language.

Output also provides an effective way to see where the "holes" are in the "Swiss cheese" of our Japanese abilities. We often don't know *what we don't know* until we try to say or write something. When we struggle to produce a given word, phrase, or structure, we then know where to focus our efforts. We can go look up a given word or ask a native speaker what phrase they'd use in a given situation. In this way, *output* can actually make our *input* tasks that much more efficient. In the beginning, there may be more holes than cheese, but you'll eventually fill in most of the gaps with enough exposure and practice.

PRACTICE WITH NATIVE SPEAKERS ONLINE

There are no shortages of language learning communities, exchange sites, and tutoring services online today, with more and more popping up every year. And with the advent of free VOIP (voice over IP) services like Skype, you can talk with native Japanese speakers right from your computer or smartphone no matter where you live.

See my recommended tutoring sites and tools here:
Learn How to Learn > Work with a Tutor

ATTEND LOCAL MEETUPS

If you prefer speaking face to face, find a local Japanese language and culture group on Meetup.com, or if you live near a university, see about volunteering to help tutor Japanese exchange students.

Find a language and culture meetup near you:
bit.ly/mjmeetup

PRACTICE ON YOUR OWN

Though it's ideal to practice with native speakers, don't let it be a barrier to starting. In cases where you don't have anyone to talk with, you can always get speaking practice on your own:

- Record an audio memo, journal entry, or video *in Japanese.*

See the *Record Yourself* section for my recommended recording tools.

- Speak to Siri, Google Assistant, or Alexa *in Japanese.*

See the next section for step-by-step instructions to set up Japanese speech input on all your devices.

- Talk to yourself *in Japanese*, whether under your breath or by pretending to be on the phone. Even practicing "speaking" in your head or imagining what you'd say in a certain situation can be helpful.

SPEAK TO YOUR DEVICES IN JAPANESE

Not too long ago, people might have though you were a few cards short of a deck if you asked your phone questions or gave it commands. Nowadays, some people do it all the time. All fears aside about AI and robots taking over the world, speaking to your device in Japanese can be a good way to squeeze in a little extra speaking practice each day. Here now are step-by-instructions for how to set up Japanese speech commands for:

- Siri
- Google Assistant
- Alexa

Speak to Siri in Japanese

To change Siri to Japanese on iOS:

1. Open *Settings* (設定) and tap *Siri & Search* (Siriと検索).
2. Under *Ask Siri* (SIRIに頼む), tap on *Language* (言語).
3. Select *Japanese* (日本語) from the list.
4. Tap *Change Language* (言語を変更).
5. Tap *Siri Voice* (Siriの声) to choose a male (男性) or female (女性) voice.

While it's good to get used to both male and female voices, I recommend choosing your own gender in the beginning so you can practice imitating those speech patterns.

To change Siri to Japanese on macOS:

1. Click the Apple icon in the upper left of the screen and select *System Preferences* (システム環境設定).
2. Click on *Siri* in the fourth row down.
3. Select *Japanese* (日本語) from the *Language* (言語) dropdown menu.
4. Choose a male (男性) or female (女性) voice.

See a list of Japanese Siri commands and questions you can use here: **bit.ly/mjsirijp**

Speak to Google Assistant in Japanese

Whenever you use Google Assistant on Android or Google Home, try speaking in Japanese instead of English. Here's how to change your Google Assistant language.

For Android phones and tablets:

1. Say "OK Google" or hold down the Home button.
2. Tap the compass icon in the bottom right.
3. Tap your profile picture in the top right and then tap *Settings*.
4. Tap *Assistant* then *Languages*.
5. Tap *Add a language* and then select 日本語 (Japanese).

For Google Home:

1. Open the *Google Home* app on your Android device.
2. Tap *Account* in the lower right corner.
3. Depending on your device, tap *Settings* or *More settings > Assistant > Languages*.
4. Tap your current language and then select 日本語 (Japanese).
5. Tap *Save Changes* and then *Yes, Change* to confirm.

See a list of Japanese Google commands and questions you can use here: **bit.ly/mjandroidga**

Speak to Alexa in Japanese

If you switch your Alexa to Japanese, you can ask questions and hear answers right in the language! Here's how:

1. Open the Alexa app on your Android device.
2. Tap the gear icon in the lower right.
3. Tap on the device you want to change.
4. Scroll down and tap *Language.*
5. Tap the dropdown menu and select 日本語 (Japanese).

See a list of Japanese commands and questions you can use here: **bit.ly/mjaap**

Improve Your Reading Skills

Unlike oral communication, which is a natural ability that emerged through human evolution, the written word is a human technology that was independently invented in the Middle East, Far East, and Mesoamerica between six and nine thousand years ago. There is fierce debate as to what culture first invented true writing, but no matter when, where, and by whom it was first created, one thing remains certain: **reading and writing are two of the most useful human tools ever invented!**

Though there are important differences between oral and written language skills, they share one important trait: the more we practice, the better we get. To that end, here are some suggestions on how to maximize your Japanese reading practice. Writing tips are then provided in the section afterwards.

LEARN TO READ KANA

Japanese is a syllabic language with 46 basic syllables. This *single* set of sounds is represented by *two* different alphabets (or more accurately, two *syllabaries*):

- ***hiragana*** (平仮名, ひらがな, lit. "simple *kana*")
- ***katakana*** (片仮名, かたかな, lit. "fragmentary *kana*")

Why, you may wonder, are there *two* writing systems representing the same darn sounds? No, it's not to torment language learners and Japanese children. It turns out that the two syllabaries are used for different linguistic purposes. More on this in the coming pages.

Why You Should Learn Kana

While you can certainly learn how to *speak* Japanese without ever learning to *read* the language, I do think it's well worth the effort to at least learn how to *read* the two syllabic alphabets. Learning how to *write* them is an added bonus, but it's certainly not a mandatory skill (in the modern world, you will mostly write Japanese by typing Roman letters). It should only take you a few days of dedicated effort to develop a functional level of recognition. And once you reach this level, you will then have the power to read all sorts of Japanese content, including children's books and even many teen comic books, since they often have little *hiragana* reading guides next to *kanji*.

Hiragana History

Each *hiragana* symbol is based on the cursive form of particular Chinese characters that carry similar pronunciations. For example:

The hiragana for *a* (あ) is based on the cursive form of 安.

The hiragana for *i* (い) is based on the cursive form of 以.

The hiragana for *u* (う) is based on the cursive form of 宇.

Where & When Hiragana Is Used

Hiragana is used in the following situations:

- **Verb endings:** The "stem" or "root" of most Japanese verbs is written in *kanji*, while its grammatical endings are written in *hiragana*. Technically, this part of a word not written in *kanji* is called *okurigana* (送り仮名, おくりがな, lit. "accompanying letters"). For example:

kaku (書く, かく, "to write") → stem (書) in *kanji* + ending (く) in *kana*

yomu (読む, よむ, "to read") → stem (読) in *kanji* + ending (む) in *kana*

- **Adjective endings:** Just like with verbs, the stem of Japanese adjectives is usually written using *kanji* while the ending is written in *hiragana*. For example:

---

hiroi (広い, ひろい, "wide")

---

utsukushii (美しい, うつくしい, "beautiful")

- **Grammatical particles:** Japanese uses a number of grammatical particles, the vast majority of which are usually written in *hiragana*. For example:

The subject particle *ga* (が)

The topic particle *wa* (は)

- **Uncommon *kanji*:** Words with *kanji* outside the official list of 2,136 "common use characters"—called *hyougaiji* (表外字, ひょうがいじ, lit. "characters from outside the table")— are usually written in *hiragana* instead of *kanji*. For example:

kaeru ("frog") is usually written かえる, not 蛙

- **Kunyomi readings:** Japanese *kanji* have two types of readings: *kunyomi* (訓読み, くんよみ, "readings of Japanese origin") and *onyomi* (音読み, おんよみ, "readings of Chinese origin"). When looking up a character in a dictionary, *kunyomi* are always written using *hiragana*, while *onyomi* are written in *katakana*.

Katakana History

Like *hiragana*, *katakana* (片仮名, かたかな) was also developed from *kanji* characters that carry similar pronunciations. In this case, they are based on individual chunks, not the cursive form of the complete character.

The katakana for *a* (ア) is based on a stylized piece of 阿.

The katakana for *i* (イ) is based on a piece of 伊.

The katakana for *u* (ウ) is based on a piece of 宇.

Where & When Katakana Is Used

The *katakana* syllabary is used as follows:

- **Writing foreign loan words:** Japanese has borrowed thousands and thousands of words from English and other European languages. Such terms are written in *katakana* to distinguish them from words of Japanese or Sino-Japanese origin. For example:

The word "coffee" is written as *kouhii* (コーヒー).

- **Writing foreign names:** Foreign proper nouns (e.g. people, places, businesses, and brands) are also written using *katakana*. For example:

"Microsoft" is rendered as *Maikurosofuto* (マイクロソフト).

- **Sound effects & onomatopoeia:** Japanese comic books usually write sound effects using *katakana*. For example:

Dokan! (ドカン, "Boom!")

- **Onyomi kanji readings:** As mentioned above, *kanji* have two types of readings: *kunyomi* (訓読み, くんよみ) and *onyomi* (音読み, おんよみ). The latter, which represents pronunciations of Chinese origin, is always written in *katakana*.

How To Learn Kana

There are numerous books, apps, and sites to help you learn *kana*. Here are just a few to get you started:

- **How Japanese Works:** I share a detailed overview of *hiragana* and *katakana* in the *How Japanese Works* PDF, including detailed notes on how to properly write and pronounce each syllable.

Download the *How Japanese Works* PDF here:
bit.ly/howjapaneseworks

- **My print-ready kana cheat sheet:** I have created a *kana* cheat sheet to accompany the overview of *hiragana* and *katakana* in the *How Japanese Works* PDF.

Download the print-ready *Kana* PDF here:
bit.ly/mjkana

- **Remembering the Kana: A Guide to Reading and Writing the Japanese Syllabaries in 3 Hours Each.** This useful guide is by James Heisig, the creator of the well-known *Remembering the Kanji* series. It provides a systematic approach to learning Japanese *hiragana* and *katakana* in a mnemonic-based approach that leverages the creative power of adult brains.

Available on Amazon here: **bit.ly/mjrtkana**

FORMAT: PAPERBACK | **PAGES:** 160 | **PUBLISHED:** 2007 | **GOODREADS:** 4/5

- **Scripts by Drops:** The Scripts app, form the makers of the popular *Drops* app, is a beautiful, fun, effective way to learn *hiragana* and *katakana* right on your iOS or Android device using an immersive, game-like approach.

Download the *Scripts* app here: **bit.ly/mjscripts**

PRICE: FREE W/ UPGRADES | **PLATFORMS:** IOS & ANDROID

LEARN TO READ KANJI

Ah yes, the big "K-word." Many language learners dread the thought of conquering *kanji* (漢字, かんじ, lit. "Chinese/Han characters"), but I promise that the journey is not nearly as difficult as you might expect if you choose the right route and tools.

Why You Should Learn Kanji

One of the most common questions I hear from beginning learners of Japanese is:

Why should I learn kanji? Can't I get by with *roumaji* and *kana*?

Learning *roumaji* and *kana* is indeed an essential *first* step in your Japanese journey as it familiarizes you with all of the sounds in the language, allows you type Japanese on your computer or smartphone, and helps you look up words in the dictionary. But neither is a substitute for learning characters:

- While you *can* find some Japanese content written solely in *roumaji* or *kana*, these materials tend to be boring, stilted, and inauthentic. Being able to read *kanji* opens up a massive pool of authentic Japanese content, and there is no better feeling than reading authentic Japanese books, blogs, etc. in the original language.

- Most Japanese restaurants—the kind of thing you fly all the way to Japan for!—write their menus and daily specials entirely in *kanji*-laden Japanese. Sure, you can always point at pictures, but wouldn't you rather be able to read the menu?

- Mastering characters boosts confidence. It takes most native speakers many years (and heaps of tedious rote learning) to learn all standard use characters, and given how hard it was for *them*, it's generally believed that foreign learners of Japanese will have an even *harder* time. But when you use the modern, adult-friendly methods I recommend, you can learn to recognize all the common-use kanji in a matter of months!

Knowing *kanji* also helps prevent ambiguity. Given all the homonyms in Japanese, content written without *kanji* is ripe for potential confusion. Here's one of my favorite such examples from the Tofugu article *Everybody Makes (Embarrassing) Mistakes*:[48]

Pan-tsu-kut-ta-koto-aru?
(パン作ったことある？ "Have you ever made bread?")

Pan-tsu-kut-ta-koto-aru?
(パンツ食ったことある？Have you ever eaten underwear?)

As you can see, the two above sentences have the same exact syllables, as shown in the top *roumaji* line. Obviously, the context will make it clear whether you're asking about making bread or eating underwear, but using *kanji* helps, too!

You will hear many people—including the Japanese themselves—go on and on about how difficult characters are to learn. Yes, just like learning to *speak* the language, learning to read and write Japanese takes time and effort. But the task ahead is not nearly as arduous as you've been led to believe, *if*:

- You focus on the highest frequency characters first.
- You learn the basic character building blocks ("radicals").
- You learn the phonetic and semantic clues radicals provide.
- You use creative mnemonics instead of rote memory.

Apply the "MED" Principle to Kanji

As discussed in the *Maintain the Habit of the Habit* section, the "minimum effective dose" (MED) principle helps prevent wasted time, effort, and energy. We talked about how for boiling water, the MED is 212° F (100° C), and going to a higher temperature doesn't make the water any *more* boiled. Similarly, when it comes to *kanji*, the MED is 2,136 characters, and you will get by just fine knowing these. Yes, there are many more *kanji* than this in existence—approximately 50,000 are listed in the *Dai Kan-Wa Jiten* (大漢和辞典, だいかんわじてん)—but lucky for us, the Japanese Ministry of Education has limited the official number of so-called "common use characters," or *jouyou kanji* (常用漢字, じょうようかんじ), to only the 2,136. Learning this smaller sub-set enables you to read the vast majority of Japanese text you will encounter. Most publications limit themselves to just these characters, using *kana* instead of *kanji* for any word with characters outside the list.

Download my print-ready PDF to see the MOE's entire *jouyou kanji* list: **bit.ly/moekanji**

And I have *even better* news for you! Though you will need to learn all 2,136 *jouyou kanji* to be fully literate, you can cut down your *initial* workload by employing the *80-20 Rule*. A *small* sub-set of highest-frequency characters accounts for a *large* percentage of the *kanji* used in most writing. Consider, for example, the following statistics for Japanese Wikipedia:

- 50% of Japanese Wikipedia is written with just 200 *kanji*.
- 75% of Japanese Wikipedia is written with just 500 *kanji*.

There are many *kanji* frequency lists available online, but most are based on newspapers, meaning that the rankings tend to be skewed toward specialized vocabulary used in business, finance, geography, crime reporting, etc. To create a less biased frequency list, a *Kanji Koohii* forum member named Shang decided to use the whole of Japanese Wikipedia as the text corpus. He then compiled the data in a nifty Google Sheet that includes KANJIDIC reference numbers, as well as *Remembering the Kanji* frame numbers and keywords. (You rock, Shang!)

View the Kanji Frequency in Wikipedia Google Sheet here: **bit.ly/mjwikjpkanji**

NOTE!

Though it makes sense to focus on the highest-frequency words and characters in the beginning, it doesn't mean that you shouldn't also spend time on vocabulary outside of these lists that fits your personal interests and unique learning needs. The guiding light throughout your Japanese journey should be interest. No matter how frequent a given set of words or characters are, they won't stick if you're studying them in isolation or using materials that bore you to tears. Frequency lists are a useful reference point, but the actual learning should come from audio, video, and text content you love.

Get "Radical"

In 1710, the emperor of the Manchu Qing Dynasty, Kāngxī Dì (康熙帝,) decreed the creation of a new and improved Chinese dictionary. Six years later, the Kāngxī Zìdiǎn (康熙字典, "Kangxi Dictionary") was published, a massive tome containing over 47,000 entries. Considering the dictionary's volume of entries, it's not particularly useful for our purposes. The dictionary *did*, however, leave one lasting convention that we can put to good use: the standard 214 *bushu* (部首, ぶしゅ, "kanji radicals").

See the complete list of 214 radicals here:
bit.ly/mjwikrad

Just as 26 letters combine to create tens of thousands of words in English, these 214 graphical building blocks combine to form tens of thousands of Chinese characters.

For example, on its own, 力 is a kanji meaning "power" or "muscle." But if we combine it with the radical 工 (meaning "craft"), we get 功 ("achievement").

Memorizing the meaning, writing, and pronunciation of radicals offers Japanese learners three key advantages:

- **Radicals save you time:** Would you rather have to learn every single stroke in each new character you encounter, or just recognize a relatively small set of familiar chunks?

- **Radicals help you create mnemonics:** Trying to learn *kanji* by pure rote memory is not only tedious, but also highly ineffective. A far more fun and effective way to remember the meaning and writing of characters it to construct vivid mental stories based on its constituent radicals. (More on this method shortly.)

- **Radicals help you guess the meaning and pronunciation of new *kanji* you encounter:** Contrary to popular belief, most Chinese characters are not pictographs. Nearly 90% are actually "pictophonetic" compounds comprised of two chunks, a "phonetic indicator" that points to the character's pronunciation, and a "semantic indicator" relating to its meaning. Though there are plenty of exceptions, these indicators enable you to make educated guesses about a character's pronunciation and meaning even if you're seeing it for the first time. Just make sure to confirm your guesses later when you have a dictionary handy.

Focus on the Highest-Frequency Radicals First

Just as high-frequency *kanji* account for the vast majority of written Japanese, so too do radicals. A small number of the 214 make up a large percentage of the 2,136 common-use characters. The following 6 radicals, for example, make up 25% of all *jouyou kanji*!

- **The "mouth" radical:** 口
- **The "water" radical:** 水 or 氵
- **The "tree" radical:** 木
- **The "person" radical:** 人 or 亻
- **The "hand" radical:** 手 or 扌
- **The "heart" radical:** 心 or 忄 or ⺗

Combined with the above 6 radicals, the following 12 account for 50% of jouyou kanji!

- **The "word" radical:** 言
- **The "sun" or "day" radical:** 日
- **The "thread" radical:** 糸 or 幺
- **The "meat" or "moon" radical:** 肉 or 月
- **The "ground" or "earth" radical:** 土
- **The "road" radical:** 辶
- **The "grass" or "plant" radical:** 艹
- **The "roof" or "crown" radical:** 宀

- **The "shell" or "money" radical:** 貝
- **The "woman" radical:** 女
- **The "village" or "wall" radical:** 阝
- **The "gold" or "metal" radical:** 金

Mind Look-Alike Radicals

When you're just starting to learn Chinese characters, you may find yourself confusing "look-alike" radicals. Not to worry: we all go through this stage! With enough exposure, your brain will get used to differentiating the smallest character details at lightning speed. But to give your brain a head start, take a moment to review some of the common offenders:

亻("person") vs 彳("step")

冫("ice") vs 氵("water")

土("earth") vs 士("scholar")

人 ("man") vs 入 ("enter") vs 八 ("eight")

刀 ("knife") vs 力 ("power") vs 勹 ("wrap")

禾 ("grain") vs 釆 ("distinguish") vs 米 ("rice")

厂 ("cliff") vs 广 ("building on a cliff") vs 疒 ("sickness")

Use "Remembering the Kanji" (RTK)

Remembering the Kanji (or "RTK" for short) was created by Dr. James Heisig. A quick search on the internet will show that RTK has both die-hard fans and vehement detractors. Personally, I think that it's one of the most effective tools for committing the meaning and writing of Chinese characters into long-term memory.

So why I am such a big fan of RTK? Because it leverages ***imaginative memory*** instead of ***visual memory***.

As Heisig points out in the introduction to *Remembering the Kanji*, trying to remember *kanji* using visual memory is like trying to memorize the shifting patterns of a kaleidoscope:

"Picture yourself holding a kaleidoscope up to the light as still as possible, trying to fix in memory the particular pattern that the play of light and mirrors and colored stones has created. Chances are you have such an untrained memory for such things that it will take some time; but let us suppose that you succeed after ten or fifteen minutes. You close your eyes, trace the pattern in your head, and then check your image against the original pattern until you are sure you have it remembered. Then someone passes by and jars your elbow. The pattern is lost, and in its place a new jumble appears. Immediately your memory begins to scramble. You set the kaleidoscope aside, sit down, and try to draw what you had just memorized, but to no avail. There is simply nothing left in memory to grab hold of. The kanji are like that. One can sit at one's desk and drill a half dozen characters for an hour or two, only to discover on the morrow that when something similar is seen, the former memory is erased or hopelessly confused by the new information."[49]

Unless you have a photographic memory (which very few people do), a *visual memory* approach will lead only to frustration and failure. Fortunately, we have a far better cognitive tool at our disposal: *imaginative memory*.

The human brain is much better at remembering *stories* than *images*, so we can use this to our advantage when learning *kanji*. In RTK, you learn how to create vivid, highly memorable stories for each *kanji*, using radicals and useful chunks (what Heisig calls "primitive elements") as the "characters" and "scenes" in your imaginative stories.

As Heisig puts it:

> "The aim is to shock the mind's eye, to disgust it, to enchant it, to tease it, or to entertain it in any way possible so as to brand it with an image intimately associated with the key word. That image, in turn, inasmuch as it is composed of primitive meanings, will dictate precisely how the kanji is to be penned—stroke for stroke, jot for jot."

You may hear some people say that this approach is "childish" or "extraneous," but such folks have obviously not used the book, didn't follow the instructions carefully, or are just masochists who enjoy torturous rote approaches.

Creating effective "imaginative memory" stories can take a little extra time *up front*, but it's well worth the investment *in the long run*. Would you rather spend a single 5 minute session *now* to fuse a character into long-term memory, or have to come back to the character again and again hundreds of times because you didn't spend enough time up front to make an effective story?

Using the RTK approach, a motivated learner can master the meaning and writing of all 2,136 *jouyou kanji* in a matter of *months*, not the many *years* or even *decades* it takes most Japanese children and non-native adult learners using traditional rote methods.

Granted, you will still need to learn how to pronounce each

character and what additional meanings each character may have (a much longer process), but this knowledge will come with sufficient exposure to authentic Japanese. Moreover, gaining the ability to recognize and produce all standard use kanji in such a short period of time provides a massive boost to confidence, unlocks oceans of kanji-based learning materials, and lays a strong, level foundation to build further knowledge upon.

One of the first things you may notice about RTK is that it does not present characters in the standard order prescribed by the Japanese Ministry of Education. This is for good reason.

As Heisig argues:

"If one's goal is to learn to write the entire list of general-use characters, then it seems best to learn them in the order best suited to memory, not in order of frequency or according to the order in which they are taught to Japanese children."

You will also notice that RTK does not include *kanji* etymologies or the original ancient pictographs. This is by design. While these drawings may be fun to look at, they aren't much help in the learning process.

As Heisig explains:

"Pictographs are an unreliable way to remember all but very few kanji; and even in those cases, the pictograph should be discovered by the student by toying with the forms, pen in hand, rather than given in one of its historical graphic forms. For another, the presentation of an image actually inhibits imagination and restricts it to the biases of the artist... The more original work the individual does with an image, the easier will it be to remember a kanji."

Another common complaint about RTK is that it doesn't include the readings of kanji in the first volume. This is *also* by design. Most textbooks and kanji resources teach *all* this information at once, with the assumption that "one is useless without the other." In reality, it's far more efficient to learn one *after* the other, concentrating first on meanings and writings—which is actually the *easier* task—and *then* continuing on to the more complicated task of learning *kanji* readings.

As Heisig puts it:

"One has only to look at the progress of non-Japanese raised with kanji to see the logic of the approach. When Chinese adult students come to the study of Japanese, they already know what the kanji mean and how to write them. They have only to learn how to read them. In fact, Chinese grammar and pronunciation have about as much to do with Japanese as English does. It is their knowledge of the meaning and writing of the kanji that gives the Chinese the decisive edge."

Here are a few quick tips and reminders to get the most out of the RTK approach:

- **RTK is NOT a dictionary:** The book is designed for *learning* Chinese characters, not simply looking them up. That said, it does include an index that helps you find specific *kanji*, primitives, and keywords.

- **Read the introduction:** If you are like me, you usually skip most book introductions and get right to the "meat." That is a mistake with RTK. In the book's introduction, Heisig goes into great detail explaining not only *how* the book works, but *why* it works.

- **Confirm the exact meaning of each keyword:** The foundation of the Heisig system is the single English keyword he has connected with each *kanji*. To ensure that you don't waste time and energy creating a story that conjures up the wrong concepts, make sure to look up any unknown keywords using Wikipedia, Google Image Search, Dictionary.com, etc. Trust me, there will likely be at least a few words you have never heard.

- **Get the free update if you have an older copy:** In 2010, the Japanese government added 196 characters to the official "general-use" list. Pre-2010 versions of *Remembering the Kanji* were actually ahead of the curve and already contained 39 of these additions. But there are still 157 additional characters you will now need to be considered “literate” in Japanese. Fortunately, James Heisig has created a free download to augment older versions of RTK.

Download the free *Newly Approved General-Use Kanji* PDF here: **bit.ly/mjrtknewjyk**

RTK Tools

Here now are my recommended resources for getting the most from the RTK approach:

- **RTK – Volume 1 (6th Edition):** *Remembering the Kanji 1: A Complete Course on How Not to Forget the Meaning and Writing of Japanese Characters* guides you through how to learn the meaning and writing of 2,200 characters, including the basic 1,945 general-use *kanji* made standard in 1981, 196 additional *kanji* added to the general-use list in 2010, and 59 *kanji* frequently used in proper names. Make sure to get the sixth edition if possible or download the free PDF supplement shared above if you get an older used copy.

Available on Amazon here: **bit.ly/mjrtk1**

FORMAT: PAPERBACK & KINDLE | PAGES: 496 | PUBLISHED: 2011 | GOODREADS: 4/5

- **Print-Ready RTK Cheat Sheet:** I have compiled all of the *kanji*, English keywords, and frame numbers from *Remembering the Kanji 1* into a convenient cheat sheet you can use for quick reference, review, or measuring your progress.

Download my print-ready RTK cheat sheet here: **bit.ly/rtksheet**

- **RTK – Volume 2:** The second book in the RTK series, *Remembering the Kanji 2: A Systematic Guide to Reading Japanese Characters*, is designed to teach the various *onyomi* and *kunyomi* readings of Japanese characters in a logical, intuitive, systematic way.

Available on Amazon here: **bit.ly/mjrtk2**

FORMAT: PAPERBACK | PAGES: 416 | PUBLISHED: 2012 | GOODREADS: 4/5

- **RTK – Volume 3:** The third and final volume in the RTK series, *Remembering the Kanji 3: Writing and Reading Japanese Characters for Upper-Level Proficiency*, helps learners master the meaning, writing, and reading of 800 advanced *kanji* needed for university and special fields.

Available on Amazon here: **bit.ly/mjartk3**

FORMAT: PAPERBACK | PAGES: 368 | PUBLISHED: 2012 | GOODREADS: 4/5

- **Official RTK App for iOS:** The *Remembering the Kanji* iOS app is intended as a companion to—not replacement for—the books. It includes all the characters, primitives, keywords, and readings included in RTK 1, 2, and 3, but lacks the explanations, tips, and stories from the books. You can, however, add in any notes or personalized mnemonics as you go.

Download the app here: **bit.ly/mjrtkapp**

PRICE: $9.99 | PLATFORM: IOS

- **Kanji Koohii:** This awesome website allows you to ① create your own "imaginative memory" stories or pick one from the community, ② utilize the "Smart Dictionary" which uses only *kanji* you've already studied, and ③ review using beautiful, SRS-optimized flashcards.

Set up a free *Kanji Koohii* account here: **bit.ly/mjkoohii**

Other Kanji Learning Tools

If RTK is not your "cup of ocha," or you want to supplement it with other tools, here are some of my favorite *kanji* apps and sites.

- **Skritter:** According to their site, Skritter users remember an average of 90.2% of characters learned after 3 semesters, while non-Skritter users only remember 39% after the same period! I love their beautiful, intuitive interface, their use of non-intrusive handwriting guidance, and the integration of "active recall," a method that requires you to actually write each character. This way, you know which characters you truly *know by heart* and which you can simply *recognize* but not yet *produce* from memory.

Try a free demo & download the app here: **bit.ly/skritter**

PRICE: $14.99/MO | PLATFORMS: WEB, IOS & ANDROID

- **Wanikani:** Created by Tofugu, *Wanikani* (鰐蟹, わにかに, lit. "Crocodile Crab") is a beautifully designed *kanji* learning website dashed with enough Koichi-style humor to help the *kanji* medicine go down more smoothly. Like the other resources I recommend, Wanikani makes extensive use of mnemonics and radicals to help you remember *kanji* more easily, as well as intelligent spaced repetition and contextual learning. Their promise is: "2,000 kanji. 6,000 vocabulary words. In just over a year." The first 3 levels are completely free, and then the service is $9 per month thereafter if you want to master all 60 levels.

Sign up for a free account here: **bit.ly/mjwanikani**

PRICE: FREE TO L3 (THEN $9/MO) | **PLATFORM:** WEB

- **Kanji Damage:** I love Kanji Damage's funny, practical, no B.S. approach to *kanji*. Their tagline is "where you can learn 1,700 kanji using Yo Mama jokes." 🤣 I also like that they rank *kanji* in terms of frequency and utility value (not the standard order presented to Japanese children in school), while also cutting out 100 infrequent *kanji* they consider "bogus." The site also does a great job of pointing out "look alike" *kanji* (with useful hints to help you keep them straight) and which *kanji* are used in compounds only.

Sign up for a free account here: **bit.ly/kanjidamage**

PRICE: FREE | **PLATFORM:** WEB

- **Read the Kanji:** Unlike many tools that just drill you on the individual readings of individual characters in isolation, *Read the Kanji* uses complete example sentences to provide context. The site also checks if you know the different readings a particular character can take on when used to express different meanings. For example, whether 家 should be pronounced *uchi* (うち, "my" or "our") or *ie* (いえ, "house") in a given context. You can study *kanji* from all JLPT (Japanese Language Proficiency Test) levels, as well as *yojijukugo* (四字熟語, よじじゅくご, "four-character phrases/idioms").

Sign up for a free trial here: **bit.ly/mjreadtk**

PRICE: $5/MO | PLATFORM: WEB

CHANGE YOUR DEVICE DISPLAY LANGUAGE

Considering how many hours a day most of us spend on our computers and smartphones, changing our device display language to Japanese is a simple but powerful way to increase our exposure to the language as we go through our normal routines. While you will likely encounter a lot of words you don't yet know, you should be able to guess your way through based on your experience using the English interface. Below you will find step-by-step instructions for switching to Japanese on the following platforms:

- iOS
- Android
- macOS
- Windows

And don't worry: if this form of immersion proves too frustrating, I've also included instructions to switch back to English.

 **NOTE!**

The following steps may differ slightly depending on which version of each operating system you are using.

iOS

To change the display language to Japanese on your iPhone, iPad, or iPod touch:

1. Open *Settings.*
2. Tap *General.*
3. Tap *Language & Region.*

4. Tap on the language next to *iPhone Language.*
5. Select 日本語 (Japanese) from the list.
6. Tap *Done* and then *Change to Japanese.*
7. The screen will then turn black and display 言語を設定中 until the process completes.
8. Your phone interface will now be in Japanese, as will any apps that support the language.

To switch back to English:

1. Open 設定.
2. Tap 一般.
3. Tap 言語と地域.
4. Tap on 日本語 to the right of iPhoneの使用言語.
5. Select English (英語) or your preferred language from the list.
6. Tap 完了 and then 英語に変更.
7. The screen will then turn black until the process completes.

Android

To change the display language to Japanese on Android:

1. Open *Settings* by swiping down from the top of the screen and tapping the gear icon.
2. Tap *General Management.*
3. Tap *Language & Input* and then *Language.*
4. Tap *Add a Language.*
5. Tap 日本語.
6. Tap *Set as Default.*

To switch back:

1. Open 設定.
2. Tap 一般管理.
3. Tap 言語とキーボード.
4. Tap 言語.
5. Drag *English* (or your preferred language) to the top of the list.
6. Tap 適用.

macOS

To change the display language on macOS to Japanese:

1. Click the Apple icon in the upper left corner of the screen and then select *System Preferences* from the dropdown list.

2. Click on *Language & Region.*

3. Click the + icon in the lower left below the list of currently installed languages.

4. Select 日本語 — *Japanese* from the list of options and click *Add.*

5. Click *Use Japanese* on the dialogue window that pops up.

6. Restart your computer to make the changes take effect. Your entire operating system will now be in Japanese, as will native macOS apps like Pages, Keynote, Photos, and any third-party apps that support Japanese.

To switch back to English:

1. Click the Apple icon once more and select システム環境設定 from the dropdown list.

2. Click on 言語と地域.

3. Drag *English* (or your preferred language) to the top of the list.
4. Click the red circle in the upper left to close settings.
5. Click on 今すぐ再起動 when the dialog box pops up to restart your computer.

Windows

To change the display language to Japanese on Windows:

1. Open *Settings.*
2. Click *Time & Language.*
3. Click *Language.*
4. Click *Add a preferred language* in the *Preferred languages* section.
5. Search for *Japanese* (日本語) and select it from the results.
6. Click *Next* and then check both the *Set as my display language* and *Install language pack* boxes.
7. Click *Download* and then *Back* once it's finished.
8. Select Japanese (日本語) from the *Windows display language* menu.

USE THE WEB IN JAPANESE

Changing your operating system using the steps above will usually make most websites display in Japanese by default. If not, you can manually change many popular sites to Japanese as follows. And don't worry: if using these websites in Japanese becomes too overwhelming, I've also included step-by-step tips to switch back.

Use Amazon in Japanese

Here's how to use Amazon in Japanese:

1. Click over to the *Amazon Japan* store.

Access Amazon Japan here:
bit.ly/mjamazonjp

---

2. Click the language dropdown menu (located just below and to the right of the search bar).
3. Select 日本語 - *JP*.
4. Click 変更する.

To switch back:

1. Simply click the language dropdown menu again.

2. Select *English - EN.*

3. Click *Save Changes.*

Use Google in Japanese

To learn Japanese through Google, I suggest the following two changes:

- **Search using Google Japan:** Using the Japanese version of Google Search will get you more relevant results for Japanese-specific content and sites.

Access the Google Japan search page here:
bit.ly/mjgooglejp

- **Change your account language to Japanese:** This will change the display language to Japanese for the Google search engine and most Google Apps.

Here's how to change your Google display language:

1. Open your Google Account (sign in first if needed).

Access your Google Account page here:
bit.ly/mjgoogleact

2. Click *Data & personalization* in the left panel.

3. Click on *Language* under *General preferences for the web* (you have to scroll down a little ways first).

4. Click the pencil icon next to your current/default language.

5. Search for *Japanese*, click on 日本語 (Japanese), and then click *Select*.

To switch back:

1. Open your Google Account page again.

Access your Google Account page here:
bit.ly/mjgoogleact

---

2. Click データとカスタマイズ in the left panel.

3. Click on 言語 under ウェブ向けの全般設定.

4. Click the pencil icon next to 日本語.

5. Search for *English* (or your preferred language), select that language from the list, and then click 選択.

If your preferred language is already displayed under *Other languages you understand* (理解できるその他の言語), you can simply click the up arrow until it gets to the top under *Default language* (既定の言語).

To change only the language of Google Search:

1. Click over to the Google Search home page.

Access the Google Japan search page here:
bit.ly/mjgooglejp

2. Click *Settings* in the lower right corner.
3. Select *Search Settings* from the popup menu.
4. Click *Languages* from the list on the left.
5. Check the radio button next to 日本語.
6. Click *Save* and then *Okay.*

Use Facebook In Japanese

To change your Facebook account language online:

1. Click the arrow icon in the upper right corner.

2. Click *Settings* in the dropdown.
3. Click *Language* in the left column.
4. Click *Edit* in the *Facebook language* row.
5. Select 日本語 from the dropdown menu under *Show Facebook in this language* (it's near the bottom).
6. Click *Save Changes.*

To switch back:

1. Click the arrow icon in the upper right again.
2. Click 設定 in the dropdown.
3. Click 言語 in the left column.
4. Click 編集する in the *Facebook*の言語 row.
5. Select *English* (or your preferred language) from the dropdown under この言語で*Facebook*を表示する.
6. Click 変更を保存.

Use Wikipedia in Japanese

Wikipedia is a language learner's paradise. Not only can you learn everything you could possibly ever wish to know about Japanese language, culture, history, etc., but you can also get highly contextual input in three key ways:

- Use Japanese Wikipedia.
- Read articles in Japanese.
- Switch the interface to Japanese.

To access Japanese Wikipedia:

1. Navigate over to Japanese Wikipedia (ウィキペディア).

Access Japanese Wikipedia here:
bit.ly/mjwikjp

2. Browse Japanese articles on the homepage, including 選り抜き記事 ("Featured Articles"), 新しい記事 ("New Articles"), and 今日は何の日 ("On This Day").
3. Search for specific Japanese articles within the search field (Wikipedia内を検索).

To change a specific article to Japanese:

1. Look for *Languages* in the left column.
2. If Japanese is available, you will see 日本語 in the list of options.
3. Click 日本語. You will now be able to read the same article in Japanese!
4. To switch the article back, simply select *English* (or your preferred language) in the left column under *In Other Languages* (他言語版).

You can also change the Wikipedia display language to Japanese as follows:

1. Log in or create a free Wikipedia account.

You can create a free Wikipedia account here:
bit.ly/mjwika

---

2. Click the gear icon next to *Language* in the left column to reveal the *Language Settings* window.
3. With the *Display* tab selected, click on 日本語.
4. Click on 設定を適用.

To switch back:

1. Click the gear icon next to 他言語版 in the left column to reveal the 言語の設定 window.
2. With the 表示 tab selected, click *English* (or your preferred language).
3. Click *Apply Settings.*

CAPTURE & STUDY ONLINE CONTENT

Finding online Japanese content is only the first step. To make the most of your online materials, you then need a system for saving, organizing, and studying that content. Here are some suggested tools.

Instapaper

Instapaper is my go-to service for saving blog posts, online articles, song lyrics, videos, etc. that I want to read or study later. I especially like the following features:

- You can save content with one click using the Instapaper browser extension.

Install the Instapaper extension for Chrome here:
bit.ly/mjipext

- Instapaper automatically strips away ads, sidebars, and other distracting content so you can focus on just the article.
- You can highlight text, add comments, or save "textshot" images for sharing longer passages where there are character limits (e.g. Twitter).
- You can organize articles into different folders.
- Instapaper automatically syncs your content between all of your devices.

Sign up for a free account here: **bit.ly/mjinstapaper**

PRICE: FREE W/ UPGRADES | **PLATFORMS:** WEB, IOS, ANDROID & KINDLE

LingQ

LingQ (pronounced "link") is a language learning system and community created by the polyglot Steve Kaufmann. The main focus of LingQ is getting extensive listening and reading input in your target language, though they do also offer language tutoring and writing correction.

Sign up for a free LingQ account here: **bit.ly/mjlingq**

Benefits of LingQ include:

- **An extensive article library:** LingQ has a wide collection of articles to choose from, most of which include both text and audio.
- **The ability to import your own content:** In addition to LingQ's library of free Japanese articles, you can also import your own content from blogs, emails, and now even Netflix subtitles!

Install the free LingQ Importer extension for Chrome here: **bit.ly/mjlingqimport**

- **Use of spaced repetition:** LingQ uses a spaced repetition system to automatically schedule reviews of your LingQs.
- **Apps for iOS & Android:** Take your "LingQing" on the go with the LingQ mobile apps.

Download the LingQ app here: **bit.ly/mjlingq**

PRICE: FREE W/ UPGRADES | **PLATFORMS:** WEB, IOS & ANDROID

Learning With Texts

Learning with Texts, or "LWT" for short, is a free, open-source tool for saving and studying online language content. While LWT lacks the lesson library, tutors, and community of LingQ, the core functionality is similar.

Here's how to use LWT:

- Download and install the free software.

Download LWT here: **bit.ly/mjlwtexts**

PRICE: FREE (OPENSOURCE) | PLATFORMS: MACOS, WINDOWS, LINUX

- Paste in any Japanese text you wish you to read.
- Add an audio URL if you have one (e.g. for podcasts).
- Look up and save new words or phrases you come across.
- Test yourself using LWT's built-in flashcards.

Feedly

Most blogs have RSS feeds which let you automatically download any new articles as soon as they are available. Feedly is a free service that lets you easily find and manage feeds all in one convenient package. You can use it online, download one of their many apps, or set up an integration with other popular tools.

Sign up for a free Feedly account here: **bit.ly/mjfeedly**
Download the Feedly app: **bit.ly/mjfeedlyapps**

READ WHAT YOU WANT!

"There is massive evidence that self-selected reading, or reading what you want to read, is responsible for most of our literacy development. Readers have better reading ability, know more vocabulary, write better, spell better, and have better control of complex grammatical constructions. In fact, it is impossible to develop high levels of literacy without being a dedicated reader, and dedicated readers rarely have serious problems in reading and writing." —Stephen Krashen, Professor Emeritus, University of Southern California

---

One of the greatest advantages of *Anywhere Immersion* over traditional language classes is that it affords you to freedom to read exactly *what* you want, *when* you want, and *where* you want. Instead of forcing yourself through boring textbooks, contrived dialogues, or stuffy literature, you can instead choose reading content that fits your interests and tickles your curiosity.

Read Japanese Movie Captions

You may be surprised to see movies mentioned here in a section about *reading*. Though we usually think of movies as a source of *listening* input, the truth is that Japanese captions can transform movies and television into a powerful form of *reading* input, too. The key here is to make sure that you are using captions in your target language, not your first. The latter—technically referred to as *subtitles* (as opposed to captions)—can be useful for increasing comprehension, but will obviously *not* help improve your Japanese reading skills.

See *Choose Your Weapons > Japanese Videos* for recommended movies and shows.

Read Japanese Blogs

Blogs are a great way to get short, interesting reading input on a wide range of subjects. Writing tends to be less formal, which can be a good *or* bad thing depending on your goals (personally, I find it useful to see how people *really* write, not just how stuffy grammar mavens *wish* they did).

Check out this collection of Japanese blogs on travel, food, and culture from FluentU: **bit.ly/mjcultureblogs**

Read Japanese Social Media Posts

Though Facebook, Instagram, Twitter, etc. can be distracting and addictive, they can *also* be a powerful source of Japanese input if used correctly. The key?

- Use the platforms *in* Japanese. By changing your interface language, you get useful reading input each time you use the apps or sites.

See *Learn How to Learn > Improve Your Reading Skills > Change Your Device Display Language* and *Use the Web in Japanese.*

- Follow teachers and native speakers to get authentic Japanese content in your feeds. Here are a few recommendations to get you started:

On Instagram, follow Miku (@miku_real_japanese):
bit.ly/mjmikuinsta

On Twitter and YouTube, follow Dogen (@dogen):
bit.ly/mjdogen

Read Japanese Comic Books

Japanese comic books—called *manga* (漫画, まんが)—are one of the best sources of reading input for language learners thanks to their highly visual style, immersive storylines, and use of *furigana* (振り仮名, ふりがな, "little *hiragana* reading guides next to *kanji*"). If you have never read any Japanese comic books, I suggest starting with a popular series such as *One Piece* (ワンピース).

For more recommended *manga*, see *Choose Your Weapons > Japanese Comics*.

Read the News in Japanese

If reading the newspaper (whether in print or online) is part of your daily routine, why not get your news in Japanese instead? Many Japanese newspapers have free web versions, which give you the added benefit of being able to use pop-up dictionaries like *Rikaikun*.

See my recommended Japanese newspapers here: *Choose Your Weapons > Japanese Newspapers*

Read Japanese Magazines

Japanese magazines are another great source of reading input, which provide a good stepping stone to longer formats like books and novels. Moreover, the frequent inclusion of photos, charts, etc. make them highly comprehensible.

For more recommendations, see *Choose Your Weapons > Japanese Magazines.*

Read Graded Readers & Bilingual Texts

Jumping right into authentic Japanese content can be a little tough for beginning learners, but there are a number of graded Japanese readers and bilingual texts that can help ease your way into full Japanese literacy.

See my recommended graded readers & bilingual texts here: *Choose Your Weapons > Japanese Books*

Read Japanese Novels

Japanese novels can be a great way to take your reading skills to the next level. You can read Japanese classics like *Wagahai wa Neko de Aru* (吾輩は猫である, わがはいはね

こである, "I Am a Cat") by *NATSUME Souseki* (夏目漱石, そうせきなつめ), modern works like *Ichi-Kyuu-Hachi-Yon* (いちきゅうはちよん, "1Q84") by *MURAKAMI Haruki* (村上春樹, むらかみはるき), or Japanese translations of popular English books like *Harry Potter* (ハリー・ポッター).

For more recommended Japanese novels, see *Choose Your Weapons > Japanese Books*.

READ AS YOU LISTEN

Whenever possible, try to find Japanese materials that have both audio *and* text. That way, you can strengthen your listening and reading skills simultaneously and build stronger connections between the spoken and written word.

Find Podcasts With Transcripts

When possible, choose podcasts with transcripts so you can read along as you listen.

See my recommended Japanese podcasts here: *Choose Your Weapons > Japanese Podcasts*

Get Both the Audio & Ebook Versions of Books

Most popular books are available in both audiobook and ebook format. When possible, get both formats so you can read along as you listen.

See my recommended audiobooks here:
Choose Your Weapons > Japanese Books

Get Books With Audio Companions

Some Japanese books (e.g. graded readers) come with companion audio CDs so you can listen along to the dialogues or stories. When searching for Japanese books, keep your eyes peeled for the following two words:

- CD付 (lit. "CD Included")
- 朗読CD (lit. "Recitation CD")

See my recommended Japanese books with audio CDs here:
Choose Your Weapons > Japanese Books

JOIN A READING CHALLENGE

For the more competitive learners among us, reading challenges are great way to maximize motivation and increase the number of books we read per year.

Join a Japanese LingQ challenge here:
bit.ly/mjlingqchallenge

Join the Goodreads annual reading challenge here:
bit.ly/mjgrchallenge

Improve Your Writing Skills

"It ain't whatcha write, it's the way atcha write it." —Jack Kerouac

In this section, you will learn:

- Why you should learn how to write in Japanese.
- How to install Japanese keyboards on your smartphone and computer.
- How to type in Japanese with the English alphabet.
- How to enter Japanese using handwriting on your touchscreen or trackpad.
- How to improve your Japanese handwriting by learning proper stroke order and calligraphy principles.
- Ways to integrate Japanese writing practice throughout your day (e.g. journalling, texting native speakers, meeting notes, and grocery lists).
- Why and how to get your writing corrected by native speakers.
- Why and how to imitate good Japanese writers.

WHY YOU SHOULD LEARN HOW TO WRITE IN JAPANESE

Learning how to write in Japanese offers many advantages to language learners:

- You can quickly look up Japanese words in dictionary apps and sites.
- You can more easily search for Japanese resources online.
- You can practice your writing and connect with friends by writing emails or text messages in Japanese.
- You can maintain a Japanese progress blog, which is a great way to increase accountability and ensure steady progress.
- You can solidify the vocabulary and structures you've seen while reading.
- Like speaking, it helps show where your gaps are in the language. Nothing reveals holes in your vocabulary like having to write things out!

INSTALL JAPANESE KEYBOARDS

Below you will find detailed, step-by-step instructions for adding a Japanese keyboard on the following mobile and desktop platforms:

- iOS
- Android
- macOS
- Windows

iOS

To add a Japanese keyboard on iOS:

1. Open *Settings* (設定).
2. Tap *General* (一般) and then *Keyboard* (キーボード).
3. Tap *Keyboards* (キーボード) and then *Add New Keyboard* (新しいキーボードを追加).
4. Scroll down and tap on *Japanese* (日本語).
5. Tap on *Romaji* (ローマ字).
6. Tap *Done* (完了).
7. If you want to change the order of your keyboards, tap

Edit (編集) and then drag *Japanese – Romaji* (日本語 – ローマ字) to the top.

To use the keyboard:

1. Make sure you are in a textfield, message, email, etc. to reveal the iOS keyboard.
2. Hold down the globe icon to the left of the spacebar.
3. Slide up to *Japanese – Romaji* (日本語 – ローマ字).

Android

To add a Japanese keyboard on Android:

1. Install the *Gboard* app.

Download the free Gboard app from the Google Play Store here: **bit.ly/mjgboard**

---

2. Tap within any text field (e.g. a new Gmail message).
3. Tap *Open features menu* > at the top of the keyboard.
4. Tap *More* ··· and then the gear icon.
5. Tap *Languages* and then *Add keyboard*.

6. Pick 日本語 (Japanese) from the list.
7. Tap Done.

To switch to the Japanese keyboard:

1. Tap within any text field.
2. Hold down the globe icon at the bottom of your keyboard.
3. Select 日本語 (Japanese).

macOS

To add a Japanese keyboard on macOS:

1. Click the Apple icon and select *System Preferences* (システム環境設定).
2. Click on *Keyboard* (キーボード).
3. Select *Input Sources* (入力ソース).
4. Click on the plus sign below the list of currently installed keyboards.
5. Select *Japanese* (日本語) from the list.
6. Click *Add* (追加).

You can then activate the Japanese keyboard in one of two ways.

- **Option 1:** Click on the flag icon in the upper right of the screen (next to the time) and select *Hiragana* (ひらがな) from the dropdown list. To switch back, click the flag again and select the keyboard you want from the list.
- **Option 2:** Use the following keyboard shortcut to cycle through to *Hiragana* (ひらがな) or back to English.

---

^ (Control) + Spacebar

Windows

To add a Japanese keyboard on Windows:

1. Click or tap the Windows symbol in the lower left corner.
2. Search for *Control Panel* and then select the app.
3. Click *Add a Language* under *Clock, Language, and Region.*
4. Click the *Add a language* tab.
5. Scroll down to *J* and click the 日本語 (Japanese) box.
6. Click *Add.*

You can then switch between English and Japanese input in one of two ways:

- **Option 1:** Hold down the following keyboard buttons at the same time:

Windows button + spacebar

- **Option 2:** Right-click on the current language in the bottom right of the toolbar (shown with *A* or あ).

HOW TO TYPE IN JAPANESE

Though writing by hand on paper has its advantages, learning to enter Japanese text on your computer and smartphone is a must for participating in the modern world and making the most of digital learning tools and resources.

Once you have set up Japanese input on your device, typing Japanese is simply a matter of spelling words out in *roumaji* and then choosing the right *kana* or *kanji*.

1. **Type in *roumaji*:** Type out the word, phrase, or sentence you want in *roumaji*. For example, if you want to write the word *taberu* (食べる, たべる, "to eat"), key in:

---

t-a-b-e-r-u

---

2. **Hit the space bar:** After typing in the correct *roumaji*, hit the space bar to bring up *kanji* options. You may also see a drop-down of suggested words that you can click on. If the first suggestion is not correct, keep hitting space until you find the right *kanji*.

3. **Hit enter:** If you type *t-a-b-e-r-u* and hit the spacebar, 食べる should show up right at the top of the list. Just hit enter to go on to the next word. However, if you need to choose different options for multiple words in a phrase or sentence, hit space until you find the character you want, then hit enter to go on to the next. Rinse and repeat until you are done with your sentence.

For the most part, you can just type in the same letters used in the standard *roumaji* chart to write most Japanese words. However, there are some important exceptions and quirks to keep in mind:

- To make double-long *a* (あ), *i* (い), *u* (う), *e* (え), and *o* (お), just type an additional *a*, *i*, *u*, *e* or *o* when typing. For example, to type お母さん (おかあさん, "mother"), enter:

---

o-k-a-a-s-a-n

- The only exception to this is the long *o* sound represented by the hiragana *u* (う). In this case, you have to type the letter *u* after the first vowel to get the right *kana* to appear. This is one of the reasons I have typed *roumaji* this way in the book instead of employing the superscript line usually used in Hepburn Rōmaji. To type 東京 (とうきょう, "Toukyou"), for example, you would enter:

---

t-o-u-k-y-o-u

- To type little vowels like ァ, ィ, ゥ, ェ, or ォ, simply type an x in front of the roumaji for that *katakana*. On Windows, you can also type the letter L. For example, to type サンティアゴ ("Santiago"), which has a small ィ, you type:

---

s-a-n-t-e-x-i-a-g-o or *s-a-n-t-e-l-i-a-g-o*

- To type double consonants, indicated in *kana* with a small *tsu* (っ, ッ), just type the same consonant twice in a row. For example, to type 結婚 (けっこん, "marriage"), you would enter:

---

k-e-k-k-o-n

- For a double consonant falling before *shi* (し, シ) or *chi* (ち, チ), enter an extra S or T respectively before typing *shi* or *chi*. For example, to type 発信 (はっしん, "dispatch"), you would enter:

---

h-a-s-s-h-i-n

- To type ぢ in *hiragana* or ヂ in *katakana*, you enter *d-i*, **not** *j-i*. Similarly, you enter *d-u*, **not** *z-u*, to type づ in *hiragana* or ヅ in *katakana*. For example, to type 続ける (つづける, "to continue"):

---

t-s-u-d-u-k-e-r-u

USE HANDWRITING INPUT

Though typing Japanese is far faster, there *are* times when handwriting can be a useful way to enter text on your device. For example, if you encounter a *kanji* character you want to look up but don't know how to pronounce, you won't be able to type it using *roumaji*. Fortunately, you can instead write out the *kanji* using your touch screen or trackpad. Here's how.

iOS: Japanese App

Unfortunately, Apple does not (yet) have a Japanese handwriting input option within the standard keyboards. But there is a simple workaround: using the handwriting input within the free Japanese dictionary app. Here what to do:

1. Download the Japanese dictionary app from the Apple App Store.

Here is a direct link to download the app:
bit.ly/mjiosjapanese

---

2. Open the app and tap in the search field.

3. Tap on the hand icon (center tab).

4. Write out the *kanji* by hand.

5. Select the one you want from the option above the box.

6. You can then copy and paste the *kanji* into other apps as needed.

iOS: Chinese Handwriting Keyboard

While iOS lacks a handwriting keyboard for Japanese, they *do* have one for Chinese. Here's how to use this option:

1. Open *Settings* (設定).

2. Tap *General* (一般) and then *Keyboard* (キーボード).

3. Tap *Keyboards* (キーボード) and then *Add New Keyboard* (新しいキーボードを追加).

4. Select *Chinese (Traditional)* or 中国語 (繁体字).

5. Select *Handwriting* (手書き).

6. Tap *Done* (完了).

To use the Chinese handwriting keyboard:

1. Make sure you are in a textfield, message, email, etc. to reveal the iOS keyboard.

2. Hold down the globe icon to the left of the spacebar.

3. Slide up to 繁體手寫 and release.

4. Draw the character and select the one you want from the menu of options above the box.

This doesn't work 100% of the time since there are some differences in writing between Traditional Chinese characters and modern Japanese *kanji*. However, it works enough of the time to be useful.

macOS

Here's how to enter kanji using the trackpad on your Mac. First, you need to turn on Trackpad Handwriting as follows:

1. Click the Apple icon and select *System Preferences* (システム環境設定).

2. Click on *Keyboard* (キーボード).

3. Select *Input Sources* (入力ソース).

4. Click on the plus sign below the list of currently installed keyboards.

5. Select *Chinese, Traditional* or 中国語（繁体字) from the list on the left and then *Trackpad Handwriting* (トラックパッド手書き認識) from the list on the right.

6. Click *Add* (追加).

You can then activate Trackpad Handwriting in one of two ways.

- **Option 1:** Click on the flag icon in the upper right of the screen (next to the time) and select *Trackpad Handwriting* from the dropdown list. To switch back, click the flag again and select the keyboard you want from the list.
- **Option 2:** Hold down the following keys at the same time to bring up the *Trackpad Handwriting* input field. Type the same combination to turn it off.

⇧ (Shift) + ^ (Control) + Spacebar

To enter a character using the *Trackpad Handwriting* input field:

1. Write the character on the trackpad.
2. Select the correct character from the list of options above the box by tapping on that part of the trackpad.
3. If you mess up or choose the wrong character, tap the backspace button in the upper right.

Android: Google Handwriting Input

The easiest way to enter Japanese by hand on Android is the free *Google Handwriting Input* app. Once installed, you can customize your settings (e.g. changing or disabling the auto-selection timing) as follows:

1. Open *Settings.*
2. Tap *Language & Input.*
3. Tap *Google Handwriting Input.*

Download the app here: **bit.ly/mjghwapp**

PRICE: FREE | PLATFORM: ANDROID

IMPROVE YOUR JAPANESE HANDWRITING

Learn the Proper Stroke Order

In the beginning, just remembering what a particular character means and what strokes go where is the priority. But don't underestimate the importance of learning proper stroke order. Being able to write the correct stroke order has many advantages:

- Using the proper stroke order helps ensure more

attractive, well-balanced *kanji*, where as improper order is one of the common causes of *Ugly Character Syndrome.*

- Proper stroke order is required to use handwriting input on your smartphone screen or computer trackpad. This input method is especially useful in cases when you know what a character looks like but not how it's pronounced.

While there are some exceptions, Chinese characters generally follow a finite set of stroke order rules:

- Top to bottom.
- Left to right.
- The first 2 strokes of square enclosures go first, then the contents, then the bottom.
- For *kanji* with bottom enclosures, write the content first, then the enclosure.

Learn Japanese Calligraphy

Whether you are interested in *shodou* (書道, しょどう, "calligraphy") as an art form or not, I highly recommend that you learn at least the basics for the sake improving your overall Japanese writing skills:

- **Calligraphy reinforces proper stroke order:** Knowing

the proper stroke order will make your life much easier in the long run (for the many reasons we just discussed), even if it requires some extra effort in the short-term.

- **Calligraphy helps you write attractive, well-balanced *kanji*:** Learning to write Chinese characters well will bring a surprising amount of praise your way. And just like Western graphologists, many Japanese people will draw connections between your *written characters* and your *inner character*.

- **Calligraphy is good for your mind, body, and soul:** Calligraphy can be extremely cathartic, providing a similar meditative effect as practicing Taichi or yoga.

TEXT WITH NATIVE SPEAKERS

Most of us already text with friends and family throughout the day, so why not repurpose the habit for learning Japanese? Here are some tools for texting with native Japanese speakers.

HelloTalk

The *HelloTalk* app allows you to practice writing and communicating with native speakers around the world. You can search for Japanese speakers by location and then interact via text or voice.

Here are some of my favorite features:

- **Correction of mistakes:** Your friends can help correct your language usage right in the app.
- **Text-to-voice:** If you can't read a given message or want to hear how it sounds pronounced, you can use the voice-to-text feature to hear it spoken aloud.
- **Voice-to-text:** Conversely, if you can't understand an audio message you receive, you can use the voice-to-text feature to convert the audio to text.
- **Favorites:** You can save any words, sentences, audio files, corrections, etc. that you'd like to review later.

Download the HelloTalk app here: **bit.ly/mjhello**

PRICE: FREE | PLATFORMS: IOS, ANDROID

LINE

You might not have heard of LINE (ライン) before, but it is in fact one of the most popular messaging apps in Japan. It has lots of great built-in features, including:

- Free messaging anywhere in the world (as well as free voice and video calls, too!).

- Free apps for all the major platforms, including iOS, macOS, Android, and Windows.
- 10,000 stickers and emoticons to spice up your messages.

Download the free LINE app here: **bit.ly/mjline**

PRICE: FREE | PLATFORMS: IOS, ANDROID, MACOS, WINDOWS

JOURNAL IN JAPANESE

Journalling in Japanese is perhaps the best way to create a sustainable daily writing habit:

- It's a great "minimum viable habit" that you can commit to everyday.
- You can do it anytime, anywhere.
- It helps you track your progress, identify mistakes, and consolidate your learning.

Use Prompts From the 5-Minute Journal

You can write whatever you want in your journal, but I highly recommend using the following prompts from *The 5-Minute Journal* since the blank page can be rather intimidating.

- Answer the following three questions first thing in the morning:

"What am I grateful for?"
ありがたいと感じていることは？

"What will I do to make today great?"
今日を素晴らしい日にするためにできることは？

"Daily Affirmation: I am..."
どんな自分になりたいか？

- Then answer the following two prompts before bed:

"What were 3 amazing things that happened today?"
今日起こった素晴らしい出来事を３つ

"How could I have made today even better?"
今日をより素晴らしい日にするためにするべきだったことは？

Try to write down at least a phrase for each. In the early

stages of your Japanese journey, you can even write in English but write down individual Japanese words you've learned. The key here, as always, is *progress*, not *perfection*.

Get a Journal App

While journalling by hand has its advantages, writing in a journal app is more ideal for our purposes:

- You can more easily share what you've written with a tutor or the Lang-8 community for correction.

See *Learn How to Learn > Improve Your Writing Skills > Get Your Writing Corrected* for tips on using Lang-8.

- You can more easily review past entries. I especially enjoy reading "On This Day" entries from years past.

For iOS & macOS, try *Day One*: **bit.ly/mjdayone**
For Android & Windows, try *Journey*: **bit.ly/mjjourney**

TAKE NOTES IN JAPANESE

Taking notes in Japanese offers many benefits to language learners:

- It provides valuable writing practice throughout your day without having to schedule special practice time.
- It makes soul-sucking meetings or classes a *little* more bearable and a *lot* more useful.
- It creates a quasi-secret code that lets you write thoughts and ideas more discretely (assuming you don't live in Japan and aren't sitting next to someone who can read Japanese).

While typing up notes on your computer will make them easier to share for correction, this is one case where I highly recommend writing by hand:

- It's less distracting to your fellow colleagues or classmates.
- It engages more of your brain and will help improve your retention of the meeting or class content.

For more on note taking, see *Learn How to Learn > Optimize Your Memory > Take Good Notes & Review Them Frequently.*

WRITE SHOPPING LISTS IN JAPANESE

Off to buy some groceries? Write out your list in Japanese! This is a great way to familiarize yourself with the Japanese terms you will need day-to-day. Here are some good places to find grocery-specific vocabulary.

Drops App

The gorgeous, gamified Drops app is a great way to learn grocery vocabulary. They have an entire section of professionally curated vocabulary just about food, with intuitive graphics and professionally recorded audio.

Download Drops here: **bit.ly/mjdrops**

PRICE: FREE W/ UPGRADES | **PLATFORMS:** IOS & ANDROID

Tuttle's Japanese Picture Dictionary

Tuttle's *Japanese Picture Dictionary* includes 1,500 high-frequency words and phrases, including an entire section dedicated to groceries, including many Japanese-specific grocery terms.

Available on Amazon here: **bit.ly/mjpictdict**

FORMAT: HARDCOVER | **PAGES:** 96 | **PUBLISHED:** 2019

START A JAPANESE LANGUAGE BLOG

Starting a blog about your Japanese language learning journey is a great way to practice writing, apply what you're learning, track your progress, get encouragement from other learners, and increase accountability.

For more on blogging, see *Master Your Day > Put Your Money & Reputation on the Line > Create Public Accountability.*

GET YOUR WRITING CORRECTED

Getting your writing corrected by native speakers will significantly accelerate the learning process and help eliminate mistakes before they become bad writing habits. You can ask a Japanese friend or tutor to look your writing over, or better yet, use Lang-8, a completely free online community where you barter correction of your Japanese by correcting writing samples submitted by those learning your native language.

Sign up for a free Lang-8 account here:
bit.ly/mjlang8

IMITATE GOOD WRITERS

My last tip for improving your writing—whether in Japanese *or* your native language—is imitating good writers. Find an author you like, read their work closely, and try to imitate their style, structure, word choice, etc. as closely as possible. It may seem silly or uncreative to imitate, but this is actually how almost *all* great artists learn their trade. They copy others until they have enough practice to start developing their own unique style.

See *Choose Your Weapons > Japanese Books* for recommended Japanese authors to use as your models.

Optimize Your Practice

MAXIMIZE YOUR MYELIN

Until very recently, most neurologists and linguists believed that acquiring complex skills like human language was a process controlled by *gray matter*, the part of our brain comprised of neurons, synapses, etc. But brain experts now know that *white matter*—the part of our nervous system made up of myelin-wrapped nerve cells—is the ultimate gatekeeper to mastery.

As Daniel Coyle puts it in *The Talent Code*:

> "...it's time to rewrite the maxim that practice makes perfect. The truth is, practice makes myelin, and myelin makes perfect . . . Every human skill, whether it's playing baseball or playing Bach, is created by chains of nerve fibers carrying a tiny electrical impulse—basically, a signal traveling through a circuit. Myelin's vital role is wrapping those nerve fibers the same way that rubber insulation wraps a copper wire, making the signal stronger and faster by preventing the electrical impulses from leaking out. When we fire our circuits in the right way—when we practice swinging that bat or playing that tone—our myelin responds by wrapping layers of insulation around that neural circuit, each new layer adding a bit more skill and speed. The thicker the myelin gets, the better it insulates, and the faster and more accurate our movements and thoughts become."

This seemingly boring fatty substance serves a crucial job in learning any skill. By insulating nerve fibers, myelin provides a major upgrade to our brain's "internet speed," vastly increasing the rate and efficiency of electrical impulses (up to 100 times faster than uninsulated nerve fibers).

Every linguistic rep makes our myelin that much thicker, and the thicker the myelin becomes, the faster we learn.

So what kind of signals create the most myelin? *Deep, deliberate practice.* The kind that challenges you. The kind that pushes you outside of your comfort zone. The kind that marks the difference between wannabes and successful learners.

ENGAGE IN DEEP, DELIBERATE PRACTICE

The difference between success and failure in language learning is not just how *much* we practice, but also *how*. Instead of simply "studying" Japanese as much as possible, we need to engage in *deliberate practice*, a special form of targeted training that:

- **Pushes us to the limits of our current abilities and comfort.** Whether intentional or not, most of us tend to focus on practicing that which proves *least* challenging to us. We stay in our comfort zones. We rest on our linguistic laurels. We try to avoid mistakes. Not so with deliberate practice. To master Japanese, we must identify and ruthlessly attack our weak points. But what this process lacks in ease and fun, it more than compensates for with efficacy and rapid progress.

- **Focuses on identifying and fixing our mistakes.** Many people want to stay in their caves, reading *manga*, watching *anime*, and listening to podcasts alone. But deep, deliberate practice requires help from others. To improve quickly, we need immediate, specific feedback on our mistakes, and we can't do that in a vacuum.

"Struggle is not optional—it's neurologically required: in order to get your skill circuit to fire optimally, you must by definition fire the circuit suboptimally; you must make mistakes and pay attention to those mistakes; you must slowly teach your circuit. You must also keep firing that circuit—i.e., practicing—in order to keep myelin functioning properly." —Daniel Coyle, *The Talent Code*

So how should we go about pushing ourselves outside our comfort zones and getting immediate, specific feedback?

Get a Japanese tutor.

Which brings us to the next section…

Work With a Tutor

WHY YOU SHOULD WORK WITH A TUTOR

I made the case earlier in the book that you don't have to attend classes or have a teacher to learn Japanese well. And I stand by this assertion. That said, working with a language tutor is a powerful way to supercharge your language learning efforts and make your *Anywhere Immersion* activities all the more effective and efficient. Here's why:

- **Tutors can help you find good materials.** What may take you hours in online searches will only take a native Japanese speaker a few minutes, especially an experienced tutor who knows where to look.

- **Tutors can point out your mistakes.** Getting feedback is an essential component of learning a language. The problem is that most Japanese friends, colleagues, or significant others won't feel comfortable pointing out your mistakes. And even if they *are*, you will probably find such correction annoying when you are focused more in the moment on *communicating* than *learning*.

- **Tutors can help keep you motivated.** Knowing that you will be talking with a tutor *tomorrow*—especially one that you are paying—will make it that much easier to put in the time toward your learning goals *today*.

WHERE TO FIND TUTORS

iTalki

iTalki is my preferred place to find Japanese tutors. The community boasts over 3 million users from more than 100 countries, and has thousands of tutors to choose from, including free language exchange partners and low-cost professional teachers. I especially like:

- Their tutor rating and review system helps you find someone who is a good fit for your interests, goals, and learning style.
- Their scheduling tool helps ensure that you and your tutor show up at the right time despite different time zones.
- You can earn free tutoring credits by referring other learners to iTalki. Each time you refer a new user, you each get $10 USD in iTalki credits, which can then be applied to iTalki lessons.

Create a free iTalki account here: **bit.ly/mjitalki**
Learn about their referral program: **bit.ly/mjitalkiref**

Verbling

Verbling has more than 7,500 teachers worldwide and offers some of the most advanced online tutoring tools. I especially like that:

- All tutors are professionally trained teachers.
- You meet with your tutor within Verbling so there is no need to install a separate third-party app (e.g. Skype).
- Their online system includes useful tools like collaborative textpads, vocabulary review, and more.
- They offer apps for iOS and Android.
- You can change the website interface to Japanese to provide more Japanese input.

Sign up for 10 lessons here and get a $30 account credit: **bit.ly/mjverbling**

LingQ

LingQ is one of my favorite tools for practicing listening and reading, acquiring vocabulary, and making sense of authentic content. But LingQ is *also* a good place to find language tutors. They don't have as many tutors as iTalki or Verbling, but the tutors they *do* have tend to be bright, enthusiastic teachers and learners. You can practice conversation on Skype or send them your writing for correction.

LingQ uses points for working with tutors, which can be purchased outright (1,000 points for $10 USD) or earned in one of four ways:

- Referring new users to LingQ.
- Adding shared content to the LingQ library.
- Hosting conversations in your native language.
- Correcting writing submissions in your native language.

If you are diligent and proactive, you can get all the tutoring and writing correction you'd ever want for free.

Sign up for a free LingQ account here:
bit.ly/mjlingq

HOW TO WORK WITH YOUR TUTOR

Once you've found a tutor or conversation partner, make sure to establish some ground rules:

- **Time:** How long will you meet each session? How flexible are you both on the start and end times? When is most convenient? When do you learn and perform best?

If possible, schedule based on your **chronotype**. See *Master Your Day > Optimize Your Timing > Honor Your Chronotype.*

- **Language use:** If you are paying a Japanese tutor, make sure they know you expect to speak Japanese only. If you are an absolute beginner in Japanese, you may need to rely on English occasionally to create context, but do your best to stick to Japanese. If you are doing a language exchange, agree to speak only the target language during each half of the session.

- **Correction:** How do you want your tutor to correct your mistakes? While some like to have mistakes pointed out *as they occur*, others want to keep the conversation flowing and discuss mistakes *after* the fact. There are pros and cons to both approaches; try out both and stick with whichever works best for you.

One particularly effective correction technique comes from the world of college basketball. Two educational researchers named Ron Gallimore and Roland Tharp studied the coaching techniques of UCLA's famed basketball coach John Wooden, named "the greatest coach of all time in any sport" by ESPN. Knowing Wooden's reputation, they had expected rousing speeches, ample praise, and stern disciplinary measures. What they observed *instead* were numerous, back-to-back, rapid-fire corrections that helped players quickly improve their performance without having to interrupt the flow of practice. In their study titled *What a Coach Can Teach a Teacher*[50], Gallimore and Tharp noted the following sequence, which they nicknamed a "Wooden":

1. Coach Wooden modeled the *correct* way to perform (what the player *should* do).

2. He then modeled the *incorrect* performance.

3. Lastly, he modeled the correct behavior again.

In shorthand, Gallimore and Tharp noted the sequence as M+, M-, M+. You can use the exact same approach in your language tutoring sessions. Instead of wasting lots of time going over a specific mistake, your tutor can simply model the correct utterance, repeat what you did wrong, and reinforce correct usage once more. This way:

- You get much more bang for your tutoring buck.

- You maintain your momentum and motivation.

- You are more likely to actually remember the corrections and use the correct word or structure next time.

- **Payment:** How much will you pay your tutor? Will you pay per hour or per session? Is there a discount for pre-paying for a bundle of lessons? Will you pay via PayPal, SquareCash, Apple Pay, etc? What is their payment email or link?

- **Preparation & follow up:** Is the tutor expected to prepare topics or materials before the session? Are *you*? Or will you just have a casual chat? Is the tutor expected to take notes and send them to you afterwards?

- **Rescheduling:** If one of you needs to reschedule, how many days or hours in advance do you prefer to be informed? Will payment be forfeited or just reapplied to the next session?

BEFORE YOUR TUTOR SESSIONS

To get the most out of your tutor sessions—and avoid the dreaded silence of those awkward "*So…what's next?*" moments—it is ideal if you and your tutor *both* prepare ahead of time:

- **Choose a topic:** The number one reason tutor sessions go bad is that one or both parties have nothing to talk about. It is, of course, just fine to go off topic, but always go *into* a session with a clear context (even if you don't end up sticking to it). Anything goes, but make sure that the main topic is something you are interested in (which usually means that it's best for you to choose your *own* topics instead of leaving the choice to your tutor). If possible, choose an article, podcast, video, etc. *ahead of time* so you and your tutor can both review the content and pick out specific words, phrases, and structures to discuss.

- **Prepare a bilingual list of words and phrases:** Go through the piece of content you chose to discuss or use a dictionary to prepare some vocabulary or expressions related to the topic. Put English in the left column, the readings in the center, and Japanese on the right. Then send the list to your tutor at least a day before the session so you can both prepare. Not only is this good for *your* Japanese, but your tutor will also get to learn some English, too. Win-win.

- **Make a list of questions:** As you listen to podcasts, watch anime, read comic books, etc., you will likely come across words or phrases that you don't understand or are unsure how to use. Keep note of these and make sure to send questions to your tutor a day ahead so they are not put on the spot during the session.

- **Share your notes.** Sending your notes to a tutor provides them with themes to discuss and likely many mistakes to correct (native speakers can spot typos and ungrammatical constructions much more quickly).

This type of tutoring is far more effective than casual chitchat and traditional classes since the entire session is focused on what *you* want to learn, not what *they* want to teach you. Moreover, the focus is on what you don't yet understand, so you don't have to waste time on material you already know. It also makes life much easier for your tutor since they then don't have to spend time and energy preparing a "lesson" in advance or trying to guess what you will find interesting.

AFTER YOUR TUTOR SESSIONS

After the tutor session, have your tutor send you:

- A list of words, phrases, and structures that come up during the call.
- A list of any mistakes you made, detailing both the incorrect and correct usage (e.g. "You said… here, but you should have said…"). In Coach Wooden format, this would look like M- → M+. For example:

**kouhii-wo suki desu.* (*コーヒーを好きです, *こうひいをすきです) →
kouhii-ga suki desu. (コーヒーが好きです, こうひいがすきです)

Optimize Your Memory

Many people claim to have "a bad memory" or be "slow at learning languages." While there certainly are differences in how easily each individual acquires, consolidates, and recalls information, I assure you that you have more than enough neural capacity to master Japanese if you are able to read this sentence. That said, there *are* some tips, techniques, and practices that will optimize your memory and make new characters, words, phrases, and structures stick.

GET A BALANCED "MEMORY DIET"

In the world of language learning, there are actually *two* main kinds of memory, not just one:

- Declarative memory
- Procedural memory

Both are essential, but traditional language study tends to focus too much on declarative memory, and not enough on its procedural counterpart. So what defines each type of memory? How are each involved in language acquisition? And how should we best optimize each?

Declarative Memory

Declarative memory stores explicit facts and events. Such memories can be consciously "declared" (i.e. explained in words), hence the term. You can think of this form of memory as knowing *what* is the case. This is the type of memory that comes to mind when most people think of "learning a language" (i.e. memorizing vocabulary and grammar rules). While declarative memory certainly has its place in language acquisition, the next type of memory is equally—if not even *more*—important when it comes to reaching fluency.

Procedural Memory

Procedural memory stores implicit skills, which are unconscious, automatic, and difficult to put into words. You can think of it as knowing *how* instead of *what*. Procedural memory, it turns out, is what allows us to create and understand grammatical sentences at rapid-fire speeds. Dr. Victor Ferreira, a psychologist at the University of California, San Diego, describes procedural memory's remarkable role in languages as follows:

> "...the core knowledge underlying human syntactic ability—one of the most creative capacities known in nature, and one that is commonly thought to depend on advanced and flexible intelligent functioning—is shaped by a specialized system of basic memory mechanisms that are themselves found in even the simplest of organisms."

DECLARATIVE MEMORY	PROCEDURAL MEMORY
Conscious	Unconscious
Easily explainable in words	Not easily explainable in words
Stores explicit information	Stores implicit knowledge
Knowing ***that*** something is the case	Knowing ***how*** to do something

Balance Is the Key

All too often, declarative memory is given too much attention in language learning, while procedural memory is given too little. This is how students can emerge from ten years of formal language study unable to have even the most basic conversation with native speakers. Sure, they can rattle off a list of vocabulary words, but they can't *use* the same words in context or *understand* them when spoken back to them. This is because they have only worked out their declarative memory muscles, leaving their procedural memory muscles weak and flabby.

Don't make the same mistake. Strive to eat a balanced "language diet" of declarative and procedural memory tasks and make sure to hit the immersion gym every day to build strong, sexy procedural memory muscles, flooding your brain with meaningful Japanese input, and communicating with native speakers every chance you get.

AVOID ROTE MEMORIZATION

"Rote memorization" is one of the unfortunate hallmarks of traditional language learning. This tedious, cure-for-insomnia approach entails force-fed memorization of new information. The learner goes through a list of words or *kanji*, for example, saying and writing each one hundreds of times, praying the whole time that the information somehow sticks. As you likely know, this approach tends to be about as ineffective as it is painful. Here's why you should avoid the rote memorization approach:

- **Rote learning does not lead to long-term retention.** Despite being able to regurgitate some *kanji* you memorized last night on today's test, you will probably find that by tomorrow, those same characters have pulled an Elvis and "left the building."

- **Rote learning is demoralizing.** There are few things worse than spending hours studying and having nothing to show for all your cognitive sweat. With so much attention given to rote memory in traditional language learning, it's no wonder so many do poorly, and many give up.

- **Rote learning ignores how the brain works.** Our brains are like cranky, penny-pinching bosses who will only authorize spending on projects that *they* find important. It does not matter how important you think a given kanji is, or how hard you try to make it stick by writing it out on the page ad infinitum. Your brain has to believe it's important before it will spend the neural resources needed for long-term retention.

Okay, so if rote memory should be avoided in language learning, how in the heck should one go about committing new information to memory? I recommend two main approaches:

- **Extensive exposure and practice in context.** Use the tips and resources throughout *Master Japanese* to flood your brain with meaningful input and create frequent opportunities to practice output (spoken and written communication) with native speakers. As you hear, read, speak, and write the language, more and more of it will get automatically stored in long-term memory without you having to consciously "memorize" words, phrases, structures, etc.

- **Use mnemonics.** Adults have a powerful shortcut at their disposals to help speed the internalization process of new information: creative mnemonics that leverage our big brains, our extensive life experience, and our gift for association.

LEVERAGE THE POWER OF MNEMONICS

Mnemonics, or *kiokujutsu* (記憶術, きおくじゅつ), are memory aids and tricks that help slippery information stick.

CULTURE CORNER

The word is derived from the Ancient Greek word μνημονικός (mnēmonikos), which means "of memory." That word in turn is derived from *Mnemosyne*, the Greek goddess of memory. But don't worry; you can harness the power of mnemonics without having to worship any ancient Greek deities.

Here are a few of the most useful mnemonic types for language learning:

- **Phrase mnemonics:** In this approach, you take the first letter of each word you're trying to remember and create a silly, memorable sentence. For example, you can remember the planets using the following:

My Very Educated Mother Just Served Us Nine Pizzas.

- **Name mnemonics:** In this technique, the first letter of each word you want to remember is combined into a memorable name or acronym. For example, here's an acronym you can use to remember the five Great Lakes:

Huron, Ontario, Michigan, Erie, Superior → H.O.M.E.S.

- **Story mnemonics:** The human brain remembers stories much more easily than random, unrelated facts. If you are struggling to remember the order of planets in the solar system, for example, you can use a story like this:

"Picture the hot SUN burning away. Suddenly it spits out a giant thermometer full of MERCURY. The thermometer is so hot it explodes, but the liquid metal quickly forms into the shape of the goddess VENUS. To cool down, she covers herself in a pile of EARTH. But she accidentally digs in the wrong yard: an angry, red-faced man comes marching over to yell at her, and throws a MARS bar at her. JUPITER, the king of the gods, sees this from above and comes down to protect the goddess. He doesn't have very good fashion sense though, and is wearing a tacky T-shirt with the letters S, U, and N (which stand for SATURN, URANUS and NEPTUNE)."

- **Music mnemonics:** This form of mnemonic leverages the power of melody and rhythm to help information stick. Probably the most famous example of this is the Alphabet Song we all learned as children.

- **Loci mnemonics:** This "mind palace" method leverages the power of spatial memory to more easily remember new information (*loci* is Latin for "places"). You picture a location you know well (e.g. your house), and then mentally "place" each fact you want to recall within discrete rooms or parts of that space.

For more about using mnemonics in language learning, read this post: **bit.ly/mjmnemonics**

USE A SPACED REPETITION SYSTEM

"There is, biologically speaking, no substitute for attentive repetition. Nothing you can do—talking, thinking, reading, imagining—is more effective in building skill than executing the action, firing the impulse down the nerve fiber, fixing errors, honing the circuit."
—Daniel Coyle, *The Talent Code*

Spaced Repetition Systems (or "SRS" for short) are flashcard programs designed to help you systematically learn *new* information—and retain *old* information—through optimally timed reviews. Instead of wasting precious study time on information you already know, SRS apps allow you to focus your time and energy on the information you haven't yet mastered.

Why You Should Use Spaced Repetition

In 1885, a German psychologist named Hermann Ebbinghaus (1850-1909) put forth a paper titled *Über das Gedächtnis* ("On Memory") in which he codified something every student already knows intuitively: new information is forgotten fast unless it's reviewed. As part of his research, he plotted how long it took him to forget new information in a graph he called the "forgetting curve."

The bad news? Ebbinghaus observed that he forgot new information almost immediately, with over half of the target information lost in just the first hour! Though his experiment was conducted only on himself (i.e. an N=1 study), his basic findings have been reproduced in more scientific studies since his time, and it's generally agreed that we forget the vast majority of new information we encounter (as much as 80%) within 24 hours.

The good news? We can use strategic repetition schedules to hack our memory and help control what sticks and for how long. Each subsequent re-exposure—if properly timed—can help push information further and further into long-term memory.

This memory-boosting method was first popularized in the language learning world by Paul Pimsleur (1927-1976), the man behind The Pimsleur Approach. His particular brand of spaced repetition was dubbed "Graduated Interval

Recall" (GIR), which he detailed in a 1967 paper titled *A Memory Schedule.*[51] He proposed the following review schedule for optimal retention and efficiency:

- **1st Review:** 5 seconds
- **2nd Review:** 25 seconds
- **3rd Review:** 2 minutes
- **4th Review:** 10 minutes
- **5th Review:** 1 hour
- **6th Review:** 5 hours
- **7th Review:** 1 day
- **8th Review:** 5 days
- **9th Review:** 25 days
- **10th Review:** 4 months
- **11th Review:** 2 years

How Spaced Repetition Systems Work

Modern SRS apps and software use even more complex scheduling algorithms than Pimsleur's GIR schedule, but lucky for us, the apps do the math so we don't have to!

And what drives the algorithm? How easily we remember each flashcard. Most SRS apps rely on self-ratings (e.g. "Easy" or "Hard"), showing "hard" cards sooner and more often than those you mark as "Easy."

How To Get the Most out of SRS

- **Use fun, interesting, personal content:** When learning through *Anywhere Immersion*, there is no excuse to use boring materials! Read and listen to content that excites you, topics that you would spend time with even in your native language. Then take chunks of this text or audio content you love and put them into your SRS deck.

- **Create context with example sentences:** Avoid creating cards with just a single word or *kanji* on the front and the reading or translation on the back. Whenever possible, use phrases or sentences to show how a given *kanji*, word, particle, or structure is used in context.

- **Create some CLOZE cards:** CLOZE deletion tests are assessments that test your knowledge and active recall by requiring you to fill in missing information. Place a complete phrase or sentence on the front of card, with one *kanji*, word, or particle missing. You then show the missing information on the back. This approach offers many advantages: ① You can create cards completely in Japanese and not have to include translations. ② The cards provide valuable reading practice. ③ They focus on active production instead of passive recognition.

The term "cloze" was coined in 1953 by W.L. Taylor, and is based on the Gestalt theory concept of "closure."

- **Add audio and photos when possible:** Images help sidestep the limitations of translation by creating a direct connection to meaning. Adding audio helps you strengthen your listening skills, too, instead of just improving reading like text-only cards.

- **Speak or write out your answers to each card:** Instead of just passively consuming your SRS flashcards, try to actively speak or write the answer to each. This better assesses and strengthens your active ability in the language.

- **Grade yourself honestly but quickly:** A lot of learners get hung up on how to rate themselves, worrying they are giving themselves an overly generous score when they don't really know the material or being too harsh on themselves when they were close but not perfect. Don't fall into the trap of spending your valuable time *deciding* what you know instead of actually *expanding* what you know.

- **Don't be afraid to delete cards:** If you come across cards that are boring, annoying, or too easy, simply delete them from your deck. Don't think about it too much. If you find yourself wanting to delete a card but are unsure if you should, just delete it and move on. You won't miss it. As Khatzumoto of *All Japanese All the Time* puts it:

"When your SRS deck starts to become more of a chore than a game, bad cards are most likely your problem."

Recommended SRS Apps & Tools

There are numerous sites and apps available today that incorporate spaced repetition. Here are a few of the best:

- **Tinycards:** Duolingo's Tinycards app is one of the most intuitive, elegant flashcards apps I've come across yet. I like that it includes just enough gamification to keep learning fun, but not so much that it gets distracting. You can choose from hundreds and hundreds of premade decks (both from Duolingo and from fellow learners), or better yet, you can create your *own* decks based on words, phrases, and sample sentences you encounter in your *Anywhere Immersion* activities. For example, I've created decks for new terms I've come across while using iOS and macOS in Japanese. Though Tinycards doesn't have all the bells and whistles of some of the other flashcards apps below, I think that the simplicity is actually a good thing since it minimizes distraction and overwhelm. No app is perfect, and there *are* things that occasionally annoy me about Tinycards, but at the time of writing, it's my go-to flashcard app.

Tinycards for iOS: **bit.ly/tinycardsios**
Tinycards for Android: **bit.ly/tinycardsandroid**

- **Memrise:** Memrise is one of the best designed SRS tools on the block, with sound science, fun methodologies, and a strong community of users. Memrise is built on the principle of "elaborate encoding" (each flashcard includes multiple touch points to help the information stick: mnemonics, etymologies, videos, audio, photos, example sentences, etc.).

Register a free Memrise account here: **bit.ly/mjmemrise**

PRICE: FREE W/ UPGRADES | **PLATFORMS:** WEB, IOS, ANDROID

- **Anki:** Literally meaning "memorization" in Japanese, *Anki* (暗記, あんき) is one of the most widely used SRS tools for language learning. And for good reason: ① you can download heaps of useful user-generated decks, ② you can use the app on every major platform, and ③ you can extensively customize the app's settings.

Register a free Anki account here: **bit.ly/mjankiapp**

PRICE: FREE ($24.99 FOR IOS) | **PLATFORMS:** IOS, ANDROID, MAC, WINDOWS, LINUX

NOTE!

If you're curious why the iOS version costs 25 buckaroos while the other platforms are free, here is Anki creator Damien Elmses' justification: "Taken alone, AnkiMobile is expensive for an app. However, AnkiMobile is not a standalone app, but part of an ecosystem, and the $17.50 Apple gives me on each sale goes towards the development of that whole ecosystem. For the price, you get not only the app, but a powerful desktop application, a free online synchronization service, and mobile clients for various platforms."

- **iKnow:** The iKnow app lets you practice listening, speaking, reading, and writing, and helps you master the 6,000 highest-frequency words using their excellent *Memory Bank* spaced repetition tool. Plus, all audio in the app is recorded by professional Japanese voice actors.

Register for iKnow here: **bit.ly/mjiknow**

PRICE: ¥1,480/MO | **PLATFORMS:** WEB, IOS & ANDROID

- **Flashcards Deluxe:** This is a good low-cost, high-quality, user-friendly alternative to Anki. The app allows you to either create your own flashcards (complete with audio and photos) or import pre-made decks from Quizlet. I especially like that you can create "multi-sided" cards that can test you multiple bits of information, instead of just binary "front" and "back" testing.

Download Flashcards Deluxe here: **bit.ly/mjfcd**

PRICE: $3.99 | PLATFORMS: IOS & ANDROID

- **Nihongo dictionary app:** Not only does the app include a built-in SRS flashcard system, but it automatically keeps track of words you've looked up or imported into the text reader. You can then quickly turn any of these words into flashcards with just one tap.

Download *Nihongo* here: **bit.ly/mjnihongo**

PRICE: FREE W/ IN-APP UPGRADES | PLATFORMS: IOS

- **Japanese dictionary app:** Prior to discovering the Nihongo app above, my favorite dictionary app was Japanese. It's still a solid option, especially for those not on iOS. It also has a built-in SRS flashcard system, and allows you to either study your own custom lists or choose from premade decks for JLTP levels, parts of speech, common subjects, *kanji*, radicals, and more.

Download *Japanese* here: **bit.ly/mjjapaneseapp**

PRICE: FREE | PLATFORMS: IOS & ANDROID

- **Skritter:** Not only does Skritter integrate spaced repetition into their app, but they take it one step further by leveraging the power of "active recall." Instead of simply reading each flashcard, the app requires that you write out your answer on the screen (which better assesses and strengthens your memory).

Try a free demo & download the app here: **bit.ly/skritter**

PRICE: $14.99/MO | PLATFORMS: WEB, IOS & ANDROID

USE "SMASHIN SCOPE"

In Tony Buzan's book *Master Your Memory*,[52] he shares twelve memory principles you can use to better encode information in long-term memory. The principles can be easily remembered (pun intended!) using the mnemonic "SMASHIN SCOPE."

Synaesthesia

We have multiple senses at our disposal: vision, hearing, smell, taste, touch, and kinesthesia (i.e. where your body is located in space and where it's moving to). Synaesthesia is the phenomenon when one sense blends with or influences another. For example, my wife "sees" numbers and letters as colors. While this occurs in some individuals automatically, we can apply the basic concept consciously to better remember new information. For maximum effect, deploy *all* of your senses in language learning.

Movement

When creating mnemonics (especially "imaginative memory" stories for remembering *kanji*), try to imagine that people and objects are moving. Our brains evolved to detect the slightest of movements, and even the *imagined* variety will help make information stick.

Association

We learn new information by associating and comparing it with what we already know. Every *past* life experience provides a foothold for *future* information to rest upon. This is, in fact, one of the reasons that adults are actually better language learners than children (they have far more life experience to draw upon when learning new things).

Another way to leverage association is changing your learning environment. When you spend time with Japanese in a variety of locations and contexts, you provide your brain with a greater number—and wider range—of attachment points for new information.

Sexuality

Our brains tune into sex-related stimuli like moths to a porch light. Some might be squeamish about leveraging sexual imagery in their heads to optimize memory, but realize that:

- Nobody else ever needs to know what sexual associations you use.
- Sexuality is a natural, hardwired component of being human.

Humor

We all love a good laugh, so why not use humor to help you learn a language? As Buzan points out:

> "The more ridiculous, absurd, funny and surreal you make your images, the more outstandingly memorable they will be."

Imagination

Try to bring back some of your childhood penchant for daydreaming, coupling it with your vastly larger pool of grown-up experiences.

Number

Adding a number to information increases specificity and efficiency, which in turn makes information more concrete and easier to recall.

 **NOTE!**

The power of numbering works hand in hand with *Order and Sequence* (see the next page).

Symbolism

Replace boring, everyday, or intangible images with more exciting, rare, or concrete equivalents to improve your memory. Using readily identifiable symbols or icons like light bulbs can also improve recall.

Color

We are hard-wired to be attracted to bright colors, hence why fast-food chains use them for their logos, signs, and food packaging. Use the same dirty tricks to make your mental imagery easier to recall.

Order & Sequence

You've probably noticed that once you're prompted with a word from a list you've previously studied but forgotten, you suddenly remember the words before and after the one in question. I often notice this same memory phenomenon when I hear a favorite song from my teen years and then immediately expect to hear the tune that happened to come next on the mixtape I made 25 years ago!

Positive Images

Our brains like to remember the positive side of life, which is why we tend to recreate overly rosy versions of history once enough time has passed:

"She was such a great girl! Why oh why did we ever break up!?"

Use this tendency to your advantage by making happy, happy, joy, joy images whenever you can.

Exaggeration

To help improve memory, exaggerate sizes, dimensions, and sounds in your mental imagery and stories:

- Make *small* things extremely **BIG**.
- Make SHORT things loooooong or TALL.
- Make *quiet* things **L-O-U-D**!

UTILIZE ALL OF YOUR INTELLIGENCES

Yes, you read that correctly: intelligence**s**. The plural is not a typo. Psychologist Howard Gardner argues in his book *Frames of Mind: The Theory of Multiple Intelligences*[53] that there are nine different categories of intelligence, not just one. And once you identify your unique strengths, you can choose learning styles, activities, and materials that best fit your temperament and preferences.

Determine your Multiple Intelligences profile by completing this free survey: **bit.ly/mjmis**

Verbal-Linguistic Intelligence (Word Smarts)

An individual with strong verbal-linguistic intelligence usually excels at reading, writing, story-telling, memorizing new vocabulary, translating, and learning foreign languages through more academic approaches.

PRO TIP

Though textbooks and language classes are certainly not a requirement to learn a language (and are often *counterproductive* for many people), those with strong verbal-linguistic intelligence may find them useful.

Logical-Mathematical Intelligence (Logic & Math Smarts)

Someone with strong logical-mathematical intelligence will tend to have good reasoning abilities and be quick to solve math equations and detect patterns in data. Although languages are certainly not math equations, learners with a proclivity for logical-mathematical thinking can benefit from a more logical, grammatical approach to the language.

PRO TIP

If mathematics is your game, consider finding yourself a math textbook in Japanese or watching Japanese math tutorials on YouTube.

Visual-Spatial Intelligence (Art Smarts)

A visually/spatially inclined person can easily manipulate images on paper, in 3-D, or in their mind's eye. If an individual also possesses strong bodily-kinesthetic intelligence, they will often excel at drawing, painting, and sculpting.

PRO TIP

Learning a Japanese art form or martial art (*in* Japanese, of course) would be a great way for those with strong visual-spacial intelligence to maximize both enjoyment *and* efficiency.

Bodily-Kinesthetic Intelligence (Body Smarts)

While most people would automatically relate bodily-kinesthetic intelligence to sports, this intelligence can lend itself to *any* activity involving fine motor movement: dance, drawing, playing an instrument, and even foreign languages.

PRO TIP

Learners with strong bodily-kinesthetic intelligence should incorporate movement as much as possible, including walking as they listen to podcasts, learning a martial art in Japanese, or finding a Japanese teacher who uses TPR ("Total Physical Response").

For more on Japanese martial arts, see *Learn How to Learn > Learn Through Action > Learn a Japanese Martial Art.*

For more about TPR, see this Wikipedia article: **bit.ly/mjwiktpr**

Musical Intelligence (Tone & Rhythm Smarts)

You probably know one or two amazing individuals who can hear a tune once and then play it back on the piano, or hum an "A" note on command. On the flip side, you probably know a few unlucky folks who scare away the family cat when trying to sing, and can never seem to keep the beat when clapping along to a song. The former group has strong musical intelligence, while the latter is weak in this area.

 **PRO TIP**

Learners with "music smarts" would benefit from studying the lyrics of Japanese songs as well as learning an instrument in Japanese.

For recommended genres and artists, see *Choose Your Weapons > Japanese Music.*

Interpersonal Intelligence (People Smarts)

An individual endowed with strong interpersonal intelligence is good at talking with people, and can pick up on subtle changes in mood that may be missed by others. Such folks often think out loud, and life has little texture unless they can interact with others.

 **PRO TIP**

While all learners should seek out native speakers to practice with, doing so is *especially* important for those with people smarts.

Intrapersonal Intelligence (Self Smarts)

Hardcore Matrix fans will remember that the Oracle had a placard in her kitchen that read:

"Temet Nosce"

The phrase is Latin for "Know Thyself." People with high intrapersonal intelligence can more easily follow the Oracle's advice. They are keenly aware of their emotional states, feelings, and motivations. They enjoy self-reflection and analysis, and are particularly good at identifying personal strengths and weaknesses.

Individuals with strong Intrapersonal Intelligence should regularly review their learning goals and study habits, and make changes when they see a contradiction between the two.

TAKE GOOD NOTES & REVIEW THEM FREQUENTLY

"I take notes like some people take drugs. There is an eight-foot stretch of shelves in my house containing nothing but full notebooks. Some would call this hypergraphia (Dostoevsky was a member of this club), but I trust the weakest pen more than the strongest memory, and note taking is—in my experience—one of the most important skills for converting excessive information into precise action and follow-up."
—Tim Ferriss

Notes are a great way to consolidate your knowledge, practice your Japanese writing skills, jot down useful words and phrases you encounter, and keep track of questions to ask your tutor.

The Advantages of Handwritten Notes

Handwritten notes provide many advantages for language learners:

- **They help identify your gaps:** When writing Japanese by hand, it becomes immediately apparent which words or *kanji* you can *recognize* but can't yet *produce* from memory.
- **They improve retention:** Writing by hand adds a kinesthetic dimension that can help improve your

memory. This seems to be especially true for those with strong *Bodily-Kinesthetic Intelligence.*

- **Then tend to be more polite in social situations.** When you're chatting with others at a party, at the table, etc., I highly recommend taking notes on paper instead of using your smartphone. The latter tends to be perceived as rude and creates too many opportunities for distraction (social media updates, new emails, etc.).

Use the Bullet Journal Method

Though any pen and paper will do to create handwritten notes in Japanese, I highly recommend using Ryder Carrol's *Bullet Journal Method.* Why? As Ryder Carrol puts it:

"In the most connected time in history, we're quickly losing touch with ourselves. Overwhelmed by a never-ending flood of information, we're left feeling overstimulated yet restless, overworked yet discontented, tuned in yet burned out. As technology leaked into every nook in my life, with its countless distractions, my methodology provided an analog refuge that proved invaluable in helping me define and focus on what truly mattered." —*The Bullet Journal Method: Track the Past, Order the Present, Design the Future* [54]

Get free Bullet Journal tips and tricks here: **bit.ly/mjbullet**
Get the Bullet Journal book here: **bit.ly/mjbulletbook**

For fellow stationary nerds, here is the notebook and pen I use personally for Bullet Journalling:

- **Leuchtturm1917 Hardcover A5 Notebook:** It has a number of features that make Bullet Journalling a cinch, including numbered pages, a blank table of contents, dotted pages, and not *one*, but *two* string bookmarks. I also like that it opens flat, has thick, ink-proof paper that doesn't bleed through, an expandable pocket, an elastic closure, stickers for labeling and archiving notebooks, and tear-out pages in the back for sharing notes.

The Leuchtturm1917 Notebook is available on Amazon here: bit.ly/mja1917

- **Uni Jetstream Multi Pen & Pencil:** One side effect of living in Japan was developing an obsession with multi pens. I've spent more yen on them over the years than I'd care to admit, but fortunately I've finally found a low-cost option I love: the Uni Jetstream. It includes a 0.5mm mechanical pencil, 0.7mm ballpoints in black, red, blue, and green, and a built-in eraser, and is only about $7!

The Uni Jetstream Multi Pen is available on Amazon here: bit.ly/mjuni

---

The Advantages of Digital Notes

Though handwritten notes are ideal for the reasons above, I should point out that audio notes and typed notes also have their advantages:

- Audio notes provide speaking practice as you make them and listening practice when you later review. They are also more convenient when one's hands and eyes are currently occupied (e.g. while driving).

- Typed notes, while not a very effective way to *capture* notes, are a great way to *consolidate* handwritten and audio notes. You can then easily search for words or phrases instead of having to flip through notebooks or scrub through audio files.

- Digital notes can be backed up and stored in the cloud so they are always available wherever you go.

Consolidate & Review Your Notes

Taking good notes is only half the battle. The most important step is actually *consolidating* and *reviewing* them on a regular basis. This process may take a little extra time *up front*, but it has many advantages in the *long run*:

- **It allows you to better organize and retrieve notes:** When your notes are tidy and well organized, you can quickly find exactly what you're looking for instead of wading through noise and distraction. Truncated, consolidated notes are also much faster to review, allowing you to focus on just the information that matters most.

- **It maximizes your understanding and retention:** The simple act of rewriting your notes increases your familiarity with the content and improves your retention.

- **It provides a context for tutor sessions:** Instead of trying to come up with new curricula for each session, you and your tutor can simply review your Japanese notes from the week, discussing the usage of new words, the meaning of unfamiliar structures, etc. Your tutor can also easily spot any mistakes in your notes; there is nothing worse than spending lots of time and energy committing mistakes to memory!

See my recommended tutoring sites and tools here:
Learn How to Learn > Work with a Tutor

Create Mind Maps

Lists are great for quick capture, but mind maps are a far better tool for consolidation and review. Why? Because they better reflect the way our brains process, store, and retrieve information. Moreover, they make it easier to organize vocabulary by relationship, category, and hierarchy, and put everything on just one page for easy review. Here are some tips on making effective mind maps:

- Start with a central topic or idea in the center, create sub-category nodes around it, and then add individual items branching off them.
- Try to use only **one word** per node. Paragraphs defeat the purpose of a mind map!
- I suggest limiting yourself to 3 hierarchical levels. You can go further if you want, but your mind map will start to get cluttered and make for a less useful tool.
- If possible, use colors to both increase retention. Remember: our brains *love* color! You can also use color to help make connections between similar words (e.g. put verbs in green, nouns in blue, etc.).

For more on mind mapping, check out Tony Buzan's book *Mind Map Mastery*: **bit.ly/mjmindmap**

Optimize Brain Health

You may be surprised to see a section about *health* in a *language* book. So what gives? Well, last time I checked, the brain resides in the body. And we acquire, produce, and understand languages in our brains. The better we nourish our gray matter through diet, exercise, and sleep, the better we will be able to learn, remember, and produce Japanese.

 **SIDE NOTE**

I should also point out here that—in addition to my career in linguistics and languages—I am a certified Functional Nutritional Therapy Practitioner (FNTP) and have worked in nutrition curriculum development for a number of years.

So how can we improve our ability to acquire a language by improving the health of our brain? There are three essential components:

- Eat a nutrient-dense, anti-inflammatory, species-appropriate diet.
- Move your body frequently, lift heavy things, and sprint occasionally.
- Get enough rest, relaxation, and high-quality sleep.

EAT A NUTRIENT-DENSE, ANTI-INFLAMMATORY DIET

What we eat affects how well we think, how well we remember, and how well we perform. When we choose foods, we should always try to *maximize* the density of nutrients (to optimally fuel our brains and bodies) and *minimize* inflammation (to keep our bodies running smoothly).

I could write an entire book on this topic, but here are just a few essential nutrition guidelines to help you optimize brain function, memory, and cognitive performance.

Focus on "Real" Food

> "Don't eat anything your great-great grandmother wouldn't recognize as food. There are a great many food-*like* items in the supermarket your ancestors wouldn't recognize as food . . . stay away from these."
>
> —Michael Pollan

We are all unique *bioindividuals*, and the specific foods ideal for *you* will vary based on factors such as your ancestry, gut health, activity level, body fat percentage, etc.

That said, there *is* at least one kind of food that everyone should eat: **real food**. What do I mean by *real*?

- Real food is—or was *once*—alive.
- Real food grows in or on the ground (i.e. it comes from an animal or plant).
- Real food is rich in nutrients and low in antinutrients.
- Real food is delicious and satisfying, but doesn't lead to addictive consumption or bingeing.

Eat Ample Amounts of Healthy Fat

"Fats from animal and vegetable sources provide a concentrated source of energy in the diet; they also provide the building blocks for cell membranes and a variety of hormones and hormone-like substances. Fats as part of a meal slow down nutrient absorption so that we can go longer without feeling hungry. In addition, they act as carriers for the important fat-soluble vitamins A, D, E, and K. Dietary fats are needed for the conversion of carotene to vitamin A, for mineral absorption and for a host of other processes." —Sally Fallon, *Nourishing Traditions*[55]

Some may be shocked to see "fat" in the same sentence as "healthy."

But an honest look at scientific literature, biology, and evolutionary anthropology shows that fat—even the supposed boogeyman *saturated* fat—is essential to health. It turns out that much of the anti-fat dogma of the past 60 years was based on shoddy science, confirmation bias, special interests, and corporate greed, *not* ironclad evidence.

For more on the history of anti-fat dogma, read *The Big Fat Surprise* by Nina Teicholz. **bit.ly/mjbfs**

Why is fat so important for learning? One key reason is that we need fatty acids to build *myelin*, the neural insulators that lead to new skills. Without fat, we can't build myelin. And without myelin, we can't learn, understand, or use a language.

Moreover, fat—in concert with cholesterol—is used to create the outer membrane of every single cell in your body, as well as sex hormones, meaning that "fat-free" foods should really be relabeled "*libido*-free!"

For more on the role of myelin, see *Learn How to Learn > Optimize Your Practice > Maximize Your Myelin* section.

So now that we've established the importance of fat in human nutrition, physiology, and brain function, what are some good sources of healthy fats?

- Animal fats from properly raised animals (e.g. fatty cuts

of meat, butter, or tallow from 100% grass-fed cows).

- Wild-caught fish and seafood (e.g. salmon, sardines, etc.).
- Organic virgin coconut oil.
- Avocados and avocado oil.
- Olives and olive oil.

 NOTE!

Avoid the following "Franken-Fats" at all costs:

- **Margarine:** Eat butter instead! It's better for you and tastes far better to boot!
- **Trans fats and hydrogenated fats and oils:** Commonly found in fast foods, processed foods, frozen foods, and baked goods.
- **Highly processed seed oils:** canola oil (a.k.a. rapeseed oil), soybean oil, safflower oil, cottonseed oil, etc. These have been cleverly branded as "vegetable oils," but they do *not* come from veggies.

These are **not** healthy fats no matter how many millions of dollars the edible oil industry spends trying to convince you otherwise! Many of these easily oxidize when exposed to heat or light and should therefore never be used for cooking. Canola oil and soybean oil are especially widespread since they're supposedly "heart healthy." They are anything but! The real reason they're used so frequently is because they're profitable to manufacture and cheap to buy.

Eat Enough High-Quality Protein

When it comes to protein, *quantity* and *quality* are equally important. Most people either eat *too little* protein or *way too much* of the wrong kind. Focus on getting protein from a variety high-quality sources, including:

- Pasture-raised ruminant animals (e.g. beef, bison, lamb, goat, etc.).
- Pasture-raised poultry and eggs.
- Wild-caught seafood.

I do *not* recommend relying heavily on protein powders, protein bars, etc. These are highly processed, usually laden with sugar, and lack many of the important vitamins, minerals, and cofactors found in real food.

Protein from animals is much more *bioavailable*—easy to digest, absorb, and utilize—than protein from plants. This doesn't mean that plant protein is inherently bad; it just means that relying *solely* upon it in one's diet is not a great recipe for optimal health.

Go Easy on Sugar, Starch & Alcohol

Sugar in its myriad forms should be kept as low as possible to help keep your energy levels consistent and your brain firing the way it's supposed to.

 **NOTE!**

Constantly elevated blood sugar can damage the hippocampus, which is involved in the storage of long-term memories.

In general, starchy vegetables and fruit are okay in moderation, but those with digestive issues or struggling with energy swings and fatigue may need to limit or avoid them altogether.

Whenever possible, buy local, in-season, organic options to maximize nutrient-density and minimize toxins, the latter of which impairs brain function.

And sorry to be a buzzkill, but alcohol acts much like sugar in the body and should be only consumed on occasion if you want to keep your brain and memorization function in tip-top shape.

(**Pro Tip:** "Tuesday" is not an occasion.)

GET ENOUGH REST, RELAXATION & SLEEP

"The best asset we have for making a contribution to the world is ourselves. If we underinvest in ourselves, and by that I mean our minds, our bodies, and our spirits, we damage the very tool we need to make our highest contribution. One of the most common ways people—especially ambitious, successful people—damage this asset is through a lack of sleep." —Greg McKeown, *Essentialism*

Don't be one of the fools who brags about how little sleep they get. I *was* such a fool through most of my twenties and early thirties, and have had to do a lot of work to repair the damage I did to my body through chronic sleep deprivation and stress. Boast instead about how rested and productive you feel because you get adequate rest!

When it comes to learning and consolidating new information, sleep is not a *nice* to have. It's a **must** have! Our brains process and consolidate memories while we're in *La La Land*, so we have to get enough high-quality sleep to finish the learning we do while awake. You can spend your entire day studying Japanese, but the hours of effort will count for little until you get a few full sleep cycles to encode the new information.

So how can we get more high-quality sleep, get to sleep more easily, and actually *stay* asleep once we doze off?

Avoid Caffeine After Noon

One of the most common causes of insomnia is consumption of caffeine too close to bedtime. We each metabolize caffeine at different rates, so you will need to do some personal experimentation to figure out how early you need to cut off consumption to avoid negatively impacting your sleep quality. To be safe, I recommend limiting caffeine consumption to just the morning to give your body plenty of time to clear the molecule from your system before bed.

 **NOTE!**

Caffeine is found in many foods and beverages, not just in coffee: energy drinks, many teas, most sodas, many energy bars, and coffee-infused ice creams, yogurts, etc. A similar molecule called theobromine is found in chocolate, so it's best to exercise the same time constraints as for caffeine-containing beverages and foods.

Limit Blue Light Exposure After Dark

Our circadian rhythms—which help control our sleep cycle—are affected by the light received by the eyes and skin. Blue light, which is naturally highest at midday and lowest at night, tells the brain that it's "daytime" and inhibits production of melatonin, a hormone associated with the onset of sleep.

Unfortunately, common household items such as televisions, computers, smartphones, and light bulbs emit lots of blue light. When viewed at night, they can disrupt our circadian rhythms, trick our bodies into thinking it's daytime, and make it much more difficult to fall asleep. To combat this problem:

- Avoid *all* screens at least 2 hours before bed, including TVs, computers, smartphones, etc.

 **PRO TIP!**

The easiest way to avoid screens before bed is making a rule not to have them in the bedroom. Set up a charging station somewhere else in the house to help make the habit stick. If you usually use your phone as an alarm, get a Philips Wake-Up Light instead. → **bit.ly/mjphilips**

- Wear blue blocker glasses after dark. Any orange-tinted construction glasses will do, but I personally use this snazzy pair from Swanwick Sleep:

Swannies Blue Light Blocking Computer Glasses:
bit.ly/mjswannies

- Set your devices to automatically shift the color and brightness of the screen based on the latitude, date, and time of day.

For your computer, install F.lux: **bit.ly/mjgetflux**

PRICE: FREE | **PLATFORMS:** MACOS, WINDOWS

For iOS, turn on *Night Shift*: **bit.ly/mjnightshift**
For Android, install *Twilight*: **bit.ly/mjtwilight**

- Turn off or dim the lights in your home if possible. Candles and salt lamps are a great sleep-friendly lighting alternative after dark.

Salt lamps are available on Amazon:
bit.ly/mjsaltlamp

Avoid TV, News & Social Media Before Bed

Do your best to avoid scrolling through social media or watching television, movies, or the nightly news before bed. Not only does this habit present the blue light issues discussed above, but it also proves problematic for sleep in another key way: exciting, disturbing, irritating, violent, or sexual content can stimulate the nervous system and make it more difficult to doze off.

Here are some sleep-friendly evening activities to consider:

- Read a book (preferably fiction to help turn off the analytical parts of your brain and ideally in print instead of on a device).

 **PRO TIP!**

To minimize exposure to blue light as you read, use a red headlamp instead of an overhead light or bedside lamp. → **bit.ly/mjheadlamp**

- Talk to your significant other or have sex, both of which are all the more likely when there isn't a TV in the bedroom!
- Take a hot bath with Epsom salts, followed by a cool shower. The hot bath relaxes, while the cool shower begins to reduce your core temperature (which helps trigger sleep).
- Sip some caffeine-free tea with raw honey and organic apple cider vinegar.
- Meditate. You can simply focus on your breath, do a body scan form head to toe, or use a guided sleep meditation.

Check out the sleep-specific meditations from Headspace: **bit.ly/mjhss**

Make Your Room as Dark & Quiet as Possible

Light and noise are both sleep saboteurs. Here's how to block out both and create a more sleep-friendly bedroom:

- **Install thick blackout curtains:** Not only do blackout curtains block out light, but they also help insulate your room and reduce noise from outside.

Blackout curtains are available on Amazon here:
bit.ly/mjcurtains

- **Wear a sleeping mask:** I recommend the Manta Sleep Mask: its formfitting design and adjustable eye cups block out all light and don't put pressure on the eyes.

The Manta Sleep Mask is available on Amazon here:
bit.ly/mjmanta

- **Use earplugs:** Any earplugs can help, but I recommend using silicon options to prevent skin irritation.

I like these silicon earplugs from EarJoy:
bit.ly/mjearplug

Turn Down the Temp

In addition to light, temperature also plays an important role in regulating our circadian rhythm. Until very recent history, our bodies were automatically exposed to cooler temperatures after the sun went down (which naturally triggered the onset of sleep). But in our modern temperature-controlled world, many of us no longer receive this crucial temperature signal. So what can we do aside from sleeping outside? Fortunately there are some easier ways to ensure a sleep-friendly temperature without living in a cave:

- **Turn down the thermostat:** Set your thermostat to automatically reduce to 55° to 65° overnight. Ideally, you want your bedroom around this temperature from the time you go to bed until you wake up, so you may need to cut the heat or open windows a few hours before bedtime. If you don't already have one, I recommend getting a Nest thermostat, a modern, intelligent device that you control right from your smartphone.

The Nest thermostat is available on Amazon here: **bit.ly/mjthermostat**

- **Get a chiliPAD:** Though they are certainly not cheap, the chiliPAD is a great option for those whose partners run significantly hotter or colder than oneself. The thin pad allows you to raise or the lower the temperature of each side of the bed, so there's no need to fight for covers or throw them off the bed.

The chiliPAD is available on Amazon here:
bit.ly/mjchilipad

WALK, PLAY, LIFT & SPRINT

"A noble soul dwells in a strong body." —Japanese Proverb

Along with eating right and getting enough sleep, exercise completes the brain health trinity. Sadly, most of us get far too little movement in our daily lives. We sit during our commutes. We sit at work. We sit when we study. We sit when we watch TV.

But sitting *itself* is not really the problem. Switching to a standing desk, for example, can be beneficial, but it doesn't solve the root problem: being sedentary.

The *real* solution is frequent, varied movement. Just as we need to eat a variety of *dietary* nutrients to survive and thrive, we *also* need to get a variety of *movement* nutrients for optimal health. Here are but a few suggested "courses":

- Take short walks throughout the day.
- Play tag or hide-and-seek.
- Play Ultimate Frisbee.
- Go for a bike ride.
- Lift weights (no more than twice a week).
- Sprint (no more than once a week).

PRO TIP!

Short, intense physical activity such as HIIT (high-intensity interval training) provides much more bang for your buck than long, low-intensity activities like jogging or long-distance running. Moreover, these latter activities present considerable "wear-and-tear" risks to your knees, shoulders, etc., and provide **no** added health benefits over brief, intense exercise. [56] [57]

Not only will movement improve your overall health, but it can *also* help supercharge language acquisition. Exercise has been linked with numerous cognitive and neurophysiological benefits, including:

- Improved short-term and long-term memory.

- Increased volume in the prefrontal cortex and medial temporal cortex, the areas that control thinking and memory.
- Increased production of growth factors (e.g. BDNF, "Brain-derived neurotrophic factor") which support the formation and preservation of brain cells and blood vessels.
- Increased blood flow to the brain, which means more oxygen for hungry brain cells and reduced damage from free radicals.
- Increased production of dopamine and other feel-good hormones.
- Improved mood and sleep quality.
- Increased discipline.
- Reduced stress and anxiety.
- Reduced insulin resistance and inflammation.

So before you begin the next chapter, take a brief break to walk outside, bust out some pushups, and prep your brain to learn even more!

CHOOSE YOUR WEAPONS

"Man is a tool-using animal. Without tools he is nothing, with tools he is all." —Thomas Carlyle

One of the greatest advantages of *Anywhere Immersion* is that it empowers you to choose your *own* tools and materials. Instead of being stuck with boring, outdated, irrelevant resources, you can choose fun, modern, personalized content. But this advantage comes with a serious potential side-effect: overwhelm and paralysis. Today's Japanese learner has a nearly infinite number of options to choose from, which can be a blessing or a curse depending on how you proceed.

The good news is that *I* have already wasted . . . I mean *invested* . . . hundreds of hours trying out hundreds of different resources so *you* don't have to. I then separated the wheat from the chaff and created a curated list of the very best Japanese resources I've found to date in this chapter.

My goal here is to help minimize decision fatigue, eliminate guesswork, and free you to spend your precious time actually *acquiring* Japanese instead of searching for learning resources.

In the coming pages, you will learn:

- How to choose resources that fit your unique interests, needs, goals, and learning style.
- Where to find high-quality Japanese media, including free and paid resources, digital and print formats, etc.
- My specific recommendations for Japanese podcasts, music, videos, video games, comics, books, magazines, reference tools, and more.

How To Choose Your Weapons

"We should remember the warning of the wise Grail knight in *Indiana Jones and the Last Crusade*: 'You must choose, but choose wisely, for as the true Grail will bring you life, the false Grail will take it from you.' Choose the highest-yield material and you can be an idiot and enjoy stunning success. Choose poorly and, as the Grail knight implied, you're screwed no matter what. You'll chase your own tail for years."
—Tim Ferriss, *The 4-Hour Chef*

Choosing the right language learning tools and resources significantly accelerates the language learning process. But more than just adding *speed*, it also adds something far more important: *fun*. The more you enjoy yourself, the more likely you are to show up each and every day, and the more easily the language will stick.

There are seven keys to choosing good resources and getting the most out of them:

- Choose topics and tools you genuinely love and will look forward to using.
- Choose quickly: don't let yourself get stuck in paralysis by analysis.
- Choose the smallest number of resources you need to reach your goals.

- Choose digital materials when possible. They're faster, cheaper, and easier to carry.
- Choose the shortest materials possible to reduce procrastination and better support repetition.
- Choose audio-based materials to focus on the foundational skills of listening and speaking.
- Use the tools you *already have* before buying more.

CHOOSE TOPICS & TOOLS YOU LOVE

"Do what you love, do it in a way that you love, and pour your heart and soul into every moment of it." —Josh Waitzkin, *The Art of Learning*

There is no single language learning approach that guarantees success for everyone, but there *is* one path that guarantees failure for all: **boredom**. It's essential that you choose topics and tools that light you up, fill you with excitement, and help you enjoy the learning journey. With so many options available today, there is no reason to force yourself through boring, uninteresting, irrelevant materials. Be discerning about what you spend your precious time, money, and energy on. When deciding on a given investment, ask yourself:

- Will I look forward to using this resource or tool? Or will I dread it?
- Does this resource or method align with my personal WHY?
- Will this help me reach my SMART goals and integrate with my daily systems?

One of the best ways to increase fun and excitement is learning Japanese as you learn *another* skill or hobby.

See the *Learn Through Action* section for more about learning Japanese through art, martial arts, and travel.

CHOOSE QUICKLY

On the other hand, do not let yourself succumb to the fool's *pursuit of perfection*. So many language learners—including a younger, more ignorant version of this author!—spent far too much time stuck in paralysis by analysis, trying to sift through the mountains of Japanese media to uncover *just the right* resources. I wasted a lot of time *looking* for resources that could have spent actually *using* the tools I already had. You, dear reader, needn't make the same mistake.

CHOOSE A SMALL SET OF CORE RESOURCES

"...the rejection of alternatives liberates us—rejection of what does not align with our most important values, with our chosen metrics, rejection of the constant pursuit of breadth without depth."
—Mark Manson, *The Subtle Art of Not Giving a F*ck*

Another common mistake many learners make is trying to use too many resources at once. This is especially true in today's world of online overwhelm. There is a near infinite number of app, websites, blogs, podcasts, videos, movies, TV shows, anime programs, magazines, manga series, books, etc. Instead of letting yourself get spread too thin, try to focus on just one or two core resources at a time.

The internet may be an all-you-can eat buffet, but that doesn't mean you have to pile everything onto your plate at once. Savor the flavors of *one* dish at a time, and then move onto the next course when you're ready.

CHOOSE DIGITAL MATERIALS WHEN POSSIBLE

I'll be honest: I have an almost fetish-level attraction to good old-fashioned paper books. Whether it's the feel of turning the pages, the weight of the book in my hands, or the smell of the paper, there's just something about the tactile nature of print books that their digital counterparts can never match. When it comes to learning a second language, however, especially one like Japanese that uses ideo-phonetic characters with multiple readings and meanings, digital materials make our lives much, much easier. Here are a few reasons why I recommend digital tools for language learners:

Digital Materials Are Faster

When I started learning Japanese in college, eBooks were still on the fringe and I did most of my reading practice in print books. Having to look up unknown words and *kanji* in a separate dictionary meant that even a single page could take *hours*, especially when going through materials that were way over my head.

Worse yet, back then, there was no easy way to enter *kanji* using handwriting input like you can now on your smartphone screen or laptop trackpad. Nope, if you encountered a *kanji* and didn't know how to pronounce (and therefore couldn't search using *roumaji*), the only way to look it up was by stroke count or radical, a glacier-pace affair that I don't miss in the slightest. Today's Japanese learner, on the other hand, can look up and save words extremely quickly using online popup dictionaries and built-in dictionaries in the Kindle and iBooks apps.

Digital Materials Are More Portable

It's a lot easier to carry around "bits" instead of "atoms." Most smartphones and tablets can store more reading and listening content than you could get through in a lifetime. Instead of killing your back and wasting valuable space in your travel bag with physical resources, you can instead carry all the Japanese content you could ever want in digital format.

Digital Materials Are Often Cheaper

Due to their lower production and distribution costs, the retail price of digital materials tends to be much lower than their paper equivalents. Best of all, you can find a lot of digital content for free online, including digitized versions of books in the public domain, books published with a Creative Commons license, etc.

CHOOSE THE SHORTEST MATERIALS POSSIBLE

Shorter Materials Are Less Intimidating & Create Small Wins

"Once a small win has been accomplished, forces are set in motion that favor another small win. Small wins fuel transformative changes by leveraging tiny advantages into patterns that convince people that bigger achievements are within reach." —Karl E. Weick

---

Long materials can be daunting, and we are more likely to put off difficult tasks. The longer we postpone, the less likely we are to ever begin in the first place. Think about it: given the option between reading a short blog post or a long novel, which would you choose? There's certainly nothing wrong with reading the novel, and I hope you do finish a Japanese text cover to cover some day, but it's better to start small than never at all. Instead of letting the fear of committing to massive undertakings hold you back, just choose something small and manageable to build momentum.

Shorter Materials Are Better Suited for Repetition

If you have children or have ever spent a great deal of time around them, you know that they love watching the same cartoon episode or rereading the same book again, and again, and again. In fact, I often wonder if this taste for repetition is an evolutionary adaptation to speed up first language acquisition…

While we adults may not enjoy repetition as much, we still benefit from its power. The shorter a material is, the easier (and less painful) it will be to repeat it.

CHOOSE AUDIO-BASED MATERIALS WHEN POSSIBLE

Many language learners fall into the trap of spending too much time reading and not enough time listening. As reading becomes easier, one spends more and more time with their nose in a book, furthering the language skill imbalance and making person-to-person interaction ever more uncomfortable. Don't let yourself fall into this trap! Ensure that you spend just as much time (if not *more*) listening to Japanese. Here are a few powerful ways to squeeze in more Japanese listening input throughout your day:

Listen To Podcasts

As I will discuss more shortly, podcasts are one of the best tools for language learning because they are usually free, they cover a wide range of topics, and they sometimes include transcripts and show notes.

See the *Podcasts* section for an extensive list of recommended podcasts and podcast tools.

Listen to the News

Listening to the news in Japanese is a great way to learn relevant, timely, high-frequency vocabulary. While *reading* the news is fine, your listening skills will get much more benefit from *listening* to it instead.

NHK Web News Easy provides audio and video companions to each article: **bit.ly/mjnhknews**

Get Audiobooks or Books With Audio Companions

If you really enjoy reading, try finding the audio version of books you want to read or books that include an audio companion CD or downloadable MP3s.

See *Choose Your Weapons > Japanese Books* for recommended resources and tools.

Use RhinoSpike To Create Audio Versions of Text-Only Content

Creating audio versions of text-only content you love is another great way to improve your Japanese listening skills. You can have a tutor record material for you, or you can use one of my favorite crowdsource tools: RhinoSpike. Here's how the free service works:

1. **Submit your text:** Simply upload some text content that you want a native Japanese speaker to record.

2. **Record for submissions in your native language:** To both help the community and push your submission ahead in line, answer a request for recordings in *your* native language.

3. **Download the finished audio file.** When a native speaker has finished recording your text submission, just download it to your computer.

Just like that, you have your own "on-demand" foreign language audio that is perfectly tailored to your interests!

Learn more about RhinoSpike and sign up for a free account at: **bit.ly/mjrhino**

USE THE TOOLS YOU ALREADY HAVE

> "Do what you can, with what you have, where you are."
> —Theodore Roosevelt

It doesn't matter how many Japanese books are on your shelf, how many Japanese apps are on your phone, or how many Japanese flashcards are in your deck, if you don't actually *use* them. Before buying or downloading yet *another* resource, take an honest look at what you already have. What books have you not finished, or even cracked open once? What apps did you download and never open? Which podcasts remain unplayed? Instead of scratching the surface of *lots* of resources, take the advice of polyglot Lindsay Williams and "squeeze every last drop" out of your language learning sponges.

Listen to my interview with Lindsay Williams here:
bit.ly/mjlindsay

Japanese Audio Courses

If you are completely new to Japanese or struggle to pronounce things properly, I highly recommend investing in an audio-based course. They can be a bit pricey, but the benefit to your pronunciation and speaking skills is worth the money. These programs do an excellent job of presenting essential words, phrases, and structures in an intuitive, building-block method, all the while getting you to speak aloud so you can activate what you learn and get used to hearing and producing the sounds of the language.

MICHEL THOMAS

The *Michel Thomas Method* is an audio-based language learning approach developed by Michel Thomas (1914 - 2005), a Polish-born polyglot who emigrated to Los Angeles in 1947 after surviving multiple Nazi concentration camps. He was awarded the Silver Star in 2004 for his work helping the U.S. Army Counter Intelligence Corps during World War II. After starting a language school in Beverly Hills, his reputation as a master teacher spread quickly, and he went on to teach a number of high-profile students.

To see Michel in action, check out *The Language Master* documentary from the BBC: **bit.ly/mjmtm**

During his years of learning and teaching languages, Michel Thomas came to believe that students should *not* try to overtly memorize new words, phrases, and patterns. Instead, the learner's brain should automatically internalize the language *if* it's broken down into sufficiently small chunks, and these tiny pieces are presented in just the right order. If done right, the learner develops the intuitive ability to then put the pieces *back together* without struggle or conscious effort.

Just Enough Grammar

Many new learners are shocked to find that—despite spending tons of time studying grammar—their conscious knowledge of the rules is all but useless in real-time communication. This is because grammar study mostly builds *declarative memory*, not *procedural memory* (the kind we need to understand and use grammar patterns). That said, I do think a *little* grammar knowledge can be useful, and The Michel Thomas Method courses do a good of providing just enough grammar tips without boring or distracting learners.

Proper Pronunciation Is Stressed Above all Else

As I often say:

"Pronunciation trumps grammar."

Proper syntax is obviously important, but you will be more easily understood if you pronounce things correctly with broken grammar, than perfect grammar pronounced with a strong, improperly stressed accent.

Sufficient Repetition Without Stagnation

While the *Michel Thomas Method* doesn't use a formulaic spaced repetition schedule, you will find that the courses offer enough repetition to help you internalize the words and structures you hear without boring you to death.

Learning Alongside Others Builds Confidence

Each Michel Thomas Method course includes a few fellow students who learn "alongside" you. I was initially skeptical of this part of the course, but I think it can be helpful for many learners (especially those who have never learned a foreign language). Why? Hearing the other learners struggle and make occasional mistakes normalizes this inevitable aspect of language learning.

Moreover, you may find that *you* sometimes know the correct answer or response when the learners in the recording *don't*. This can be very encouraging, helping give you the extra psychological juice you need to keep going.

Get the Michel Thomas Method *Total Japanese Foundation Course* on Amazon here: **bit.ly/mjmtmtf**

Buy digital versions of Michel Courses online: **bit.ly/mjmtmsite**

Download the iOS app here: **bit.ly/mjmtmios**
Download the Android app here: **bit.ly/mjmtmandroid**

NOTE!

The Michel Thomas Method courses for Japanese are not taught by Michel himself as he passed away before they were made. However, the instructors—Helen Gilhooly and Niamh Kelly—follow the Michel Thomas method closely in the materials, and are both professional Japanese teachers with extensive teaching experience.

PIMSLEUR

Pimsleur is one of the most popular self-study language learning programs on the planet. The system was developed by the late Dr. Paul Pimsleur, an applied linguist, and professor of French and foreign language education at UCLA, Ohio State University, State University of New York at Albany, and Ruprecht Karl University of Heidelberg. He was also a founding member of the ACTFL (American Council on the Teaching of Foreign Languages). The Pimsleur Approach promotes three core principles:

The Power of Anticipation & Active Recall

The extremely passive nature of most language classes, with students simply listening to—or repeating after—the teacher, is a highly ineffective way to build memories and develop fluency.

To address this problem, Dr. Pimsleur developed a "challenge and response" approach, which requires students to translate a phrase into the target language when given a prompt in English. He believed that this anticipatory approach strengthens memories and better reflects real-life conversations.

Spaced Repetition

Paul Pimsleur's version of spaced repetition is called "Graduated Interval Recall" (G.I.R.). Like other spaced repetition systems, Pimsleur audio courses present the same vocabulary items and phrases in progressively longer intervals, refreshing your memory just when you are about to forget.

Core Vocabulary

The Pimsleur Approach presents only the most common words first (approximately 500 new words per level). As discussed earlier in the guide, a very small number of words account for the vast majority of spoken and written material in a language so it makes sense to master the highest-frequency terms first.

Get the Level 1 CD set on Amazon here:
bit.ly/mjapimsleur

GLOSSIKA

Glossika is a science-based, audio-focused language learning platform created by the polyglot Mike Campbell. He speaks numerous languages to an extremely high level (including some of Taiwan's indigenous languages spoken by few non-native speakers), a feat he has accomplished using the very methods embodied in Glossika's architecture.

Mike designed Glossika to overcome many of the common problems with traditional language learning tools. Instead of focusing on reading and isolated vocabulary, the system uses a more natural, sentence-based approach that focuses on training your ears and mouth and getting your brain used to the underlying patterns and "deep semantics" of a language.

Register for Glossika here: **bit.ly/mjglossika**

PRICE: $30/MO | **PLATFORM:** WEB

Listen to my interview with Mike here: **bit.ly/mjmikecampbell**

Japanese Podcasts

Despite the myriad advantages podcasts offer language learners, I am often surprised how many people have never heard the word "podcast," or at least have never listened to one themselves. Podcasting is getting more and more popular with each passing year, but here's quick primer if you're completely new to the medium:

- In essence, podcasts are audio shows that you can download or stream *whenever* and *wherever* you want.
- You can think of podcasts as on-demand radio. Just as many now watch TV shows and movies on Netflix, Hulu, etc. instead of watching them live on television or at the theater, many now listen to podcasts instead of having to wait for a radio show to be broadcast live over the air.
- The word "podcasting" is a portmanteau that combines the *pod* from "iPod" with the *casting* from "broadcasting." However, podcasts are *not* specific to Apple devices and can be enjoyed on any smartphone, media player, or computer.

For more on podcasting, check out Common Craft's simple video explanation here: **bit.ly/mjccpod**

WHY PODCASTS ROCK

So why are podcasts so great for language learning? Here are but a few of the many advantages over other media types:

Podcasts Are Almost Always Free

While some podcast makers offer premium content and tools on their companion sites, the podcasts themselves are free.

Podcasts Are Usually Short

Podcasts tend to be relatively short, making them easier to repeat again and again.

Podcasts Are Diverse

As of writing, there are more than 700,000 active podcast programs in existence, with a total of 29,000,000 +podcast episodes. From professionally created shows to do-it-yourself programs recorded in someone's bedroom, there is a massive pool of topics to choose from.

Podcasts Are Convenient

Podcasts are distributed via RSS or XLM feeds, meaning that new content can be automatically download in your podcast app or "podcatcher" as soon as they become available. No need to constantly check for new content or manually update your shows.

Podcasts Let You Optimize Your Time

Though video and reading resources are helpful, they have one major limitation: you can't really do anything else while you watch or read. With podcasts, on the other hand, you can make use of otherwise wasted time to acquire Japanese. This is a historically significant, game-changing technological revolution! As the psychologist Jordan Peterson puts it:

> "For the first time in human history, the spoken word has the same reach as the written word... That's a Gutenberg revolution. Except it's even more extensive, because the problem with books and videos is that you can't do anything else while you're doing them... But if you're listening to a podcast, you can be driving a forklift or long haul truck. Or you can be exercising or doing the dishes. And so what that means is that podcasts free up, say, two hours a day for people to engage in educational activities that they wouldn't otherwise be able to engage in... So podcasts hand people one-eighth of their life back to engage in high-level education."

Some Podcasts Include Transcripts

Some of the better language podcasts come equipped with transcripts, making it easier to look up new words and follow along as you listen.

TAKE ACTION!

In the Apple Podcasts app for iOS:

1. Play a podcast episode.
2. Slide up to reveal "Episode Notes." If a transcript is included by the provider, it will appear here.
3. Tap "Show" or "Hide" to the right to display or remove show notes.

In the Apple Podcasts app for macOS Catalina (and newer):

1. Play a podcast episode.
2. Click the "i" (Information) icon in the upper right corner to reveal episode notes.

In older versions of iTunes:

1. Select "Podcasts" from the dropdown menu in the upper left.
2. Hover over an episode with your cursor, and select the ··· icon on the right and click on "Podcast Info."
3. Select the "Description" tab. If a transcript is not included, you can always paste in your *own* transcript here.

RECOMMENDED PODCAST APPS

There are numerous podcast apps to choose from. Here are a few of my favorites to help get you started.

Apple Podcasts App

The Apple Podcasts app is certainly not the fanciest option available, but it's a solid option for three reasons:

- The app is free.
- The user interface is simple and intuitive.
- Your podcasts are automatically synced between all your Apple devices (iPhone, iPad, Mac, Apple Watch, and Apple TV), and you can pick up where you left off when switching between devices.

Learn more about how to listen with the Apple Podcasts app on any Apple device: **bit.ly/mjapplepodcasts**

PC users can download and listen to Apple Podcasts using iTunes for Windows: **bit.ly/mjitunesms**

Overcast

The Overcast podcast app has a number intelligent features that help you get more from your audio content:

- **Smart Speed:** This nifty feature saves time without distortion by shortening pauses and silence in podcasts.
- **Voice Boost:** This helpful tool automatically equalizes every podcast, ensuring clear audio and equal volume.
- **Custom playback speeds:** You can adjust by small increments, not just the standard ½ or 2X.

Download the Overcast app here: **bit.ly/mjovercast**

PRICE: FREE WITH IN-APP UPGRADES | **PLATFORM:** iOS

Pocket Casts

Pocket Casts is a great cross-platform option, with a clean, user-friendly interface, an optional dark theme, custom skip times, and variable playback speeds.

Download Pocket Casts here: **bit.ly/mjpocketcasts**

PRICE: FREE WITH IN-APP UPGRADES | **PLATFORMS:** IOS, ANDROID, MACOS & WINDOWS

Spotify

The popular music streaming service Spotify has recently planted its flag in the spoken word world, and is quickly becoming one of the top podcast platforms.

Get the Spotify app: **bit.ly/mjgetspotify**

PRICE: FREE WITH IN-APP UPGRADES | PLATFORMS: IOS, ANDROID, MACOS & WINDOWS

Google Podcasts

Android users should check out Google Podcasts, one of the newest and most promising podcast apps on the market. Some of the best features include:

- The ability to pause on one device and resume on another using Google Assistant.
- Automatic silence removal to shorten episode lengths, especially for those who pause a lot in their speech.
- Adjustable playback speed.

Download the Google Podcasts app here: **bit.ly/mjgpa**

PRICE: FREE | PLATFORM: ANDROID

RECOMMENDED JAPANESE PODCASTS

I could create an entire book on nothing but recommended Japanese podcasts, but for the sake of brevity and actionable intel, here is but a short sampler of Japanese podcasts to whet your appetite and help you get started. I've included a mix of learner podcasts and those intended for native Japanese speakers to keep things interesting.

 TIP!

One common problem with learner podcasts is that they often spend way too much time speaking *in* English *about* Japanese. While this can help you wrap your head around the language, it does little to actually improve your ability to *understand* or *use* Japanese. I therefore suggest skipping ahead to just the dialogue portion of each episode and moving on to podcasts intended for Japanese native speakers as soon as possible.

JapanesePod101

JapanesePod101 produces some of the highest quality learner podcasts and tools available:

- They include resources for absolute beginners, beginners, intermediate learners, and advanced learners.
- Each episode includes show notes with a complete transcription in *kanji*, *kana*, and *roumaji*, and an English translation.

- With a membership, you get unlimited access to nearly 3,000 audio and video episodes.
- You can use their lesson checklist to keep track of which episodes you've already listened to, and create a custom podcast feed that automatically downloads episodes for only *your* level.
- They have spaced repetition flashcards, *kanji* study tools, pronunciation and accent review tools, a grammar bank, and more.
- You can learn on the go using the Innovative Language app.

Create a free lifetime account: **bit.ly/mjjpod101**
Download the Innovative app: **bit.ly/mj101app**

Manga Sensei

Manga Sensei (漫画先生, まんがせんせい) brings you short doses of Japanese, five minutes at a time. The show is hosted by John Dinkel, an entrepreneur and interpreter who first learned Japanese as an LDS missionary in Japan. He quickly became obsessed with the language and culture, and loves sharing the lessons he's learned along the way.

To learn more about John, make sure to check out my interview with him on *The Language Mastery Show*.

Subscribe to the *Manga Sensei* podcast: **bit.ly/mjmsp**
Listen to my interview with John: **bit.ly/mjjohnd**

Bilingual News

Bilingual News, or *Bairingaru Nyuusu* (バイリンガルニュース), provides a weekly overview of current events and news in casual, unedited Japanese and English. Each episode starts with cohost Mami (マミ) presenting in Japanese, and then cohost Michael (マイケル) providing the translation in English. They then discuss the topic bilingually. I especially appreciate that they offer detailed transcripts and timestamps for each episode through the companion app.

Subscribe to the podcast here: **bit.ly/mjbnpod**
Download the transcript app here: **bit.ly/mjbnapp**

Tofugu Podcast

Koichi and the gang at *Tofugu* have been pumping out top-notch Japanese learning materials for years, and I was delighted when they decided to start a podcast in 2016. Koichi has a wonderful sense of humor, a delightfully sarcastic wit, and a direct, succinct way of explaining Japanese patterns and concepts.

Subscribe to the *Tofugu Podcast* here:
bit.ly/mjtofugupod

Nihongo con Teppei

There is a lot to like about the *Nihongo con Teppei* podcast: each episode is short (usually about four minutes), presented *only* in Japanese (with no distractions in English), and tailored for language learners (with words pronounced in a slow, clear way). The show is hosted Teppei, a popular Japanese teacher on iTalki who has taught over 750 lessons to date. Since he is learning English and Spanish *himself*, he knows exactly what it's like to learn a language, and uses the same methods to teach his native language that he employs to learn foreign tongues.

Subscribe to the *Nihongo con Teppei* podcast here:
bit.ly/mjteppei

Japanese LingQ

Though the *Japanese LingQ Podcast* is no longer updated, all the past episodes are still available online. Each episode has a full transcript (which you can mine for new vocabulary within the LingQ site or app). I also like that each episode goes right into the Japanese dialogue, with no trite English introductions or grammar dissections—or rather *distractions*—in English.

Browse the archives here: **bit.ly/mjlingqjp**
Sign up for a free LingQ account here: **bit.ly/mjlingq**

Learn Japanese Pod

Learn Japanese Pod is the brainchild of Alex (a musician, composer, and experienced expat), Asuka (a native Japanese speaker and professional radio announcer), and Beb (a composer and rockstar). They cover vocabulary, grammar, and a wide range of language topics in a fun, clear way.

Subscribe to Learn Japanese Pod here:
bit.ly/mjljp

NHK World's Yasashii Nihongo

The *Yasashii Nihongo* (やさしい日本語, やさしいにほんご) podcast provides free, easy Japanese lessons in seventeen different world languages, including: Arabic (アラビア語), Bengali (ベンガル語), Burmese (ビルマ語), Chinese (中国語), English (英語), French (フランス語), Hindi (ヒンディー語), Indonesian (インドネシア語), Korean (ハングル), Persian/Farsi (ペルシャ語), Portuguese (ポルトガル語), Russian (ロシア語), Spanish (スペイン語), Swahili (スワヒリ語), Thai (タイ語), Urdu (ウルドゥー語), and Vietnamese (ベトナム語).

Visit the Yasashii Nihongo website and scroll down to the language you want to subscribe to: **bit.ly/mjyasashii**

NHK Radio News

NHK Radio News (NHKラジオニュース) is another useful offering from Japan's national public broadcaster. You can stream the episodes online or subscribe to the show in your favorite podcast app.

Visit the NHK Radio News site to stream or grab their podcast RSS feed: **bit.ly/mjnhkrn**

Cross Cultural Seminar

Though Cross-Cultural Seminar podcast (大杉正明先生とスーザン岩本さんの英会話講座) is intended for Japanese native speakers learning English, the content is perfectly relevant to English speakers learning Japanese. In fact, I often find such "reverse learning" to be the most interesting form of input and practice. Though the show is no longer updated, but the entire archive is still available online and in Apple Podcasts.

Browse episodes online: **bit.ly/mjccseminar**
Subscribe in Apple Podcasts: **bit.ly/mjccsitunes**

女子だけ体育館に集合

In each episode of the *Joshi Dake Taiikukan-ni Shuugoo* (女子だけ体育館に集合, じょしだけたいいくかんにしゅうごう) podcast, four women meet up at the gym in Kobe to chat on a wide range of topics. Though the show is targeted at women listeners, I think it is a great way for *all genders* to expand their vocabulary and get used to authentic Japanese.

Browse episodes online: **bit.ly/mjjoshi**
Subscribe in Apple Podcasts: **bit.ly/mjjoshiitunes**

JAPANESE PODCAST DIRECTORIES

When you are ready to branch out, here are some tools for browsing additional Japanese podcasts:

Apple Japan

If you simply browse for Japanese podcasts in the Apple Podcasts app, you will mostly find shows intended for Japanese *learners* (e.g. JapanesePod101). This is a good place to start, but I highly recommend moving onto authentic Japanese content as soon as possible. In iTunes (available for Windows and older versions of macOS), the easiest way to find such content is changing the country/region setting to Japan in iTunes as follows:

1. Select "Podcasts" from the dropdown menu in the upper left and click the "Store" tab at the top.

2. Scroll down all the way down, click on the round flag icon in the bottom right, and click on "Japan" in the "Asia Pacific" section.

3. Choose from the treasure trove of Japanese language podcasts now available! You can subscribe to shows, download episodes, or simply stream within iTunes.

4. Normally you would need a Japanese credit card or iTunes Japan gift card to purchase items from the

iTunes Japan Store, but since podcasts are free, you can subscribe and download using your home country account.

If you are running macOS Catalina or newer, iTunes is no longer available (it was replaced with three separate apps in fall of 2019: Apple Podcasts, Apple Music, and Apple TV apps). While greatly improved in many respects, the new Apple Podcasts app lacks the country icon at the bottom of the screen that allowed you to quickly change one's country or region. You *can* still change your country in your account settings, but it's a hassle and cancels any existing podcast subscriptions you have in your home country account. The good news is that you can now simply search for a specific podcast, host, or episode in the Apple Podcasts app and download it without having to change one's country settings.

NHK Radio

NHK offers numerous programs on a wide range of topics. You can listen to shows about news, sports, weather, politics, music, pop culture, and more.

Access the NHK Radio site here:
bit.ly/mjnhkradio

TBS Radio Podcasts

The *good* news is that TBS Radio offers tons of free Japanese news and entertainment shows, covering politics, pop culture, comedy, relationships, and even motor sports for the gear-heads out there. The *bad* news is that the content can only be accessed using their free app called ラジオクラウド (Radio Cloud), which can only be downloaded from the Japan iTunes Store. Likewise, you can only stream or download the content if you are in Japan or using a Japan-based VPN.

Browse TBS Radio's shows here: **bit.ly/mjtbs**
Download the ラジオクラウド app here: **bit.ly/tbsrc**

Japanese Music

The two Chinese characters in the word for music, *on* (音, おん) and *gaku* (楽, がく), literally mean "sound" and "fun" respectively. I think this says a lot about the power of music in language learning! Not only is music inherently enjoyable, but it can actually help improve retention. Try it yourself: just add a simply melody to any phrase or sentence you're struggling to remember, and boom, you will be able to recall it much more easily. Moreover, learning the lyrics of Japanese music helps you get reading and listening input at the same time.

JAPANESE MUSIC GENRES

Here are some of the more popular genres of music in Japan, as well as some tips on which are better suited for language learning.

Enka

Enka (演歌, えんか) employs the "pentatonic" scale, giving it a somewhat similar sound to blues, and there is even further similarity given that both genres tend to focus on stories of loss and loneliness. Interestingly, *enka* had its beginnings as a way for Meiji era political activists to voice their opinions without breaking anti-dissent laws.

Folk Rock

Japan has some excellent folk rock, or *fouku rokku* (フォークロック, ふぉうくろっく). The genre is perfect for language learners since singer-songwriters tend to pronounce their ballads more clearly than many other genres.

Hip-Hop

Japanese hip-hop—or *hippu hoppu* (ヒップホップ, ひっぷほっぷ)—tends to have rather simple lyrics, which makes the genre a great tool for language learning.

J-Pop

Japanese Pop—or *jei poppu* (ジェイポップ, じぇいぽっぷ)—is arguably the most popular genre of music in Japan, and probably the easiest to approach for non-native speakers since their lyrics tend to be clearly pronounced.

J-Rock

Japanese Rock—or *nihon no rokku* (日本のロック, にほんのろっく)—ranges from fairly light pop rock to quite intense heavy metal. The former tends to be better for language learning since you can actually hear what the singer is saying, while the latter can be less helpful (screaming tends to be a less-than-ideal form of language input).

WHERE TO GET JAPANESE MUSIC

With the plethora of music streaming services available today, it's easier than ever to listen to Japanese music artists and genres you love *anywhere, anytime*. But you can still buy MP3s or CDs individually too if you prefer.

Apple Music

Apple Music has tons of Japanese artists, albums, and songs to choose from. Though you can buy individual songs and albums, a subscription to Apple Music is well worth the money since it unlocks an important feature for language learners: **song lyrics**! Not all songs in Apple Music have lyrics, but many do. Here's how to access them:

- In the Apple Music app on iOS, play a Japanese song and then tap the lyrics icon (a speech bubble with a quotation mark inside) in the lower left. The mobile version automatically syncs the lyrics to the song, highlighting each phrase as it's sung karaoke style!

 **PRO TIP!**

Didn't quite catch part of a lyric? Or want to practice singing aloud after the singer? You can quickly repeat a line (or jump to a different part of the song) by tapping on any section of the song's lyrics.

- In the Apple Music app on macOS, click the lyrics icon in the upper right corner to reveal a sidebar with the song's lyrics. Unfortunately, the lyrics are not synced to the music the way they are in the iOS version.

You can browse popular Japanese artists using the link below, or search within the Apple Music app on your iPhone, iPad, Mac, AppleTV, or Apple Watch. Note that you may need to search for specific artists or albums using romanized names.

Browse Japanese artists available in Apple Music here: bit.ly/mjitunesmusic

---

Amazon Prime Music

If you already have an Amazon Prime account, you can stream or download thousands of Japanese songs and albums using *Prime Music*. I especially like that:

- **Many songs have built-in lyrics:** If available for the song you're listening to, you will see the word *Lyrics* (or 歌詞 if your device is in Japanese) on the right. Just swipe up on the hamburger icon in the middle, and then read along as you listen. Karaoke right in your pocket!

- **You can listen offline:** Those who travel a lot will

especially appreciate the fact you can download songs, albums, and playlists for offline playback.

- **You get unlimited skips:** Most streaming services limit the number of songs you can skip in a row, but with Amazon Music, you can skip to your heart's content!

Learn more about Amazon Music here:
bit.ly/mjamazonmusic

Download the Amazon Music app here: **bit.ly/mjamapps**

PRICE: FREE FOR PRIME MEMBERS | **PLATFORMS:** IOS, ANDROID, MAC, WINDOWS & MORE

Amazon Japan

If you want to buy Japanese music Amazon, your best bet is switching to the Amazon Japan store. They have a wide variety of CDs and digital downloads to choose from, but I suggest sticking with MP3s (MP3音楽ダウンロード) to avoid overseas shipping fees.

Browse digital downloads available in the Amazon Japan store:
bit.ly/mjamazonmp3

Line Music

If you already use LINE for messaging (as many people in Japan do), LINE MUSIC can be a great way to rock out. Unfortunately, the service is only available in Japan or using a Japan-based VPN.

Sign up for a Japan Line account here:
bit.ly/mjlinemusic

For more on using a virtual private network, see *How to Use a VPN* in the *Video* section.

SoundCloud

SoundCloud is a good source for smaller indie artists, DJ sets, and J-Pop remixes. You can stream for free online or using the SoundCloud app.

Create a free account here: **bit.ly/mjsoundcloud**
Download the SoundCloud app here: **bit.ly/mjsca**

Spotify

Spotify is one of the most popular "freemium" music streaming services and has one of the best selections of Japanese music. You can listen for free with ads, or upgrade to remove ads, listen offline, and even get Hulu for free (which is one of the best platforms for watching Japanese *anime*, by the way).

Sign up for Spotify and download the free apps here:
bit.ly/mjspotifyapp

To get started, check out this J-Pop and J-Rock playlist:
bit.ly/mjspotifyjp

TuneIn

TuneIn is another freemium streaming service that allows you to hear Japanese radio anywhere in the world, right from your device. Use the link below to browse Japanese music by genre (e.g. Hip Hop, Indie, J-Pop, etc.) or radio station.

Browse Japanese music on TuneIn here:
bit.ly/mjtimusic

YouTube

YouTube is the second largest search engine in the world after Google (its parent company), and you can find heaps of Japanese songs, music videos, and playlists.

Browse Japanese music here: **bit.ly/mjytmusict**
See recommended playlists here: **bit.ly/mjytmusicl**

Kinokuniya

Though best known for books, *Kinokuniya* (紀伊国屋, きのくにや) *also* sells CDs. They have branches all over the world, and they can always order something for you if it's not in stock at your local store.

Find a Kinokuniya branch near you:
bit.ly/mjkinokuniya

WHERE TO FIND JAPANESE LYRICS

While *listening* to Japanese music can be fun and effective, you will get even more benefit if you study the lyrics:

- Lyrics help increase comprehension (we only learn when we understand).
- Lyrics highlight new words and structures you're not yet familiar with.

Amazon Music

To reveal lyrics in the Amazon Music app, simply swipe up on the = icon in the middle of the screen.

Learn more about Amazon Music here:
bit.ly/mjamazonmusic

Apple Music

For Apple Music, tap the lyrics icon in the lower left on iOS or in the upper right in macOS.

Learn more about Apple Music lyrics here:
bit.ly/mjapplemusiclyrics

Anime Lyrics

As the name implies, Anime Lyrics is a good place to find lyrics for anime theme songs. But they *also* have lyrics for many popular J-Pop songs, too. Best of all, they have a built-in pop-up *kanji* dictionary (just make sure to click the "View Kanji" link first to display lyrics in Japanese script). You can search for a specific song or browse through the titles, grouped by genre and title.

Browse Japanese songs and find lyrics here:
bit.ly/mjanimelyrics

Shazam

You might have used Shazam to identify a song title you don't know, but the app also a cool feature you might not be aware of: real-time karaoke style lyrics! Simply tap the center button to identify the song, then select *Lyrics* (歌詞) at the top to display that song's words. To see the entire song's lyrics, tap *See Full Lyrics* (歌詞全体を見る).

Download the free Shazam app here: **bit.ly/mjshazam**

PRICE: FREE | **PLATFORMS:** IOS & ANDROID

RECOMMENDED ARTISTS & BANDS

Musical taste is a very personal thing, and you will need to try out a wide range of Japanese artists to find who resonates with you most. To help you start your journey of musical exploration, here is a shortlist of some of Japan's top bands, musicians, and singers (arranged in alphabetical order).

TIP!

For more Japanese music artist recommendations, check out the *r/japanesemusic* subreddit. It's a great place to find recommended albums, songs, and music videos. → **bit.ly/mjredditjm**

AMURO Namie

Known to some as the "Queen of J-Pop," *AMURO Namie* (安室奈美恵, あむろなみえ) began her music career as a teen idol member of the Super Monkeys, but went on to have an über successful solo career, winning "Album of the Year" at the 50th Japan Record Awards.

Bump of Chicken

Since their founding in 1994, *Bump of Chicken* (バンプ・オブ・チキン) has grown into one of Japan's top rock bands, with fourteen singles and five albums under their belts.

Their tunes are frequently used as theme songs in television shows and video games, so you will likely come across their work in your various immersion activities.

B'z

Pronounced *beezu* (ビーズ, びいず), B'z is one of Japan's most well-known rock bands. If you ever visit Hollywood's RockWalk, you will find the signatures and handprints of the band's guitarist, *MATSUMOTO Takahiro* (松本孝弘, まつもとたかひろ) and vocalist, *INABA Koushi* (稲葉浩志, いなばこうし). With 80 million records sold, nearly 50 number-one singles, and 24 number-one albums, B'z is a must for hard rock fans.

Dabo

Unlike most Japanese hip-hop that tends to be rather "poppy," *Dabo* (ダボ, だぼ) represents a sound and message more reminiscent of American rap.

FLOW

Formed in the late 90s, *Flow* (フロウ, ふろう) is a "mixture rock" band (ミクスチャー・ロック, みくすちゃあろっく) whose music has been featured in many popular Japanese anime, including *Naruto* (ナルト, なると) and *Koukyou Shihen Eureka Sebun* (交響詩篇エウレカセブン, こうきょうしへんえ

うれかせぶん, "Psalms of Planets Eureka Seven").

Glay

Ranked number seven on Music Station's best selling Japanese music artists of all time, *Glay* (グレイ, ぐれい) is known for music spanning a wide range of genres, including pop, rock, reggae, and even gospel.

HAMASAKI Ayumi

Known by her fans as *Ayu* for short, *HAMASAKI Ayumi* (浜崎歩, はまさきあゆみ) is often called the "Empress of Pop" given her nearly 50 million record sales and the influence she's had on other artists in Japan and Asia.

Happy End

Although *Happy End* was only together for three years (1970 to 1973), they continue to receive praise and notoriety for their unique, highly influential sound. You can hear their song *Kaze-wo Atsumete* (風をあつめて, かぜをあつめて, "Gather the Wind") in the movie "Lost in Translation."

HIKAWA Kiyoshi

Starting out his career with supporters like *KITANO Takeshi* (北野武, きたのたけし), *HIKAWA Kiyoshi* (氷川清志, ひかわき

よし) quickly rose in popularity, coming to be known as "The Prince of Enka." His real name is *YAMADA Kiyoshi* (山田清志, やまだきよし), and you will sometimes see him referred to as simply *KIYOSHI* (written in all capital letters) in his non-enka endeavors.

Hime

Literally meaning "Princess," *Hime* (姫, ひめ) creates a unique blend between traditional Japanese music and modern hip-hop. She is well known for her efforts to empower Japanese women, and fight back against the stereotypical portrayal of women in Japan.

Jero

Jero (ジェロ, じぇろ)—a.k.a. Jerome Charles White—is one of my heroes. Hailing from Pittsburgh, Pennsylvania, Jero is the first African-American *enka* (演歌, えんか) singer in Japanese music history. His interest in the art form was sparked at an early age by his Japanese grandmother, who had met his grandfather (an American serviceman) at a dance in post World War II Japan. By blending his two cultural backgrounds, Jero has managed to revitalize *enka*, a genre that had previously seemed doomed for extinction.

KAWAGUCHI Kyougo

If you like bittersweet folk, you will love *KAWAGUCHI Kyougo* (河口恭吾, かわぐちきょうご). One of his best known songs—and one of my all time favorites of *any* genre or language—is *Sakura* (桜, さくら, "Cherry Blossoms").

King Giddra

Debuting in 1993, *King Giddra* (キングギドラ, きんぐぎどら) is considered one of the primary pioneers of Japanese hip-hop. The three-member group (MC K Dub Shine, MC Zeebra, and DJ Oasis) was heavily influenced by Public Enemy, and like the U.S. group, uses hip-hop as a platform for addressing social problems. If you're curious, the group named itself after the three-headed dragon creature in Godzilla of the same name.

KITAJIMA Saburou

One of Japan's most well-known *enka* singers, *KITAJIMA Saburou* (北島三郎, きたじまさぶろう) is best known for *Namida-Bune* (なみだ船, なみだぶね, "Boat of Tears"), released in 1962, and *Kyoudai Jingi* (兄弟仁義, きょうだいじんぎ, "Brothers Humanity & Justice"), released in 1965. Growing up poor in the aftermath of World War II, he is no stranger to the woes of Japan's working class, and much of his work aims to tell their story. And like many men of his generation, he doesn't let age stop him: in 2010, he released *Fuufu Isshou* (夫婦一生, ふうふいっしょう, "Couple of a Lifetime") at the age of 73!

KOUDA Kumi

Final Fantasy X-2 fans should already be familiar with *KOUDA Kumi* (倖田來未, こうだくみ) as her songs were used extensively in the game. While she initially represented a more conservative look and sound, she evolved into a more provocative artist. To date, she has sold more than 18 million records.

L'Arc-En-Ciel

Beginning as a "visual kei" group (ヴィジュアル系) using makeup and costumes somewhat akin to Kiss, *L'Arc-en-Ciel* (which means "The Rainbow" in French) gave up the gags shortly after their major label debut in 1994.

MISORA Hibari

With her passing in 1989, the world lost one of the Japanese music industry's most prolific artists. *MISORA Hibari* (美空ひばり, みそらひばり) was the first woman in Japan to be awarded the "People's Honor Award" (awarded only after her death, sadly) and has sold more than 80 million records. Her most famous song is *Kawa-no Nagare You Ni* (川の流れの

ように, かわのながれように, "Like the Flow of The River"), which has been remade by many notable artists, including *The Three Tenors*, *Teresa Teng* of Taiwan, and *Mariachi Vargas de Tecalitlan* of Mexico.

Mr. Children

Mr. Children is difficult to classify, with one foot in J-Pop and another in Folk Rock. Their song *Kuruma no Naka de Kakurete Kisu o Shiyou* (車の中でかれてキスをしよう, くるまのなかでかくれてきすをしよう, "Let's Hide Away in the Car and Kiss") is one of my favorite songs.

OKABAYASHI Nobuyasu

Called "Japan's Bob Dylan" and "The God of Folk" by some, *OKABAYASHI Nobuyasu* (岡林信康, おかばやしのぶやす), is one of Japan's best-known folk singers. Once a Christian, he later began to question his beliefs, looking for escape and expression in his music.

ONITSUKA Chihiro

If you've watched *Trick* (トリック) before, you will be familiar with *ONITSUKA Chihiro's* (鬼束ちひろ, おにつかちひろ) song *Gekkou* (月光, げっこう, "Moonlight"), her hauntingly beautiful debut single used in the show's closing credits (another one of my all-time faves).

Rhymester

One of the first hip-hop groups in Japan, *Rhymester* (ライムスター, らいむすたあ) consists of three members: MC Mummy-D, MC Utamaru, and DJ Jin. Though their first works were not well received by critics, they have gradually become popular with rap and rock fans alike. Rhymester is well-known for political and social satire, with frequent criticism of both the Japanese and U.S. governments.

Sambomaster

Named after the Russian martial art Sambo, *Sambomaster* (サンボマスター, さんぼますたあ) has a number of hits, and is frequently tapped for theme songs in Japanese anime, dramas, and video games. For example, their song *Kimi-wo Mamotte, Kimi-wo Aishite* (君を守って君を愛して, きみをまもってきみをあいして, "I Protect You, I Love You") was used as the closing theme of *Bleach* from episode 215 through 229.

SMAP

SMAP (スマップ, すまっぷ) is one of Japan's best-known boy bands. Their upbeat sound is exemplified by their best-selling single *Sekai-ni Hitotsu-Dake no Hana* (世界に一つだけの花, せかいにひとつだけのはな, "The One and Only Flower in the World").

Japanese Videos

"Languages are about people. If you don't have real people, films and TV are the next best thing." —Katie Harris, *Joy of Languages*

Staring at pixels might not ever replace living abroad, but videos can at least create a highly immersive, engaging forms of language learning input you can enjoy anywhere in the world. Moreover, the strong visual context makes video a more comprehensible form of input than reading alone. And speaking of reading: when you turn on subtitles in your target language, video becomes a source of reading input, not just listening.

In this section, you will find:

- Tips for choosing videos that fit your level, preferences, and interests.
- How to increase your comprehension and get more out of video-based language learning.
- How to stream Japanese videos using free and paid services.
- How to watch Japan-only content anywhere in the world using a Virtual Private Network (VPN).

- Why DVDs are still a useful language learning tool even in the era of streaming services.
- Recommended *anime* series, TV shows, and movies to get you started.

HOW TO CHOOSE THE RIGHT VIDEOS

Choose Videos That Fit Your Interests

Video can be one of the most enjoyable forms of Japanese language input, but not if you are forcing yourself through uninteresting content. A general guideline to follow: **if you would not watch something *in English*, don't force yourself through it *in Japanese*.**

Choose (Mostly) Comprehensible Videos

With enough effort, patience, and courage, you can watch *any* videos you want, regardless of your current Japanese ability level. That said, it's much more enjoyable—and much more effective from a language learning perspective—to choose content that you can *mostly* understand. It's like *Goldilocks and the Three Bears*: you want your video "porridge" to be not too hard, not too easy, but just right.

In my experience, an ideal comprehension level is about 70

to 80%. Below this, your video porridge will probably be too "cold." You'll either have to stop the video too frequently to look up unknown words or you will have to soldier on not really understanding what's happening. This makes it difficult to get into the "flow" of the story, the video will quickly become tedious and uninteresting. It will take a significant amount of motivation and discipline to keep going, which transforms video-based language learning from an inherently fun activity to laborious language study. On the other hand, if you know almost every word in the video, then your video porridge is too "hot." On this end of the spectrum, you're really just watching TV, not learning a language.

HOW TO INCREASE COMPREHENSION

Unfortunately, you will rarely find "perfect porridge" in the wild. Especially when just starting out in Japanese, most of the video content you find will be beyond a comprehension level of 70 to 80%. But don't despair! There are a number of ways to increase comprehension and better follow the flow of the story.

Read About the Movie or Show Before Watching

Most streaming services will have a brief description about the TV show or movie, which is a good place to start. But if you don't mind spoilers, you can usually find more in-depth descriptions and plot synopses using IMDB or Wikipedia (especially the Japanese version).

Access IMDB (the Internet Movie Database): **bit.ly/mjimdb**
Access the Japanese version of Wikipedia: **bit.ly/mjwikijp**

Watch With English Subtitles First

If you have the time and energy to rewatch the same movie or episode multiple times, try the following order of operations to maximize your learning:

1. Watch with English subtitles on the first time through so you clearly understand what's happening.
2. Watch again with Japanese subtitles on (if available) to strengthen your vocabulary, practice reading, and better connect the spoken and written word.
3. Watch once more with no subtitles to strengthen your listening skills and immerse yourself in the story.

Use the *Language Learning With Netflix* Extension

The *Language Learning with Netflix* extension for Google Chrome provides a wealth of useful language learning tools right within the browser version of Netflix. When enabled, the extension adds interactive subtitles, a nifty pop-up dictionary, and adjustable playback speed, all of which help you understand TV shows and movies that might otherwise be beyond your reach.

Install the free LLN Chrome extension here:
bit.ly/mjllnetflix

Import Netflix Subtitles To LingQ

LingQ has long been one of my favorite tools for importing blogs and other online content for language study. But they recently made their Chrome import extension tool *even* more useful: you can now import subtitles directly from Netflix!

Install the Chrome extension: **bit.ly/mjlingqimport**
Learn more about importing subtitles: **bit.ly/mjlingqsubs**

Get Help From a Japanese Tutor

One of the best ways to get more out Japanese videos is enlisting the help of a tutor:

1. Ask your tutor to help find Japanese videos, TV shows, movies, *anime*, etc. that fit your level and interests.

2. Choose an episode to watch, and then schedule two tutor sessions to discuss it: one session *before* you watch to preview the storyline and a second session *after* to go over any language or plot points you didn't understand.

3. Put a reminder on your calendar to watch the same episode again in a few months. This will provide valuable repetition, deepen your learning, and provide a valuable progress check. Nothing motivates more than seeing and feeling progress.

See my recommended tutoring sites and tools here: *Learn How to Learn > Work with a Tutor*

Keep a Dictionary & Notepad Handy

As you watch a show or movie, look up or jot down a few key words and phrases that you want to learn. Don't worry about catching every new word (as mentioned above, this will interrupt the flow too much), but try to catch a few useful or interesting terms or structures.

See my recommended Japanese dictionary apps here: *Choose Your Weapons > Japanese Reference Tools.*

WHERE TO STREAM JAPANESE VIDEOS

From free ad-supported websites to premium streaming services, there are tons of ways to (legally) watch Japanese anime, dramas, and movies online today. Here is a shortlist of the best video tools I've found to date, arranged in alphabetical order.

Amazon Prime Video

If you are an Amazon Prime member, you can access a fair number of Japanese TV shows and movies on Amazon Prime Video. As of writing, there are 605 Japanese titles available for streaming, 33 of which are available for free to Prime Members (the balance being available for rent). Not a massive number, but hey, this is plenty of content to immerse yourself in Japanese right from your TV or smartphone, transforming otherwise wasted time into productive language learning. There are even a few Japanese language Prime Originals (日本オリジナル), which were previously available only in Japan but are now available to stream outside the country.

If you're not yet an Amazon Prime member, sign up here: **bit.ly/mjprime**

The Japanese version of Amazon Prime Video has a much wider selection of Japanese content, including popular TV dramas like *Trick* (トリック) and many *Prime Originals* only available in Japan. You can also watch popular *American* shows and movies with Japanese subtitles. The bad news? You will need a separate Amazon Japan Prime account to access the content, as well as a Japan-based VPN if you don't live in Japan. Also, many of the Japanese videos lack Japanese *or* English subtitles, so much of the content will be beyond reach unless you are at an advanced level.

Amazon Prime Video can be streamed through your browser online or using one of the many Prime Video apps, available on the following platforms:

- Apple, Google, and Amazon devices
- Most Smart TVs, Blu-ray players, set-top boxes
- PlayStation, Xbox & Wii
- Roku

Download the Amazon Prime Video app here:
bit.ly/mjprimeapps

The easiest way to find Japanese content on Amazon Video is searching for "Japanese" in any of the Prime Video apps above or using the following filters within the web version (a feature not yet available in the app):

Movies & TV > Foreign & International > By Original Language > Japanese > Prime Video

---

This filter limits content to Japanese movies and TV shows that Prime members can stream for free. You can then further filter search results by:

- Genre
- Actor
- Director
- Average Customer Reviews
- Decade

Go directly to my recommended filter settings here: **bit.ly/mjprimejp**

As of writing, Amazon Prime Video only supports English subtitles for Amazon.com users. If you want to watch content with Japanese subtitles, you will unfortunately need to set up a separate Prime account on Amazon.co.jp.

To turn on English subtitles:

1. Select the *Subtitles and Audio* button (the speech bubble with 2 lines).
2. Select *English*.
3. If you like, select *Subtitle Settings* to customize the font size, color, etc.
4. Tap or click anywhere outside the subtitle menu to return to your video.

If you want to practice your listening comprehension, try turning off English subtitles:

1. Select the *Subtitles and Audio* button again.
2. Select *Off* under Subtitles.

See my specific show and movie recommendations in the *Recommended TV Shows* and *Recommended Movies* sections.

Apple TV & iTunes

Apple has a decent number of Japanese titles, which you can easily stream on any Apple device (iPhone, iPad, Mac, or Apple TV). You can rent content or buy it outright if you intend to rewatch many times.

See Japanese movies available on the iTunes U.S. store here: **bit.ly/iTunesJapaneseMovies**

See Japanese movies available on the iTunes Japan store here: **bit.ly/iTunesJapaneseMoviesJP**

Unfortunately, you will first need to jump through quite a few extra hoops to purchase content from the Japanese iTunes Store, but the access to so much great Japanese content is worth the effort.

You can see detailed instructions for setting up a Japan iTunes Store account here: **bit.ly/mjitunesaccount**

Crunchyroll

With 45 million registered users and over 2 million subscribers, Crunchyroll is the world's most popular destination for anime. With the basic service, you can stream for free in a web browser, but you can remove advertisements, get access to the full library, stream videos in high resolution, and watch on other platforms when you upgrade to premium ($6.95 a month with a 14-day free trial).

Sign up for a free Crunchyroll account: **bit.ly/mjcrunchy**
Download the Crunchyroll app: **bit.ly/mjcrunchyapp**

GoGoAnime

GoGoAnime offers a vast selection of free, high-quality anime organized by genre and popularity.

Browse popular Japanese anime series here: **bit.ly/mjgogo**

GoodDrama

GoodDrama is one of the best places to find Japanese TV series completely free. And unlike most free sites of this nature, the videos are fairly well organized, complete with detailed descriptions, user ratings, and cast listings.

Browse Japanese TV shows and movie on GoodDrama here: **bit.ly/mjdrama**

Hulu

Hulu is one of the best destinations for high-quality Japanese *anime*. They also have a decent number of Japanese films to choose from.

CULTURE CORNER

A bit of fun trivia for you: the name "Hulu" is based on two Chinese words with the same basic pronunciation but different tones, *húlú* (葫蘆, "bottle gourd") and *hùlù* (互錄, "interactive recording"). According to the company blog: "The primary meaning interested us because it is used in an ancient Chinese proverb that describes the Hulu as the holder of precious things. It literally translates to "gourd," and in ancient times, the Hulu was hollowed out and used to hold precious things. The secondary meaning is "interactive recording". We saw both definitions as appropriate bookends and highly relevant to the mission of Hulu."

You can find Japanese content on Hulu in two ways:

- Click *Search* in the upper right and enter a specific title you're looking for. Note that you will need to enter the name in English, not Japanese.

- Select *Browse* in the upper left and then choose either *Anime* or *International.*

Most Japanese content on Hulu automatically plays with Japanese audio and English subtitles. However, be aware that many anime *also* have a version with English dubbing (which we obviously want to avoid for the purposes of learning Japanese). To tell which is which, look for *Sub* instead of *Dub* at the beginning of the show title.

Kanopy

Kanopy is a fantastic way to watch movies for free. All you need is a library card! Once registered, you can:

- Watch up to seven movies per month for free (credits refresh on the 1st of each month).
- Watch on your computer, TV, or mobile device with the Kanopy apps for iOS, Android, Roku, Apple TV, Chromecast, and Amazon Fire Tablet.
- Save movies to your personal watchlist.

I especially like that Kanopy has a number of Japanese

classics that are difficult to find on other streaming services (e.g. Seven Samurai).

Learn more about Kanopy and get the free app here: **bit.ly/mjkanopy**

Netflix

Netflix may be associated most with binge-worthy series like *House of Cards* and subtle romantic preambles ("Netflix and chill?"), but it can actually become a fantastic Japanese language learning tool, too, *if* used correctly:

- You can choose from hundreds of Japanese-language *anime*, TV shows, and movies.
- You can watch some English-language movies and TV shows with Japanese subtitles.
- You can change the interface to Japanese.

The easiest way to find Japanese-language content on Netflix is to simply type "Japanese" into the search field or browse within the following categories:

- Japanese Movies
- Japanese Dramas

- Japanese TV Shows
- Japanese Anime

Many of the Japanese *anime*, TV shows, and movies on Netflix support both Japanese *and* English audio and subtitles (especially "Netflix Originals" which are indicated with a Netflix logo in the upper left corner of the thumbnail). Here's how to change the audio and subtitle settings to fit your learning goals and preferences:

1. Click the *Audio & Subtitles* box in the lower right corner of the screen.
2. Select *Japanese* in the left *Audio* column.
3. Select *English*, *Japanese [CC]*, or *Off* in the right *Subtitles* column.

I also recommend changing the Netflix interface language to Japanese so that you not only get useful Japanese input while watching movies or shows, but *also* highly contextual reading practice *between* the videos. Here's how:

1. On the login page, select *Manage Profiles*.
2. Select the pencil icon on your profile image.
3. Select 日本語 from the Language dropdown.
4. Select *Save* and then *Done*.

A few tips and clarifications before you make the change to put you at ease:

- If you're new to Netflix, it's probably a good idea to use it in English first to get the hang of how to use the site or app.
- The change to the interface language only affects *your* profile. So don't worry about freaking out your spouse, parents, children, roommates, or the acquaintances freeloading on your Netflix account.

If you find that using Netflix in Japanese is too difficult for your current level, you can switch back to English as follows:

- Go to the login screen and select プロフィールの管理.
- Select the pencil icon on your profile image again.
- Select *English* from the 言語 dropdown.
- Select 保存 ("Save") and then 完了 ("Done").

See my specific show and movie recommendations in the *Recommended TV Shows* and *Recommended Movies* sections.

There are two awesome language learning tools you can use to supercharge Netflix:

- **Language Learning with Netflix:** This Google Chrome extension adds interactive subtitles, a pop-up dictionary, and adjustable playback controls. Install it here → **bit.ly/mjllnetflix**
- **LingQ Importer:** This Chrome extension allows you to import Netflix subtitles directly into your LingQ account. Install the extension here → **bit.ly/mjlingqimport**

TED

TED was once an invite-only conference in Monterey, California attended by the who's who of technology, education, and design (which is what "TED" stands for by the way). Fast forward three decades and TED is now a massive worldwide community of lifelong learners that holds local TEDx events all over the world. While I highly recommend attending a TED event in person if possible (I attended TEDxTaipei and TEDxOlympia and loved both), most talks are recorded and posted online where anyone in the world with an internet connection can view them. So this is all fine and dandy, but how can TED videos be used for learning Japanese? I have three main suggestions:

- **Watch TED Talks with Japanese subtitles:** As of writing, there are 2,625 TED videos on TED.com with Japanese subtitles, including TED Talks, TEDx Talks, and TED-Ed videos. That ought to keep you busy for a while! First filter talks by Japanese language, and then further refine your search by topic (technology, entertainment, design, business, science, and global issues), duration, or event type.

Browse all TED Talks with Japanese subtitles here: **bit.ly/mjtedsub**

- **Use TED's cool interactive transcripts:** All TED Talks have nifty interactive transcripts that let you to click on a phrase and jump right to that part of the video! To view Japanese subtitles, simply click the "Transcripts" tab below the video and select 日本語.
- **Watch Japanese TEDx Talks:** While most TED Talks around the world are presented in English to maximize their global reach and impact, there *are* a decent number of talks in Japanese, too.

Check out this list of 5 inspirational TEDx Talks from *Japanese Level Up*: **bit.ly/mjtedx**

Viki

Viki is another great way to stream Japanese TV shows and movies for free. You can stream online or watch in one of the many apps. If your'e curious, the name "Viki" is a portmanteau of the words "video" and "wiki," a nod to the fact that subtitles are crowdsourced from the Viki community.

Stream on the Viki site here: **bit.ly/mjviki**
Download the Viki app here: **bit.ly/mjvikiapps**

YouTube

YouTube probably has enough Japanese language content to keep every language learner busy for the next million years. From language lessons, to Japanese music videos, to Japanese commercials, to Japanese video game playthroughs, there is something to fit every taste and goal. Like Japanese resource selection in general, choosing what to watch can quickly get overwhelming. To help you get started, here are a few of the best YouTube channels for learning Japanese:

- **Miku Real Japanese:** Miku is a native Japanese speaker and teacher passionate about helping foreigners learn natural Japanese. Each of her videos focuses on a useful phrase, term, or construction, and she is particularly good at pointing out common mistakes made by English speakers learning the language. She is also very active on Instagram for those who prefer that platform instead of YouTube.

Watch Miku's videos on YouTube here: **bit.ly/mjytmiku**
Follow Miku on Instagram here: **bit.ly/mjigmiku**

- **Nihongo no Mori:** *Nihongo no Mori* (日本語の森, にほんごのもり, lit. "Japanese Forest") offers loads of Japanese videos and language lessons for various ability levels, all organized by JLPT level. Most have subtitles or at least useful on-screen prompts to help increase comprehension and help you practice your listening *and* reading skills.

Watch Nihongo no Mori's videos on YouTube here: **bit.ly/mjytmori**

- **Dogen:** Kevin O'Donnell, known online as *Dogen*, is an American originally from Washington State who first came to Japan as part of the JET Programme. Hmmm, why does that sound familiar...? While working as an Assistant Language Teacher, he spent all of his free time studying, practicing, and writing Japanese, activities that have led to an impressive level of fluency, excellent pronunciation, and native-like mannerisms. His advanced language skills and comedic timing have amassed him an impressive following on YouTube and Twitter, where he shares hilarious, insightful videos on the idiosyncrasies of the Japanese language and culture.

Watch Dogen's videos on YouTube here: **bit.ly/mjytdogen**
Watch Dogen's on Twitter here: **bit.ly/mjtwitterdogen**

Tales From Archipel

Archipel—a Japanese YouTube channel popular with fans of Japanese culture, gaming, and *manga*—recently started a new series called *Tales from Archipel* designed for Japanese language learners. Each episode has a complete transcript, accurate translations, and a full glossary!

Subscribe to their channel: **bit.ly/mjarchipelyt**
Read transcripts on Medium: **bit.ly/mjarchipel**

HOW TO USE A VPN

Some online video content is available only to IP addresses located within Japan. If you already live in the country, great. But what about the folks learning Japanese overseas? Fortunately, technology comes to the rescue. Using a Japan-based VPN (Virtual Private Network), you can access this content anywhere in the world. As an added benefit, VPNs create a far more secure internet experience, especially when using non-secure networks at coffee shops, airports, etc. I've tried quite a few VPNs in the past few years, but *ExpressVPN* is my favorite so far. I especially like their slick apps for iOS, macOS, Windows, and Android that let you quickly change your server location with just a few clicks.

Sign up and download the ExpressVPN apps here:
bit.ly/mjvpn

Once installed, I suggest using the following settings as many streaming services now block basic VPN protocols:

1. Click the hamburger icon in the upper left.

2. Click *Preferences.*

3. Select *UDP - OpenVPN.*

WHY YOU SHOULD CONSIDER DVDS

Though online streaming has largely replaced DVDs, physical media still has many advantages for language learners:

- **More subtitles options:** When streaming Japanese content, you usually only have the option to watch with English subtitles. But if you get a DVD, you can often choose Japanese subtitles instead.
- **Faster repetition:** Using the scene selector in the DVD menu, you can easily go back and repeat the same scene a few times to increase comprehension and retention.
- **Bonus content:** Many DVDs include extra content like director commentaries which can provide even more Japanese input.

Okay, so now that I've made the case for DVDs, where in the heck can you find Japanese language options?

The Library

Your local library will likely have at least a few Japanese language movies on DVD.

Browse Japanese titles available at your local library using WorldCat here: **bit.ly/mjworldcat**

Amazon & Amazon Japan

Your home country Amazon store will likely have a small selection of Japanese DVDs, but you'll find many more in the Amazon Japan store. Note that you will need to pay international shipping and that the region settings may not work with your computer or DVD player.

Browse DVDs available on Amazon Japan here:
bit.ly/mjajdvd

Play Asia

Though Play Asia can be a bit pricey, they do have a wide range of Japanese language content (indicated with a Japanese flag in the upper right corner of the listing).

Browse Japanese DVDs available on Play Asia here:
bit.ly/mjpadvd

RECOMMENDED ANIME SERIES

Japan has produced a dizzying quantity of *anime* over the years; nearly 10,000 titles according to Japan's *Media Art Database* (メディア芸術データーベース, めでぃあげいじゅつでえたあべえす).

Lest you succumb to "analysis paralysis," here now is a shortlist of my personal favorites to help you get started.

Each listing includes:

- A brief overview of the series.
- A direct link to stream the show.
- A content rating (e.g. TV-14).
- The genre.
- The release date.
- A rating from Rotten Tomatoes or IMDB.

Cowboy Bebop

Set in 2071, *Cowboy Bepop* (カウボーイビバップ, かうぼういびばっぷ) follows the adventures of a small group of intergalactic bounty hunters. The award-winning show is regarded around the world as one of the best *anime* series of all time (Rotten Tomatoes gives it a score of 100%!), with a masterful combination of animation, character development, and music.

Stream on Hulu here: **bit.ly/mjhulucb**

RATING: TV-14 | GENRE: SCI-FI | RELEASE DATE: 1998 | TOMATOMETER: 100%

Hunter X Hunter

Like many of the shows here, *Hunter x Hunter* (ハンターハンター, はんたあはんたあ) began as a *manga* series and was later developed into an *anime* series. The show centers on young Gon as he tries to pass the "Hunter Examination," a series of increasingly challenging skill tests that require brains, brawn, and cooperation/competition with other examinees, many of whom are trying to kill you…

Stream on Hulu here: **bit.ly/mjhuluhxh**

RATING: TV-14 | GENRE: ADVENTURE | RELEASE DATE: 2011 | IMBD: 8.7/10

One Piece

Beginning first as a successful *manga* series, *One Piece* (ワンピース, わんぴいす) follows pirate wonder boy Monkey D. Luffy and his motley crew of fellow "straw hat pirates" through their various adventures in pursuit of the ultimate treasure called the "One Piece."

Stream on Hulu here: **bit.ly/mjhuluop**

RATING: TV-14 | GENRE: ACTION | RELEASE DATE: 1999 | IMBD: 8.6/10

Samurai Champloo

Set in Japan's *Edo Jidai* (江戸時代, えどじだい, "Edo Period"), *Samurai Champloo* (サムライチャンプルー, さむらいちゃんぷるう) mixes fighting action, comedy, and Japan's seemingly insatiable obsession with food!

Stream on Hulu here: **bit.ly/mjhulusc**

RATING: TV-MA | GENRE: ACTION | RELEASE DATE: 2004 | TOMATOMETER: 88%

Space Brothers

A must for any fans of NASA or space travel, *Uchuu Kyoudai* (宇宙兄弟, うちゅうきょうだい, "Space Brothers") is about two brothers who both dream of going into space when they grow up. The older brother, *NANBA Mutta* (南波六太, なんばむった), promises to lead the way, but as fate would have it, the younger brother, *NANBA Hibito* (南波日々人, なんばひび

と), is the one who ends up becoming an astronaut first. Not happy with where his life is heading, Mutta rekindles his dream and works his tail off to get accepted into Japan's space program. I especially like the use of real day-to-day Japanese in this anime, not the less-than-useful mobster and superhero language you hear in many *anime* series.

Stream on Hulu here: **bit.ly/mjhulusb**

RATING: TV-14 | GENRE: DRAMEDY / SCI-FI | RELEASE DATE: 2012 | IMDB: 8.1/10

The Studio Ghibli Collection

Studio Ghibli (スタジオジブリ, すたじおじぶり) is known around the world for their delightfully whimsical animated films.

CULTURE CORNER

"Ghibli" is the Italian word for the Mediterranean wind that comes from the Sahara, a name that the studio director *MIYAZAKI Hayao* (宮崎駿, みやざきはやお) picked because the studio would "blow a new wind through the anime industry."

I like nearly everything Studio Ghibli creates, but here are my favorites:

- **Spirited Away:** *Sen to Chihiro no Kamikakushi* (千と千尋の神隠し, せんとちひろのかみかくし)

Purchase the DVD on Amazon here: **bit.ly/mjprimesa**

RATING: PG | GENRE: DRAMA | RELEASE DATE: 2002 | TOMATOMETER: 97%

- **Princess Mononoke:** *Mononoke Hime* (もののけ姫, もののけひめ)

Purchase the DVD on Amazon: **bit.ly/mjmononoke**

RATING: PG-13 | GENRE: ACTION | RELEASE DATE: 1999 | TOMATOMETER: 92%

- **My Neighbor Totoro:** *Tonari no Totoro* (となりのトトロ, となりのととろ)

Purchase the DVD on Amazon: **bit.ly/mjtotoro**

RATING: G | GENRE: FAMILY | RELEASE DATE: 1988 | TOMATOMETER: 94%

As of writing, Studio Ghibli titles are not available on any U.S. streaming services, but that will change in spring 2020 with the launch of *HBO Max*!

The Vision of Escaflowne

Unlike most Japanese learners I know, I actually got interested in anime *after* I began studying Japanese. And it was *Tenkuu no Esukafuroune* (天空のエスカフローネ, てんくうのえすかふろうね, "The Vision of Escaflowne") that got me hooked. The 26-episode series follows the trials and tribulations of high school-aged heroine and budding psychic *KANZAKI Hitomi* (神崎ひとみ, かんざきひとみ) after she is mysteriously transported to the planet Gaea.

Buy on Amazon Prime Video here: **bit.ly/mjprimevoe**

RATING: TV-14 | **GENRE:** SCI-FI / ACTION | **RELEASE DATE:** 1996 | **IMDB:** 7.8/10

Aggretsuko

Aggretsuko, or *Aguresshibu Retsuko* (アグレッシブ烈子, あぐれっしぶれつこ, "Aggressive Retsuko"), is a popular new Netflix Original *anime* centered around the life of Retsuko, an underappreciated and overworked office worker who self medicates with death metal karaoke. Oh, and all of the characters in the show are animated animals…

Stream on Netflix here: **bit.ly/mjaggretsuko**

RATING: TV-14 | **GENRE:** COMEDY | **RELEASE DATE:** 2019 | **IMDB:** 8.0/10

RECOMMENDED TV SHOWS

Japanese TV series, or *terebi bangumi* (テレビ番組, てれびばんぐみ) are another great way to learn Japanese through video.

While *anime* and movies can be great, I find that TV shows tend to be more useful for language learning since they model common, everyday vocabulary (some *anime* and films feature archaic samurai talk or gangster slang that won't be particularly useful or appropriate for most learners).

Here now are some of my favorite programs, arranged in alphabetical order.

Each recommendation includes:

- A brief overview of the show.
- A direct link to stream it online.
- A content rating (e.g. TV-14).
- The genre.
- The release date.
- A rating from Rotten Tomatoes or IMDB.

Documental

If you enjoy comedy, psychology, and competition, *Documental* (ドキュメンタル) is a great way to practice your Japanese while getting some laughs along the way. The premise of this Japanese Amazon Original is simple: he who laughs last wins money! The show pits ten of Japan's top comedians against each other in a closed room, with each of them attempting to simultaneously make the other nine laugh while they themselves keep a completely straight face. If a comedian smiles or laughs, they lose their entry fee of ¥1,000,000 (approx. $9,000 USD). But whoever manages to go the longest without cracking up, leaves with ¥10,000,000 (approx. $90,000 USD)!

The series is produced by *MATSUMOTO Hitoshi* (松本人志, まつもとひとし), a.k.a. *Matchan* (松ちゃん, まっちゃん), a popular comedian and TV host in Japan. He created the show title by combining the words "documentary" (キュメンタリー) and "mental" (メンタル), since the series uses a documentary style to highlight the mental battles between the "comedic fighters" who agree to enter the room and put their hard-earned yen on the line.

Stream on Prime Video here: **bit.ly/mjdocumental**

RATING: 13+ | **GENRE:** COMEDY | **RELEASE DATE:** 2018 | **IMBD:** 7.9/10

Terrace House

Terrace House (テラスハウス, てらすはうす) is an unscripted TV show that follows the lives of six strangers (three men and three women) who live together in a house outfitted with dozens of cameras that run 24 hours a day.

Stream on Netflix here: **bit.ly/mjnfth**

RATING: TV-14 | GENRE: REALITY | RELEASE DATE: 2016 | IMBD: 8.3/10

Japanese Style Originator

Each episode of *Japanese Style Originator*, or *Wafuu Souhonke* (和風総本家, わふうそうほんけ), is centered around a Japanese cultural icon (e.g. tempura, tea, tofu, temples, gardens, etc.), with quizzes on proper etiquette, historical trivia, etc. Don't worry if you don't do very well on the *kentei* (検定, けんてい, "proficiency tests"); neither do most of the show's Japanese panelists! I especially like the segments in which they highlight a traditional Japanese *shokunin* (職人, しょくにん, "artisans" or "craftsmen").

Stream on Netflix here: **bit.ly/mjnfjso**

RATING: TV-G | GENRE: TALK-SHOW | RELEASE DATE: 2008 | IMBD: 8.3/10

Samurai Gourmet

Given its silly title, I nearly skipped over Samurai Gourmet, or *Nobushi no Gurume* (野武士のグルメ, のぶしのぐるめ). But now that I've binged the entire first season, I must admit that it's one of my new favorites. The show follows *KASUMI Takeshi* (香住武, かすみたけし), a recently retired "salary man" who now uses his ample free time to eat and drink to his heart's delight. In each episode, he struggles with various cultural faux pas, which he overcomes with the help of his new inner persona, a masterless samurai who lives life on his own terms.

Stream on Netflix here: **bit.ly/mjnfsg**

RATING: TV-PG | **GENRE:** COMEDY / CUISINE | **RELEASE DATE:** 2017 | **IMBD:** 8.3/10

Trick

Trick (トリック) is one my all-time favorite Japanese shows, and one I re-watch regularly. The series stars two of my favorite Japanese actors, *NAKAMA Yukie* (仲間由紀恵, なかまゆきえ) as *YAMADA Naoko* (山田奈緒子, やまだなおこ), a highly skilled but chronically broke magician, and *ABE Hiroshi* (阿部寛, あべひろし) as *UEDA Jirou* (上田次郎, うえだじろう), a physics professor who is initially skeptical of magic. Together, the unlikely duo goes around Japan debunking cult leaders and con artists who use elaborate magic tricks to swindle people out of their money. The show itself goes on for 3 seasons, but there is also a follow-up special, and two movies.

Stream on Prime Japan here: **bit.ly/mjprimetrick**

GENRE: COMEDY / MYSTERY | RELEASE DATE: 2000

Tokyo Girl

Toukyou Joshi Zukan (東京女子図鑑, とうきょうじょしずかん, lit. "Tokyo Girls Guide"), is a comedy-drama centered around *SAITOU Aya* (斎藤綾, さいとうあや), who dreamed of moving to Tokyo as a high school student living in the *inaka* (田舎, いなか "countryside"). She finally makes it to the big city years later and lands a job at a fashion agency. But she soon realizes that reality doesn't exactly unfold with the same glamor and material trappings she had dreamed of back in Akita Prefecture (秋田県, あきたけん)...

Stream on Prime Video here: **bit.ly/mjprimetg**

RATING: 13+ | GENRE: DRAMEDY | RELEASE DATE: 2018 | IMBD: 8.0/10

RECOMMENDED MOVIES

With a history reaching back to the early 1900s, *Nihon eiga* (日本映画, にほんえいが, "Japanese cinema") accounts for one of the most significant film industries in the world, both in *quantity* (forth largest based on the number of annual feature films) and *quality* (four Academy Awards to date for the "Best Foreign Language Film," the most in all of Asia). In addition to the standard movie genres you're used to (action, comedy, drama, etc.), Japan has a number of unique movie classifications, including:

- **Jidaigeki:** Set during the *Edo Jidai* (江戸時代, えどじだい, "Edo Period") or earlier, *jidaigeki* (時代劇, じだいげき) are period dramas about the lives of samurai, craftsmen, farmers, and merchants of the day.
- **Gendaigeki:** Set in modern day, *gendaigeki* (現代劇, げんだいげき) are the opposite of *jidaigeki*.
- **Shomingeki:** *Shomingeki* (庶民劇, しょみんげき) films focus on the lives of everyday, working class people, and have a more realistic, gritty quality than *gendaigeki*.
- **Samurai Cinema:** Considered a subgenre of *jidaigeki*, this genre is also known as *chambara* (チャンバラ, ちゃんばら), a word that imitates the sound of swords clashing.
- **J-Horror:** Representing the scariest collection of films on

the planet in my opinion, J-Horror films such as *The Ring* (リング, りんぐ) are known around the world.

- **Kaiju:** Literally meaning "strange beast," *kaiju* (怪獣, かいじゅ) films center around immense monsters such as *Godzilla* (ゴジラ, ごじら).

- **Yakuza Films:** Japan makes heaps of movies about Japanese mobsters, a genre called *yakuza eiga* (ヤクザ映画, やくざえいが).

Below is a diverse collection of Japanese movies I recommend, including award-winning films, heart-warming dramas, samurai classics, and everything in between.

- Films are arranged in alphabetical order by English titles.

- Direct links are included to watch each movie.

- Ratings, genres, release dates, and ratings are included for each (either from Rotten Tomatoes or IMDB).

13 Assassins

Tired of seeing the senseless rape and murder of their fellow countrymen, thirteen samurai join forces to assassinate Lord *MATSUDAIRA Naritsugu* (松平斉承, まつだいらなりつぐ), the Shogun's younger brother, hence the film's name *Juu-san-nin-no Shikaku* (十三人の刺客, じゅうさんにんのしかく, "13 Assassins"). The film stars *YAKUSHO Kouji* (役所広司, やくしょこうじ) of "Shall We Dance" fame.

Stream on Hulu here: **bit.ly/mjhulu13**

RATING: R | GENRE: DRAMA / ACTION | RELEASE DATE: 2011 | TOMATOMETER: 95%

Akira

Akira (アキラ, あきら) is a genre-defining *anime* film set in a dystopian future city called Neo-Tokyo. The story centers on *KANEDA Shoutarou* (金田正太郎, かねだしょうたろう), the leader of a local *bousouzoku* (暴走族, ぼうそうぞく, "biker gang"), and his friend *SHIMA Tetsuo* (島鉄雄, しまてつお), who emerges with powerful telekinetic powers after surviving a terrible motorcycle accident.

Stream on Hulu here: **bit.ly/mjhuluakira**

RATING: R | GENRE: ANIME / SCI-FI | RELEASE DATE: 1988 | TOMATOMETER: 88%

Before We Vanish

Before We Vanish, called *Sanpo Suru Shinryakusha* (散歩する侵略者, さんぽするしんりゃくしゃ, lit. "Strolling Invaders") in Japanese, is a mind-twisting sci-fi thriller about three aliens who visit Earth to prepare for a mass invasion. Their approach? Taking possession of human bodies and leaving death and destruction in their tracks.

Not recommended for easily disturbed viewers!

Stream on Hulu here: **bit.ly/mjhulubwv**

RATING: R | GENRE: SCI-FI | RELEASE DATE: 2017 | TOMATOMETER: 78%

Departures

Departures, titled *Okuribito* (送り人, おくりびと) in Japanese, is about a young cellist in Tokyo who moves back to his rural hometown with his wife after his symphony is shut down. Taking a complete change of course in his life, he takes a job at a *sougiya* (葬儀屋, そうぎや, "funeral parlor") and finds himself handling dead bodies instead of expensive cellos.

The film is directed by *TAKITA Youjirou* (滝田洋二郎, たきたようじろう) and stars *YAMAZAKI Tsutomu* (山崎努, やまざきつとむ), *HIROSUE Ryouko* (広末涼子, ひろすえりょうこ), and *MOTOKI Masahiro* (本木雅弘, もときまさひろ).

It movie won "Best Foreign Language Film" at the 2009 Oscars, and "Picture of the Year" at the 32nd Japan Academy Awards.

Rent or buy on Prime Video: **bit.ly/mjdepartures**

RATING: PG-13 | GENRE: DRAMA | RELEASE DATE: 2009 | TOMATOMETER: 79%

Hafu

This thought provoking documentary follows the lives of five Japan residents who have a Japanese parent and a parent from another country. Called *hafu* (ハフ, "half") in Japan, multiethnic, multicultural individuals can face significant challenges in a country that has historically seen itself as mono-ethnic.

Stream on Prime Video here: **bit.ly/mjprimehafu**

GENRE: DOCUMENTARY | RELEASE DATE: 2016 | IMDB: 7.2/10

Hanabi

Literally meaning "Fireworks," *Hanabi* (花火, はなび) is held by many as director-actor-comedian KITANO Takeshi's (北野武, きたのたけし) masterpiece. Like most of his films, it portrays KITANO as a violent tough guy, in this case, a former police detective who borrows money from the Yakuza to help pay for his wife's leukemia treatments. The film bears many similarities to his earlier (and also well-regarded) film *Sonatine* (ソナチネ, そなちね).

Rent or buy on Prime Video here: **bit.ly/mjprimehanabi**

RATING: R | GENRE: DRAMA | RELEASE DATE: 1997 | TOMATOMETER: 96%

Ikiru

Meaning "To Live" in Japanese, *Ikiru* (生きる, いきる) is a touching *KUROSAWA Akira* (黒澤明, くろさわあきら) classic about death, living for a purpose, and the absurdities of Japanese bureaucracy. The film stars *SHIMURA Takashi* (志村喬, しむらたかし), of *Seven Samurai* fame, this time portraying a stoic *bureaucrat* instead of a stoic *warrior*.

Rent or buy on Prime Video: **bit.ly/mjprimeikiru**

RATING: PG | GENRE: DRAMA | RELEASE DATE: 1956 | TOMATOMETER: 100%

Stream *Ikiru* for free on Kanopy:
bit.ly/mjkanopy

In This Corner of the World

In This Corner of the World, or *Kono Sekai no Katasumi ni* (この世界の片隅に, このせかいのかたすみに), is an animated film based on a *manga* of the same name. The movie's main character, *Suzu* (すず), is a kind-hearted young woman who does her best to make ends meet and overcome the domestic difficulties of life during World War II.

Stream on Netflix here: **bit.ly/mjnfitc**

RATING: PG-13 | GENRE: ANIME / DRAMA | RELEASE DATE: 2016 | TOMATOMETER: 97%

Jiro Dreams of Sushi

Jiro Dreams of Sushi is one of my all-time favorite documentaries. The film, directed by David Gelb, centers on *ONO Jirou* (小野二郎, おのじろう), an 85-year-old sushi master, and his two sushi chef sons, *Yoshikazu* (禎一) and *Takashi* (隆士). *Jirou* is the owner of *Sukiyabashi Jiro* (すきやばし次郎), a 10-seat, reservation-only sushi restaurant located in a Tokyo subway station (not exactly where you'd expect to find a Michelin 3-star restaurant!).

Stream on Netflix here: **bit.ly/mjnfjds**

GENRE: DOCUMENTARY | RELEASE DATE: 2011 | TOMATOMETER: 99%

Kikujiro

Though *Kikujiro no Natsu* (菊次郎の夏, きくじろうのなつ, "Kikujiro's Summer") may be light on character development or plot depth, the film more than makes up for it with beautiful views of Japan, amazing piano music by Joe Hisaishi, and plenty of Beat Takeshi's dry comedy.

Rent or buy on Prime Video: **bit.ly/mjkikujiro**

RATING: PG-13 | GENRE: DRAMEDY | RELEASE DATE: 2000 | TOMATOMETER: 60%

Ninja Scroll

Ninja Scroll, or *Juubee Ninpuuchou* (獣兵衛忍風帖, じゅうべえにんぷうちょう, lit. "Juubee the Wind Ninja"), centers on *KIBAGAMI Juubee* (牙神獣兵衛), a vagabonding ninja with a fast wit and even faster sword skills. The historical action thriller is set in feudal Japan with an intricate plot full of ninja goodness. **Note: the film is full of violence and sex, so it's probably not the best choice if you will be watching with children or sensitive individuals.**

Stream on Netflix here: **bit.ly/mjhuluns**

RATING: NR | GENRE: ANIME / ACTION | RELEASE DATE: 1993 | TOMATOMETER: 93%

Rashomon

Rashoumon (羅生門, らしょうもん) explores the darker side of human nature, depicting four differing accounts of a woman's rape and her husband's murder. The film was directed by *KUROSAWA Akira* (黒澤明, くろさわあきら) and stars *MIFUNE Toshirou* (三船敏郎, みふねとしろう) and *SHIMURA Takashi* (志村喬, しむらたかし).

Rent or buy on Prime Video: **bit.ly/mjprimerashomon**

RATING: G | **GENRE:** ACTION / DRAMA | **RELEASE DATE:** 1954 | **TOMATOMETER:** 100%

Stream *Rashomon* for free on Kanopy: **bit.ly/mjkanopy**

Seven Samurai

Seven Samurai, or *Shichi-nin no Samurai* (七人の侍, しちにんのさむらい), was the first Japanese movie to gain international acclaim, and is considered by some to be *KUROSAWA Akira's* (黒澤明, くろさわあきら) masterpiece. It stars *SHIMURA Takashi* (志村喬, しむらたかし), as *SHIMADA Kanbei* (島田勘兵衛, しまだかんべい), the leader of the samurai group, and *MIFUNE Toshirou* (三船敏郎, みふねとしろう) as *Kikuchiyo* (菊千代, きくちよ), an unpredictable wannabe-samurai.

Rent or buy on Prime Video here: **bit.ly/mjprimess**

RATING: G | GENRE: ACTION / DRAMA | RELEASE DATE: 1954 | TOMATOMETER: 100%

Stream *Seven Samurai* for free on Kanopy: **bit.ly/mjkanopy**

Tampopo

Tampopo (タンポポ, たんぽぽ, lit. "dandelion") is a tour de force of Japanese cuisine. The Japanese comedy ties multiple story lines together in an almost Tarantino-esque style, with every sub-story involving the love of food.

Rent or buy on Apple TV: **bit.ly/mjtampopo**

RATING: NR | GENRE: COMEDY | RELEASE DATE: 1985 | TOMATOMETER: 100%

Tokyo Story

Tokyo Story, or *Toukyou Monogatari* (東京物語, とうきょうものがたり) in Japanese, is widely considered to be director *OZU Yasujirou's* (小津安二郎, おずやすじろう) greatest creation. The movie speaks volumes about Japan's conflict between filial piety (a traditional cultural ideal throughout

East Asia) and modern lifestyles focused more on an individual's work and personal satisfaction.

Rent or buy on Prime Video here: **bit.ly/mjprimets**

RATING: NR | GENRE: DRAMA | RELEASE DATE: 1953 | TOMATOMETER: 100%

Stream *Tokyo Story* for free on Kanopy: **bit.ly/mjkanopy**

Yojimbo

Youjinbou (用心棒, ようじんぼう, lit. "Bodyguard") stars *MIFUNE Toshirou* (三船敏郎, みふねとしろう) as a masterless samurai, or *rounin* (浪人, ろうにん), who uses his cunning mind and warrior arts to help a town riddled with the violence and corruption of two warring clans. The heads of both clans end up hiring him for protection, unaware he is playing both sides.

Rent or buy on Prime Video here: **bit.ly/mjprimeyojimbo**

RATING: NR | GENRE: DRAMA / ACTION | RELEASE DATE: 1961 | TOMATOMETER: 97%

Japanese Video Games

Video games, called *terebi geemu* (テレビ・ゲーム, てれびげえむ) in Japanese, can be an excellent tool for language acquisition:

- They don't require as much motivation or discipline as many other forms of input.
- They are designed around human psychology, providing just the right mix of challenge and reward.
- Many games incorporate a good mixture of listening and reading input.

But before we get to my Japanese video game tips and recommendations, a brief public service announcement.

The very thing that makes video games supremely effective for language learning (i.e. they're designed to be as fun as possible) *also* makes them potentially problematic for those who struggle with addiction. I have more than a few friends who have destroyed their health and relationships playing video games, so please *only* use them if you know you can limit their use and still maintain a healthy life *outside* of the game. Remember that you are using the game to enable you to better communicate with real, living, homo sapiens out in the physical world.

WHERE TO GET JAPANESE VIDEO GAMES

Beware that some video game consoles are are region-free, while others will only work with *either* Japanese games or those in your home region. For example, the Sony PlayStation 4, the Sony PlayStation Vita, and the Microsoft Xbox One will all play Japanese imports. However, if you own a Nintendo 3DS or Wii U purchased outside of Japan, they won't play Japanese games.

Amazon Japan

Amazon Japan is the first place I suggest looking for Japanese games and consoles as they often offer good prices, competitive international shipping, and a much wider selection than competing online retailers. You can use Amazon Japan in either Japanese or English (I suggest the latter first to get used to navigation and then switching to the former to provide another source of reading input).

Browse Japanese video games and consoles on Amazon Japan: **bit.ly/mjajtvgames**

Ebay

Ebay is another good option for finding Japanese video game imports at reasonable prices. You can filter by platform, brand, genre, release year, condition, price, and whether you want to bid or buy outright.

Browse Japanese video games available on Ebay here: bit.ly/mjebayvg

---

Play Asia

As the name implies, Play Asia specializes in video games and content from Asia. You can find Japanese titles for all the major platforms, including:

- Sony PlayStation 3 & 4
- Sony PlayStation Vita
- Microsoft Xbox One
- Microsoft Xbox 360
- Nintendo Switch
- Nintendo 3DS

Note: Japanese language products are shown with a Japanese flag in the upper right corner of the listing.

Browse Japanese video games available on Play Asia here: **bit.ly/mjpatvgames**

RECOMMENDED NINTENDO GAMES

Many Nintendo games allow you to change the language to Japanese, even if you bought the game outside of Japan. However, keep in mind that most Nintendo games and consoles have region controls, so you won't be able to play a game bought in Japan on your home country platform, and vise versa. There are many great Nintendo games, but here are just a few to get you started.

Xenoblade Chronicles 2

Xenoblade, or *Zenobureido* (ゼノブレイド, ぜのぶれいど), is a long-form JRPG (Japanese Role Playing Game) perfect for intermediate to advanced learners.

Available on Amazon here: **bit.ly/mjxeno**

PLATFORM: NINTENDO SWITCH | **RATING:** TEEN | **GENRE:** RPG | **RELEASE DATE:** 2018

The Legend of Zelda: Breath of the Wild

The Legend of Zelda, or *Zeruda no Densetsu* (ゼルダの伝説, ぜるだのでんてつ), is an excellent option for less advanced Japanese learners because there is a lot less reading involved than more text-heavy RPGs, there are *furigana* readings above *kanji*, and you can take your time to read most dialogs. There are numerous editions of Zelda, but the latest and greatest is called *Breath of the Wild* (ゼルダの伝説ブレス オブ ザ ワイルド).

Available on Amazon here: **bit.ly/mjzelda**

PLATFORM: NINTENDO SWITCH | RATING: 10+ | GENRE: ADVENTURE | RELEASE DATE: 2017

RECOMMENDED PLAYSTATION GAMES

The Sony PlayStation (or PS for short) is an excellent option for those wanting to immerse themselves in Japanese using video games. A few things to keep in mind about the PlayStation:

- Due to region controls, Japanese PS2 games will not work on non-Japanese consoles. PS3 and PS4 consoles, on the other hand, are region free and can be played on consoles purchased in any region.

- Many Japanese PS3 and PS4 games give you the option to play using Japanese audio with English subtitles, Japanese audio with Japanese subtitles, and English audio with Japanese subtitles.

Ni No Kuni II

Created in partnership with Studio Ghibli, *Ni no Kuni* (二ノ国, にのくに, lit. "Second Country") delivers the perfect blend of story, art, and music that you'd expect from Ghibli. In fact, they tapped one of my all-time-favorite Japanese artists and composers for the score: Joe Hisaishi.

Available on Amazon here: **bit.ly/mjninokuni**

PLATFORM: PS4 | RATING: TEEN | GENRE: RPG | RELEASE DATE: 2018

Final Fantasy XV

Final Fantasy is one of the most popular video game series of all time. It's a great option for upper-intermediate learners, though less advanced learners can definitely make their way through thanks to the intelligent game design and layout.

Available on Amazon here: **bit.ly/mjffxv**

PLATFORM: PS4 | RATING: TEEN | GENRE: RPG | RELEASE DATE: 2016

Yakuza 0

Yakuza 0, or *Ryuu ga Kotoku Zero* (龍が如く0, りゅうがことくぜろ, lit. "Like a Dragon 0: ") is the sixth game in Sega's Yakuza series, acting as a sequel to the previous five games. The story is set in 1988 within fictionalized versions of Tokyo and Osaka.

Available on Amazon here: **bit.ly/mjyakuza0**

PLATFORM: PS4 | RATING: MATURE | GENRE: ACTION | RELEASE DATE: 2017

Japanese Reference Tools

The modern Japanese learner has an unprecedented variety of Japanese dictionaries and reference tools to choose from. Here are a few of my favorites to help you get started, but just be careful not to spend more in your dictionary than with authentic content or actual human beings.

DICTIONARY APPS

Nihongo

I've tried dozens of dictionary apps and sites over the years, but Nihongo is currently my go-to dictionary for Japanese. The app was developed by Chris Vasselli, a software developer (formerly of Box, Subspace, and IBM) and Japanese learner who has really thought the user experience through. He has managed to overcome many of the problems with competing Japanese dictionary apps and continues to improve and adapt the app based on user feedback. I especially like:

- The focus on using the app to work through authentic Japanese content.
- The auto-creation of flashcards based on words you've looked up.

- The ability to add photos to definitions/flashcards (an idea he says was inspired by reading *Master Japanese*).
- The prominent display of *Common*, *Uncommon*, or *Rare* next to terms so you know the usage and relative utility of a new word.
- The cool Safari extension that adds furigana to kanji on web pages.
- The "Clippings" feature which allows you to easily read and study authentic content.
- The "Contained in Clippings" feature on relevant dictionary entries so you can refer back to the source.

If you are studying Japanese and use an iPhone, iPad, or iPod Touch, I highly recommend checking the app out. I don't get a single penny (or yen!) from recommending it; I just love the app and want to support Chris' ongoing effort to make the best Japanese dictionary app and self-study tool possible.

Download Japanese here: **bit.ly/mjnihongo**

PRICE: FREE WITH IN-APP UPGRADES | **PLATFORMS:** IOS

Japanese

What the *Japanese* app lacks in creative naming it makes up for in elegance, convenience, and power. Here are some of the features I love:

- It offers Japanese handwriting input! This alone is reason to download the app.
- It has a cool Text Reader tool for pasting in content from blogs, emails, text messages, etc.
- It's completely free. And not "free" with in-app upgrades for the good stuff. No, 100% F-R-E-E.
- It's available on *both* iOS and Android. Some of my earlier favorites were only available on iOS, which was fine for *me* as an iPhone user but it left me feeling bad for my Android brothers and sisters...
- It has a clean, intuitive, modern interface.
- It has 180,000 dictionary entries and 58,000 example sentences, which you can access quickly using the lightning fast search.
- It includes *kanji* breakdowns for compound words, with the meanings and readings of each individual character.
- It includes conjugations charts for verbs and adjectives,

and lets you search for verbs and adjectives in their conjugated form (instead of having to "de-inflect" them first like some other dictionaries).

- You can organize your saved words into custom folders and then study them using built-in spaced repetition flashcards.
- It has pre-populated vocabulary lists for parts of speech, JLPT level, and more.

Download Japanese here: **bit.ly/mjjapaneseapp**

PRICE: FREE | PLATFORMS: IOS & ANDROID

Apple's Built-in Dictionary

Many Apple users don't realize that they already have access to excellent foreign language dictionaries right out of the box. But you have to enable them first in settings. To turn on the dictionary in On macOS:

1. Open the *Dictionary* (辞書) app in your *Apps* folder.
2. Click *Dictionary* (辞書) in the menu and then *Preferences* (環境設定).
3. Check the box next to ウィズダム英和辞典 ("Wisdom Japanese-English Dictionary").

TIP!

Though the ウィズダム英和辞典 dictionary is intended for native speakers of Japanese, it includes a great deal of detail not usually included in learner dictionaries that you might find useful.

Once enabled, you can then search for terms within the dictionary or use the following two ways to look up Japanese words you encounter online or in other apps:

- Highlight a word and type the following keyboard shortcut:

^ (Control) + ⌘ (Command) + D

- Highlight a word and tap with three fingers on the Trackpad. Note that this option must be enabled first: Open *System Preferences* > click *Trackpad* > check the box next to *Lookup & Data Detectors.*

To enable the dictionary in iOS:

1. Open the *Settings* (設定) app.
2. Tap on *General* (一般).
3. Tap *Dictionary* (辞書).

4. Scroll down and tap on *Japanese-English* (日本語-英語).

Once it's enabled, you can then look up Japanese words (or see the Japanese translation of English terms) as follows:

1. Tap and hold on a word until a popup appears.
2. Tap on *Look Up* (調べる). Note that in some apps you may need to tap the right arrow first to reveal the look up button.
3. Tap on a definition to expand the entry.

Learn more about the Apple Dictionary: **bit.ly/mjappledict**

PRICE: FREE (BUILT-IN) | PLATFORMS: IOS & MACOS

Tagani Jisho

Though the design is a bit dated, *Tagaini Jisho* has a number of useful features:

- Powerful search filters for vocabulary, *kanji*, parts-of-speech, JLPT level, etc.
- *Kanji* stroke order animations.
- Custom tags and notes for entries.
- Built-in flashcards.

- Print-friendly templates for foldable pocket booklets perfect for offline study.

Download *Tagani Jisho* here: **bit.ly/mjtagani**

PRICE: FREE | **PLATFORMS:** MACOS, WINDOWS & LINUX

ONLINE DICTIONARIES & ENCYCLOPEDIAS

Tangorin

There is a lot to like about *Tangorin* (単語林ｵﾝﾗｲﾝ和英辞書), a free online dictionary offering:

- The ability to use multiple inputs, including English, *roumaji*, *kana*, *kanji*, etc.
- The ability to create your own custom vocabulary lists and export them to apps like Anki SRS.
- The ability to view the "plain" and "polite" conjugations of verbs and adjectives in different tenses, voices, etc.
- The inclusion of see stroke order diagrams for every *kanji*, as well as JLTP level tags.
- The ability to customize your display options to display

or hide *roumaji* or *furigana*, highlighting, example sentences, etc.

Access Tangorin online here:
bit.ly/mjtangorin

Jisho

Jisho is a powerful online dictionary created to help you understand authentic Japanese content, texts, and grammar patterns. Here are some of my favorite features:

- The ability to search using English, *roumaji*, or Japanese.
- The ability to draw in *kanji* that you don't know how to pronounce or type.
- The ability to look up *kanji* using radicals.
- The ability to look up words using voice-to-text.
- The auto-conversion of Japanese years into the Gregorian calendar equivalent (e.g. 昭和五十五 is 1980).
- The auto-conversion of Japanese numbers (e.g. 一千万 is 10,000,000).
- The use of hashtags to filter search results (e.g.

add **#verb** to show only verb search results or **#jlpt-n2** to show only kanji from the N2 level of the JLPT exam).

Access Jisho online here:
bit.ly/mjjisho

ALC's Eijirou on the Web

Eijirou (英辞郎, えいじろう) is an online dictionary provided by *ALC* (アルク), a popular English language education website in Japan. This was the dictionary of choice used by my fellow translators when I worked for the Japanese government as it includes lots of phrases, collocations, and technical terms not found in many other dictionaries. If you can't find a word using the other dictionaries listed above, chances are that you will find it here.

Access ALC's Eijirou site here:
bit.ly/mjeijirou

Japanese Wikipedia

Japanese Wikipedia has articles on just about every topic imaginable. Best of all, many of these articles are *also* written in English (and many other world languages), so you can check your understanding and increase your comprehension. Remember: **we learn when we understand**.

See *Learn How to Learn > Improve Your Reading Skills > Use the Web in Japanese* for more on using Japanese Wikipedia.

BROWSER EXTENSIONS

Rikaikun

This aptly named pop-up dictionary—*rikai* (理解) means "understand"—allows you to bring up definitions and readings by simply hovering your cursor over words, individual *kanji*, or *kanji* compounds you encounter online. One of my favorite features is the ability to de-inflect verbs and adjectives to their base form.

To get a more detailed view of individual *kanji*, just hit the ENTER or SHIFT key while hovering over a character. The expanded view shows you:

- The character's different meanings.
- The character's *onyomi* (音読み, おんよみ) and *kunyomi* (訓読み, くんよみ) readings.

- The *kanji* frame number from *Remembering the Kanji* and other popular *kanji* dictionaries.

In addition to Japanese-English translations, the extension also supports:

- Japanese-French
- Japanese-German
- Japanese-Russian
- Japanese-Thai
- Japanese-Vietnamese

Install the Rikaikun Chrome extension here:
bit.ly/mjrikaikun

LingQ Importer

Use the LingQ browser extension to quickly add online content to your LingQ library from blogs, websites, and even Netflix subtitles! You can then work through the content within your LingQ account, using the built-in dictionaries to look up and save new vocabulary, or see previously LingQed words highlighted in yellow.

Install the LingQ Chrome extension here:
bit.ly/mjlingqimport

For more about LingQ, see *Learn How to Learn > Improve Your Reading Skills > Capture & Study Online Content*.

Instapaper Browser Extension

Use the Instapaper browser extension to quickly save Japanese articles to your account for a clutter-free, offline reading experience.

Install the Instapaper Chrome extension here:
bit.ly/mjipext

For more about Instapaper, see *Learn How to Learn > Improve Your Reading Skills > Capture & Study Online Content*.

PAPER DICTIONARIES

Tuttle's Japanese Picture Dictionary

Tuttle's gorgeous *Japanese Picture Dictionary* includes 1,500 high-frequency words and phrases, grouped into 40 useful topics you will encounter in Japan including greetings, dining, transportation, shopping, work, school, social media, more. I especially like the following features:

- Hundreds of color photographs to help improve retention.
- All terms include the word in Japanese script, *roumaji*, and English.
- Example sentences that how the words are used in context.
- Companion audio recordings (available for free online) recorded by native Japanese speakers.
- Brief introductions to Japanese pronunciation, grammar patterns, etc.

Available on Amazon here: **bit.ly/mjpictdict**

FORMAT: HARDCOVER | **PAGES:** 96 | **PUBLISHED:** 2019

Kodansha's Furigana Japanese Dictionary

For those wanting a physical Japanese dictionary, you can't do much better than the *Furigana Japanese Dictionary* from *Kodansha*. It includes:

- The most frequently used words in English and Japanese.
- Learner-specific explanations on usage, formality, etc.
- Usage notes for commonly confused Japanese words and expressions.
- Thousands of example sentences and phrases.

Available on Amazon here: **bit.ly/mjfuriganadict**

FORMAT: HARDCOVER & PAPERBACK | PAGES: 1,285 | PUBLISHED: 1999

PHRASEBOOKS

Lonely Planet Japanese Phrasebook & Dictionary

Lonely Planet's excellent phrasebooks are not just for travelers. They happen to be one of the best sources of high-frequency, high-yield vocabulary and grammar patterns available. And best of all, *Lonely Planet* includes phrases written in Japanese script, unlike most phrasebooks that only include English and *roumaji*. Lonely Planet offers two versions, a convenient pocket-sized phrasebook and dictionary or a version that also includes an audio CD so you can hear and mimic native pronunciation.

Get the phrasebook here: **bit.ly/mjlppb**

FORMAT: PAPERBACK | **PAGES:** 272 | **PUBLISHED:** 2018

Get the phrasebook + audio CD here: **bit.ly/mjlppbcd**

FORMAT: PAPERBACK & CD | **PAGES:** 272 | **PUBLISHED:** 2015

The Ultimate Japanese Phrasebook

The *Ultimate Japanese Phrasebook* is packed with useful features for language learners:

- It includes 1,800 example sentences.
- It includes all three scripts: *kanji*, *kana*, and *roumaji*.
- It includes a companion audio CD with sentences read out by professional voice actors.

Available on Amazon here: **bit.ly/mjaujpb**

FORMAT: SOFTCOVER | **PAGES:** 320 | **PUBLISHED:** 2012

GRAMMAR GUIDES

Making Sense of Japanese

Written by former Harvard professor Dr. Jay Rubin, *Making Sense of Japanese: What the Textbooks Don't Tell You* does an excellent job of demystifying the Japanese language, showing that contrary to myth, the language is neither vague nor illogical. He does an especially good job in the book of explaining the difference between the topic particle *wa* (は) and the subject particle *ga* (が), a common sticking point for Japanese learners. Highly recommended.

Available on Amazon here: **bit.ly/mjmakingsense**

FORMAT: PAPERBACK | PAGES: 144 | PUBLISHED: 2013

How Japanese Works

My *How Japanese Works* guide includes 350+ pages on the basic workings of the Japanese language, from grammar, to vocab, to pronunciation.

Download the PDF here: **bit.ly/howjapaneseworks**

PRICE: FREE | FORMAT: PDF | PLATFORMS: ALL

Tae Kim's Guide to Learning Japanese

Get Tae Kim's clear, concise grammar explanations on his *Guide to Japanese* website, using his iOS or Android app (*Learning Japanese with Tae Kim*), or in his print book.

Visit the site here: **bit.ly/mjtkgtj**

PRICE: FREE | **FORMAT:** WEB, IOS & PRINT | **PLATFORMS:** ALL

A Dictionary of Japanese Grammar

A Dictionary of Japanese Grammar, or *Nihongo Bunpou Jisho* (日本語文法辞典, にほんごぶんぽうじしょ, lit. "Japanese Grammar Dictionary"), is a 3-volume series with extremely detailed explanations of Japanese grammar usage and lots of useful example sentences. The three volumes include:

- *A Dictionary of Basic Japanese Grammar*
- *A Dictionary of Intermediate Japanese Grammar*
- *A Dictionary of Advanced Japanese Grammar*

Available on Amazon here: **bit.ly/mjgrammardict**

FORMAT: PAPERBACK | **PAGES:** 636 | **PUBLISHED:** 1989

Japanese Newspapers

For those wanting to get their news fix in Japanese, here are some recommended *shinbun* (新聞, しんぶん, "newspapers") sites and apps.

NEWSPAPERS FOR LANGUAGE LEARNERS

NHK News Web EASY

NHK News Web EASY, or *Yasashii Nihongo-no Nyuusu* (やさしい日本語のニュース, やさしいにほんごのにゅうす) was originally created to provide younger Japanese readers with a more approachable reading experience. But it's great for adult language learners, too. Some of the useful features include:

- Audio recordings and videos so you can practice listening *and* reading.
- Use of *furigana* (振り仮名, ふりがな), the little *kana* readings above *kanji* (which you can toggle on or off).
- Simplified vocabulary and grammar.

Access NHK News Web EASY online here:
bit.ly/mjeasynews

News in Slow Japanese

As the name implies, *News in Slow Japanese* provides news stories at a slower rate to help language learners pick out new words and gradually improve their listening skills. The site also includes lots of extra learning tools for premium subscribers.

Access *News in Slow Japanese* here:
bit.ly/mjslownews

Bilingual News

Bilingual News, or *Bairingaru Nyuusu* (バイリンガルニュース), provides a weekly overview of current events and news in casual, unedited Japanese and English. Each episode starts with cohost Mami (マミ) presenting in Japanese, and then cohost Michael (マイケル) providing the translation in English. They then discuss the topic bilingually. I especially appreciate that they offer detailed transcripts and timestamps for each episode through the companion app.

Subscribe to the podcast here: **bit.ly/mjbnpod**
Download the transcript app here: **bit.ly/mjbnapp**

NATIONAL JAPANESE NEWSPAPERS

For those ready to tackle non-learner Japanese newspapers, here are Japan's top two daily papers.

Yomiuri Shimbun

With over 14 million subscribers, the *Yomiuri Shimbun* (読売新聞, よみうりしんぶん) has the largest readership of *any* print newspaper in the world according to the *World Association of Newspapers*.

Read the *Yomiuri Shimbun* online here: **bit.ly/mjyomiuri**

FORMAT: PRINT, ONLINE | FREQUENCY: DAILY | POLITICAL SLANT: CONSERVATIVE

Asahi Shimbun

First published in 1879, the *Asahi Shimbun* (朝日新聞, あさひしんぶん) is one of Japan's oldest and largest newspapers (second only to the *Yomiuri Shimbun*).

Read the *Asahi Shimbun* online here: **bit.ly/mjasahinews**

FORMAT: PRINT, ONLINE | FREQUENCY: DAILY | POLITICAL SLANT: LIBERAL

Japanese Comics

I was late to the comic book party, not getting into Japanese *manga* (漫画, まんが) until well into my language learning journey. I hope *you* don't make the same mistake: comics are one of the most immersive forms of reading input and one of the best ways to improve your Japanese reading skills, especially in the awkward intermediate phase when novels are bit too daunting but learner specific materials are too easy.

WHY YOU SHOULD READ COMICS

Here are a few of the reasons *manga* are so well suited for Japanese learners:

Comics Present More Colloquial Language

Perhaps the greatest advantage of Japanese comic books is that they tend to use less formal language than textbooks, newspapers, etc., offering you a unique chance to *see* Japanese words that you would normally only *hear*.

Comics Provide a Vivid Visual Context

Not only are the illustrations fun to look at in their own right, but they also help provide a context for the words you are reading. The clearer the context, the easier it is to figure out what's going on, make new connections, and commit Japanese words and phrases to memory.

Many Manga Include Furigana

Most manga include *furigana* (振り仮名, ふりがな) reading guides next to or above *kanji*. Not only will this help you learn how characters are pronounced, but it also makes it much faster to look up new words and *kanji* in a dictionary. You can of course use handwriting input on your smartphone or trackpad, but it's far faster to just type in the reading using *roumaji*.

Manga Covers an Extremely Wide Range of Topics

As I have said (and will continue to say many times to come), interest is one of the most important factors of sticking with a language long enough to reach fluency. And with so many genres and topics available, you are bound to find a *manga* that fits your particular set of interests.

Most Manga Series Include Numerous Volumes

Many *manga* go on for dozens—if not hundreds—of volumes. This means that once you find a particular series you like, there should be enough content to keep you busy for quite some time.

TYPES OF MANGA

Kodomo Muke Manga

Aimed at children below 10, *kodomo muke manga* (子供向け漫画, こどもむけまんが) usually have simple stories focused on imparting a moral lesson.

Shounen & Shoujo Manga

Created for predominantly younger audiences between 10 and 18, *shoenen manga* (少年漫画, しょうねんまんが, "boy manga") and *shoujo manga* (少女漫画, しょうじょまんが, "girl manga") tend to have simple story lines and focus on mystical plots and superhero adventures. Because of this, the genre is actually rather popular with older professionals as well (who often read them for brainless reading relaxation during their daily commutes).

This is probably the best manga genre for Japanese learners since the contexts are usually easier to decipher, and thanks to the liberal use of *furigana* pronunciation guides. Notable examples include:

- **Hunter x Hunter** (ハンターハンター)
- **One Piece** (ワンピース)
- **Naruto** (ナルト)

Seinen & Josei Manga

Intended for readers from 18 to 30 years old, *seinen manga* (青年漫画, せいねんまんが) and *josei manga* (女性漫画, じょせいまんが) tend to include deeper plots and more nuanced language usage than their *shounen* and *shoujo* counterparts. The one downside for non-native learners is that such *manga* tend to lack *furigana* pronunciation guides. Notable examples of the genre include:

- **Akira** (アキラ)
- **Berserk** (ベルセルク)
- **20th Century Boys** (20世紀少年)

WHERE TO GET JAPANESE COMICS

Amazon Japan

Amazon Japan has a wide selection of Japanese *manga* and graphic novels, which you can filter based on genre (e.g. 少年, 青年, etc.), publisher, series, format, average customer rating, release date, and more.

Browse Japanese comics and graphic novels available on Amazon Japan here: **bit.ly/mjajmanga**

Kinokuniya

If you want to browse rows and rows of Japanese comics, consider visiting *Kinokuniya* (紀伊国屋, きのくにや) if there is a branch near you. Alternatively, you can order comics using their website.

Find a Kinokuniya branch near you: **bit.ly/mjkinokuniya**
Shop for comics in their online store: **bit.ly/mjkos**

Box of Manga

Box of Manga is a great way to get a consistent supply of high-quality, level-appropriate, low-cost used *manga* delivered right to your door. The service was founded by Charles (an American who learned Japanese by reading *manga*) and his Japanese significant other Eri.

When selecting your box, you can choose from the following levels:

- **Beginner (JLPT levels 5 and 4):** You will get *manga* with a small amount of text, relatively few *kanji*, and use of *furigana* readings throughout.
- **Intermediate (JLPT levels 4 and 3):** You will receive *manga* with a moderate amount of of text and *kanji*, with

furigana readings for most characters.

- **Advanced (JLPT levels 2 and 1):** You will get text-heavy *manga* with lots of *kanji*. Only less frequently used characters will include *furigana*.

When you sign up for a six-month subscription, you get 40% off your first box!

Sign up for Box of Manga here:
bit.ly/mjboxofmanga

Play Asia

Play Asia sells a wide variety of *manga*. Japanese language products are shown with a Japanese flag in the upper right corner of the listing. 🇯🇵

Browse Japanese comic books available on Play Asia here:
bit.ly/mjpabm

RECOMMENDED JAPANESE COMICS

There are tons of *manga* series to choose from, but here are but a few suggestions to help you get started.

Crayon Shinchan

Crayon Shinchan (クレヨンしんちゃん, くれよんしんちゃん). centers around the life of a 5-year-old, albeit a rather precocious one who acts and talks like an *oyaji* (親父, おやじ, "old man"). The humor can be crude at times (which may or may not fit your sensibilities), but I like that the comic includes lots of day-to-day scenarios and high-frequency language.

Available on Amazon Japan here:
bit.ly/mjajcrayon

One Piece

Representing the best selling *manga* series of all time, *One Piece* (ワンピース, わんぴいす) has earned its fame through its enjoyable art, entertaining storyline, and unique collection of characters. The manga's protagonist is *Monkey D. Luffy* (モンキー・ディ・ルフィ, もんきいでぃるふぃ), a teenage pirate who gained the bizarre ability to stretch his limbs to extreme lengths after consuming a supernatural fruit. Together with his motley crew of Straw Hats Pirates, they navigate the globe in search of the ultimate treasure, called the "One Piece."

Available on Amazon Japan here:
bit.ly/mjajonepiece

Vagabond

Vagabond (バガボンド, ばがぼんど) paints a fictionalized portrayal of *MIYAMOTO Musashi* (宮本武蔵, みやもとむさし), one of Japan's most famous swordsman and *rounin* (浪人, ろうにん, "masterless samurai," lit. "wanderer"), who lived from 1584 to 1645. Even if you're not particularly interested in martial arts or Japanese history, I highly recommend it given its beautiful illustrations and exciting plot.

Available on Amazon Japan here:
bit.ly/mjvagabondmanga

Japanese Magazines

Finding content that fits your specific interests is an essential part of *Anywhere Immersion*, and magazines afford a level of niche granularity not afforded in many other forms of print media. Best of all, many magazines now offer at least some of their articles for free online.

WHERE TO GET JAPANESE MAGAZINES

Amazon

The good news is that you can read digital magazines right on your Kindle or in any of the many Kindle apps. The bad news is that you can only purchase Kindle titles from your home country Amazon store (meaning the selection of Japanese magazines will be limited).

Browse Japanese magazines available in Kindle format on Amazon: **bit.ly/mjamazonzashi**

Amazon Japan

For the best selection of Japanese magazines, check out the offerings on Amazon Japan. You will pay a little extra for shipping overseas, but the reading practice is worth it! As mentioned above, note that you cannot buy the Kindle version of Japanese magazines outside of Japan.

Browse Japanese magazines on Amazon Japan here: **bit.ly/mjajmags**

Kinokuniya

One of the best places to get Japanese magazines is the international bookstore chain *Kinokuniya* (紀伊国屋, きのくにや). If you happen to live near a branch, you can have fun browsing the magazine racks in person. But if you don't, you can always just get a Kinokuniya Japanese Magazine Subscription instead, called a *zasshi teiki koudoku* (雑誌定期購読, ざっしていきこうどく).

Find a Kinokuniya branch near you: **bit.ly/mjkinokuniya**
Get a Kinokuniya magazine subscription: **bit.ly/mjkmag**

RECOMMENDED MAGAZINES

There hundreds of Japanese magazines to choose from, but here are some of my recommendations for getting started.

Hiragana Times

The *Hiragana Times* is a bilingual magazine designed for language learners. It presents every article in both Japanese and English, with *furigana* reading guides for all *kanji*. You can get the magazine in print, digital format, or both.

Learn more about the magazine and subscribe here:
bit.ly/mjhtimes

Aera

Aera (アエラ, あえら) is a weekly current events magazine published by the *Asahi Shimbun* (朝日新聞, あさひしんぶん). The magazine includes a large quantity of photos, which makes it a great choice for non-native speakers needing a little extra visual context.

Available on Amazon Japan:
bit.ly/mjaera

National Geographic, Japanese Edition

The Japanese version of National Geographic (ナショナル・ジオグラフィック日本版, なしょなるじおぐらふぃっくにほんごばん) is a great option for language learners:

- It contains lots of pictures.
- It contains topics relevant to an international audience.
- You can read the same basic articles in the English version to confirm your understanding.

Available on Amazon Japan:
bit.ly/mjnatgeo

Nikkei Trendy

Nikkei Trendy, or *Nikkei Torendii* (日経トレンディ, にっけいとれんでぃ), is a monthly magazine targeted focused on consumer trends and targeted at business people in their 30s and 40s.

Available on Amazon Japan:
bit.ly/mjajnt

Japanese Books

Japan is one of the most literate societies on the planet, with a literacy rate of 99% and nearly 80,000 new titles published each year. So you will have no shortage of books to sink your teeth into (but don't *actually* sink your teeth into books; that will damage your teeth *and* your books).

TEXT DIRECTION

In modern Japan, text is printed in either the traditional vertical format, or the modern horizontal format depending on the publisher, format, or target audience.

Traditional Vertical Text

Traditionally, Japanese was written from top to bottom, right to left (just like Chinese, which should come as no surprise since Japan borrowed its writing system from China). Called *tategaki* (縦書き, たてがき, lit. "vertical writing"), the standard is still used for most Japanese books.

 **NOTE!**

When reading books published in the *tategaki* format, beware that the "front" cover is on the opposite side of English books.

Modern Horizontal Text

While many Japanese books continue to use *tategaki*, some are now printed using *hidari yokogaki* (左横書き, ひだりよこがき, lit. "left horizontal writing"), the same direction and order used in English books. The *hidari yokogaki* format is particularly common in documents and websites.

JAPANESE BOOK FORMATS & SOURCES

Below are the most common book formats used in Japan, and some recommended sources for each.

Audiobooks

There are two popular providers of audiobooks in Japan:

- **Audiobook.jp** is the largest provider of audiobooks in Japan. They have an excellent selection of titles, decent prices, and offer the option to preview titles right in your browser. They also have a 30-day free trial to give the service a thorough test drive.

Browse audiobooks available on Audiobook.jp here: **bit.ly/mjabjp**

- **Audible Japan** has a decent number of Japanese titles and they allow you to sample the audio of most books (click the サンプルを聴く button below each book).

Browse audiobooks available on Audible Japan here: **bit.ly/mjaudiblejp**

Companion Audio CDs

In Japan, you will also find a number of print books come with companion audio CDs called *roudoku shii dii* (朗読ＣＤ, ろうどくしいでぃい, "read aloud CD").

Browse books available with companion audio CDs on Amazon Japan here: **bit.ly/mjajbookscd**

Kindle & eBooks

In Japanese, eBooks are called *denshi bukku* (電子ブック, でんしぶっく, lit. "electric book"). They are particularly useful for language learners since you can quickly look up and copy unknown words. On Amazon, the Kindle version of a book is referred to as *kinderu ban* (キンドル版, きんでるばん).

Browse Japanese Kindle books available on Amazon here: **bit.ly/mjkindle**

Bunkobon

One of the most common book formats you will see in Japan is *bunkobon* (文庫本, ぶんこぼん), low-cost pocket-sized paperbacks printed in size A6 (105×148mm or ≈4"×6").

Browse bunkobon-format books available on Amazon Japan here: **bit.ly/mjajbunko**

Shinsho

At 10.3 cm (4.1") × 18.2 cm (7.2"), *shinsho* (新書, しんしょ, lit. "new book") books are low-cost, mass market paperbacks slightly larger than *bunkobon*.

Browse *shinsho* titles available on Amazon Japan here: **bit.ly/mjajshinso**

Tankoubon

Tankoubon (単行本, たんこうぼん, "standalone books") are independent works that are not part of a larger series. It is one of the main format categories you will see on Amazon Japan. Unless otherwise indicated with the word "softcover" (ソフトカバー, そふとかばあ), most *tankoubon* are in "hardcover" format.

Browse *tankoubon* books available on Amazon Japan here:
bit.ly/mjajtanko

WHERE TO BUY JAPANESE BOOKS

Amazon & Amazon Japan

Your home country Amazon store may have a small selection of Japanese books, but you will find a near infinite selection if you use the Amazon Japan store instead. The one major bummer is that you cannot purchase Kindle books from the Japan store if you live outside of Japan.

Browse Japanese books on Amazon Japan here:
bit.ly/mjajbooks

Kinokuniya

If you want to browse stacks of Japanese books, your best bet is *Kinokuniya* (紀伊国屋, きのくにや), a bookstore chain with 80 branches worldwide. But even if you don't live near a branch, you can always order using their online store.

Find a Kinokuniya branch near you: **bit.ly/mjkinokuniya**
Shop for books in their online store: **bit.ly/mjkos**

WHERE TO GET JAPANESE BOOKS FOR FREE

A Brief Guide to World Domination

If you are a fan of Chris Guillebeau's work (the creator of The *Art of Non-Conformity*, "a home for unconventional people doing remarkable things"), check out the free Japanese version his book *A Brief Guide to World Domination.*

Download the free PDF of *A Brief Guide to World Domination* (日本語版) here: **bit.ly/mjwd**

Aozora

Literally meaning "Blue Sky Library," *Aozora Bunko* (青空文庫, あおぞらぶんこ) offers a massive range of free Japanese eBooks online.

Browse free Japanese eBooks on Aozora Bunko here:
bit.ly/mjaozora

Kankomie

The Kankomie site has a wonderful collection of traditional folk stories which are not only *narrated* but also animated! That means you can get a clear visual context as you listen and improve both your reading and listening skills at the same time. Note that you will need to have Adobe Flash installed and might need to allow it to run on the site first.

Browse the folk stories available on Kankomie here:
bit.ly/mjkankomie

Project Gutenberg

Project Gutenberg aims to collect, organize, and preserve public domain texts. They have quite a few Japanese titles to choose from, and they allow you to download the book files in multiple formats, including Mobi (for use on Kindle), ePub (for use on iOS devices), HTML, plain text, and more.

Browse Japanese titles available on Project Gutenberg here:
bit.ly/mjgutenberg

Your Local Library

Many larger libraries have collections of books in various foreign languages, including Japanese. You can use *WorldCat* to find books at a library near you.

Browse book titles on WorldCat here:
bit.ly/mjworldcat

Wikisource

Wikisource houses public domain or freely licensed literature, books, and other text-based content.

Browse free Japanese eBooks on Wikisource here:
bit.ly/mjwikisource

RECOMMENDED GRADED READERS & LITERATURE COMPILATIONS

White Rabbit's Graded Reader App

White Rabbit's Japanese Graded Reader app for iOS and Android has many advantages:

- Read Japanese right in your pocket without having to lug around books.
- Enjoy reading Japanese stories without a dictionary thank to *furigana* readings for all *kanji*, contextual illustrations, and simplified grammar, vocabulary, and plots.
- Practice your listening skills with the narrations recorded by Japanese professional voice actors.

White Rabbit's Graded Reader app here: **bit.ly/mjwrgr**

PRICE: FREE W/ IN-APP UPGRADES | **PLATFORMS:** IOS & ANDROID

Japanese Graded Readers

The Japanese Graded Reader series (レベル別日本語多読ライブラリー, れべるべつにほんごたどくらいぶらりい) is an excellent way for Japanese learners to build their reading skills step-by-step. Here's what I like:

- The series includes five levels (from Level 0 for beginners to Level 5 for Intermediate learners).
- The stories cover a wide variety of genres, including folktales, fiction, biographies, history, culture, and more.
- There are *furigana* readings next to all *kanji* used in the books.
- The books include audio CDs so you can improve your listening skills, too.

See the graded readers available on Amazon here: **bit.ly/mjagraded**

Read Real Japanese Essays

Read Real Japanese Essays is edited by Janet Ashby and narrated by *MATSUNAGA Reiko* (松永玲子まつながれいこ). The book includes 8 essays by popular, contemporary authors, written in vertical text. Each essay comes with:

- Detailed translations and a Japanese-English dictionary.
- Learner notes on nuance, usage, grammar, and culture.

- Profiles of each writer.
- A free companion audio CD.

Available on Amazon here:
bit.ly/mjrrjessays

Read Real Japanese Fiction

Read Real Japanese Fiction is edited by Michael Emmerich and narrated by *MATSUNAGA Reiko* (松永玲子まつながれいこ). The book includes 6 short stories written in vertical text. Each story comes with:

- Detailed translations and a Japanese-English dictionary.
- Learner notes on nuance, usage, grammar, and culture.
- Profiles of each writer.
- A free companion audio CD.

Available on Amazon here:
bit.ly/mjrrjf

Breaking Into Japanese Literature

Created by Giles Murray, *Breaking Into Japanese Literature* includes classic works by authors like *NATSUME Souseki* (夏目漱石, そうせきなつめ) and *AKUTAGAWA Ryuunosuke* (芥川龍之介, あくたがわりゅうのすけ). The book covers over half of all standard use *kanji*, each of which is explained at the bottom of each page. You can also hear the stories read aloud by professional Japanese voice actors online.

Available on Amazon here: **bit.ly/mjbjplit**
Stream the audio readings here: **bit.ly/mjbjplitaudio**

Exploring Japanese Literature

Also created by Giles Murray, this book includes works by literary geniuses like *MISHIMA Yukio* (三島由紀夫, みしまゆきお), *TANIZAKI Junichiro* (谷崎潤一郎, たにざきじゅんいちろ), and *KAWABATA Yasunari* (川端康成, かわばたやすなり). I especially like the "mini-biographies" and "mini-prefaces" which give the reader just enough background to better understand and appreciate each work.

Available on Amazon here:
bit.ly/mjexplorelit

Short Stories in Japanese: Penguin Parallel Text

Penguin has been making parallel texts for many decades, but until recently, they steered clear of Japanese (no doubt because of the unique publishing challenges involved with vertical text, non-Latin characters, and the little *furigana* readings. Their first Japanese bilingual text brings learners eight short stories, many of which have never been translated into English before. Authors include literary giants like *MURAKAMI Haruki* (村上春樹, むらかみはるき) and *YOSHIMOTO Banana* (吉本ばなな, よしもとばなな).

While the book lacks some of the useful reference features found in *Read Real Japanese* and *Breaking Into Japanese Literature* (e.g. line reference numbers, built-in dictionaries, and author biographies), the quality of the stories makes this book well worth a go.

Available on Amazon here:
bit.ly/mjshortstories

RECOMMENDED JAPANESE NOVELS

A list of excellent Japanese novels would fill an entire book in its own right, but here are just a few of my favorites to help you dip your toes into Japanese literature.

TIP!

Each of the following novels have been translated into English, so you can read both version to check your understanding and increase comprehension.

Norwegian Wood

Norwegian Wood, or *Noruwei no Mori* (ノルウェイの森, のるうぇいのもり), is one of *MURAKAMI Haruki*'s (村上春樹, むらかみはるき) most famous works. The novel is told from the perspective of *Tooru* (トオル, とおる), a quiet bookworm from Kobe who looks back on his life as a college student in Tokyo during the late sixties, especially his romantic relationships with two polar opposites: the gorgeous yet emotionally unavailable *Naoko* (直子, なおこ), and the vivacious, outgoing *Midori* (緑, みどり).

Available on Amazon here: **bit.ly/mjamazonnw**

PAGES: 296 | **GENRE:** ROMANCE | **PUBLISHED:** 1987 | GOODREADS: 4/5

Kokoro

Kokoro (こころ) is one of *NATSUME Souseki*'s (夏目金之助, なつめ そうせき) best known works. Though the title literally translates to "heart" in English, readers should note that the term has the implied meaning here of "feeling" or "the heart of things." The book is a commentary on the changing values and roles seen in Japan following the Meiji Restoration.

Available on Amazon here: **bit.ly/mjakokoro**

FORMAT: KINDLE, AUDIO, PRINT | **PAGES:** 263 | **PUBLISHED:** 1914 | **GOODREADS:** 4/5

Kitchen

Kitchen (キッチン, きっちん) is the debut work by *YOSHIMOTO Banana* (吉本ばなな, よしもとばなな)—whose birth name is *YOSHIMOTO Mahoko* (吉本 真秀子, よしもとまほこ) if you're curious—an award winning author from Tokyo. The novel explores motherhood, love, loss, and the power of the kitchen, as seen through the eyes of the heroine *SAKURAI Mikage* (桜井みかげ, さくらいみかげ).

Available on Amazon Japan: **bit.ly/mjajkitchen**

FORMAT: PAPERBACK | **PAGES:** 200 | **PUBLISHED:** 1998 | **GOODREADS:** 3.8/5

THANK YOU!

ありがとう

I hope you have enjoyed reading *Master Japanese* as much as I enjoyed writing it. Before you close the book and yell out *yatta* (やった, "I did it!"), I have three small favors to ask:

Send Me Your Feedback

I am a big believer in *kaizen* (改善, かいぜん, "constant improvement") and regularly update the book based on reader feedback. If you have any suggestions for additions, changes, or improvements, please send me a quick email.

Email me with "Master Japanese Feedback" in the subject line: john@languagemastery.com

---

Rate the Book on Amazon or GoodReads

If you enjoyed the book, I would greatly appreciate a review on Amazon or GoodReads. As you know, Japanese learners have to wade through a lot of noise to find good resources. I want to help more people spend their time actually *learning*

Japanese instead of searching for good tools. Ratings help other learners find *Master Japanese* and get the help they need to climb Japanese Mountain.

Rate on GoodReads here: **bit.ly/mjgoodreads**
Rate on Amazon here: **bit.ly/mjprint**

Join my *Mastery Monday* Newsletter

Join my free weekly newsletter to get language learning tips, tools, and resources to help you along your language learning journey. You also unlock access to my *Quick Start Guide* and useful 1-pagers for popular languages.

Join my free newsletter here:
bit.ly/mjmasterymonday

Wherever your Japanese journey leads, I wish you fun, fulfillment, and success.

Sincerely,

John Fotheringham

REFERENCES

[1] Paine, Thomas. *Common Sense.* bit.ly/mjacommonsense

[2] Ferriss, Timothy. *The 4-Hour Workweek: Escape 9-5, Live Anywhere, and Join the New Rich*. Harmony, 2009. Print. bit.ly/mja4hww

[3] "Not Lost in Translation: The Growing Importance of Foreign Language Skills in the U.S. Job Market." *New American Economy.* 1 March 2017. PDF. bit.ly/flsjobs

[4] Mårtensson, J. et al. "Growth of language-related brain areas after foreign language learning." *NeuroImage* 63.1 (2012): 240. bit.ly/mjgrowth

[5] Kormi-Nouri, R., Moniri, S., & Nilsson, L. "Episodic and semantic memory in bilingual and monolingual children." *Scandinavian Journal of Psychology* 44.1 (2003): 47-54. bit.ly/bilingualmemory

[6] Bialystok, E., Craik, F.,Klein, R., Viswanathan, M. "Bilingualism, Aging, and Cognitive Control: Evidence From the Simon Task." *Psychology and Aging* 19.2 (2004): 290-303. bit.ly/bilingualaging

[7] Bialystok, E., Craik, F., Freedman, M. "Bilingualism as a protection against the onset of symptoms of dementia." *Neuropsychologia* 45.2 (2007): 459–64. bit.ly/bilingualdimentia

[8] Burchard, Brendon. *The Motivation Manifesto: 9 Declarations to Claim Your Personal Power*. Hay House, 2014. bit.ly/mjmotivation

[9] Herman, Todd. *The Alter Ego Effect: The Power of Secret Identities to Transform Your Life*. HarperBusiness, 2019. Kindle. bit.ly/mjalterego

[10] Levitt, Steven D. & Dubner, Stephen J. *Think Like a Freak: The Authors of Freakonomics Offer to Retrain Your Brain*. William Morrow, 2014. Print. bit.ly/mjtlaf

[11] Young, Scott. *Ultralearning: Master Hard Skills, Outsmart the Competition, and Accelerate Your Career*. HarperBusiness, 2019. Print. bit.ly/mjultra

[12] Waitzkin, Josh. *The Art of Learning: An Inner Journey to Optimal Performance*. Free Press, 2008. bit.ly/mjaaol

[13] Campbell, Joseph. *The Hero with a Thousand Faces*. New World Library, 2008. Print. bit.ly/mj1000faces

[14] Vogler, Christopher. *The Writer's Journey: Mythic Structure For Writers*. Michael Wiese Productions, 2007. Print. bit.ly/writerjourney

[15] Campbell, Joseph. *Sake and Satori: Asian Journals — Japan*. New World Library, 2002. Print. bit.ly/sakesatori

[16] Coyle, Daniel. *The Talent Code: Greatness Isn't Born. It's Grown. Here's How*. Bantam, 2009. Print. bit.ly/mjtalent

[17] Hawke, Mykel. *The Quick and Dirty Guide to Learning Languages Fast*. Racehorse, 2019. Print. bit.ly/mjquickdirty

[18] Clear, James. *Atomic Habits: An Easy & Proven Way to Build Good Habits & Break Bad Ones*. Avery, 2018. Kindle. bit.ly/mjatomichabits

[19] Currey, Mason. *Daily Rituals: How Artists Work*. Knopf, 2013. Print. bit.ly/mjrituals

[20] Farber, Barry. *How to Learn Any Language*. MJF Books, 2006. bit.ly/mjhtlal

21 Jonathan B. Spira, Joshua B. Feintuch. *The Cost of Not Paying Attention: How Interruptions Impact Knowledge Worker Productivity.* Basex, 2005. bit.ly/mjattention

22 *Pomodoro Technique.* Wikipedia, 10 July 2018. Web. bit.ly/mjwikpomodoro

23 McKeown, Greg. *Essentialism: The Disciplined Pursuit of Less.* Currency, 2014. Print. bit.ly/mjessential

24 Breus, Michael. *The Power of When: Learn the Best Time to Do Everything.* Little, Brown, and Company, 2016. Kindle. bit.ly/mjawhen

25 Mazza, Stéphanie & Gerbier, Emilie & Gustin, M.-P & Kasikci, Zumrut & Koenig, Olivier & C Toppino, Thomas & Magnin, Michel. "Relearn Faster and Retain Longer: Along With Practice, Sleep Makes Perfect." *Psychological Science* 27.10 (2016): 1321–1330. bit.ly/practicesleep

26 Payne JD, Tucker MA, Ellenbogen JM, Wamsley EJ, Walker MP, Schacter DL, et al. "Memory for Semantically Related and Unrelated Declarative Information: The Benefit of Sleep, the Cost of Wake." *PLOS ONE* 7.3 (2012): e33079. bit.ly/memorysleep

27 Duhigg, Charles. *The Power of Habit: Why We Do What We Do in Life and Business.* New York: Random House, 2012. Print. bit.ly/mjhabitpower

28 Haidt, Jonathan. *The Happiness Hypothesis: Finding Modern Truth in Ancient Wisdom.* Basic Books, 2006. bit.ly/mjahappiness

29 Baumeister, R. F., Bratslavsky, E., Muraven, M., & Tice, D. M. "Ego depletion: Is the active self a limited resource?" *Journal of Personality and Social Psychology* 74.5 (1998): 1252-1265. bit.ly/mjegodepletion

[30] Kondo, Marie. *The Life-Changing Magic of Tidying Up: The Japanese Art of Decluttering and Organizing*. Ten Speed Press, 2014. Print. bit.ly/mjkonmari

[31] Rubin, Gretchen. *Better Than Before: Mastering the Habits of Our Everyday Lives*. Kindle. Crown, 2015. bit.ly/mjabtb

[32] Ferriss, Timothy. *The 4 Hour Body: An Uncommon Guide to Rapid Fat Loss, Incredible Sex and Becoming Superhuman*. Harmony, 2010. bit.ly/mj4hb

[33] Pressfield, Steven. *Turning Pro: Tap Your Inner Power and Create Your Life's Work*. Black Irish Entertainment, 2012. bit.ly/mjturnpro

[34] Eyal, Nir. *Hooked: How to Build Habit-Forming Products*. Portfolio, 2014. bit.ly/mjhooked

[35] Rubin, Gretchen. *The Four Tendencies: The Indispensable Personality Profiles That Reveal How to Make Your Life Better*. Harmony, 2017. bit.ly/mj4tendencies

[36] Manson, Mark. *The Subtle Art of Not Giving a F*ck: A Counterintuitive Approach to Living a Good Life*. Harper, 2016. bit.ly/mjasangf

[37] Lewis, Benny. *Fluent in 3 Months: How Anyone at Any Age Can Learn to Speak Any Language from Anywhere in the World*. HarperOne, 2014. Print. bit.ly/mjafi3m

[38] Croll, James & Lee, Patricia Lee. *Report of the French Second Language Commission - A Comprehensive Review of French Second Language Programs and Services Within the Anglophone Sector of the New Brunswick Department of Education*. New Brunswick: French Second Language Commission, 2008. PDF. bit.ly/mjnbf

[39] Wyner, Gabriel. *Fluent Forever: How to Learn Any Language Fast and Never Forget It*. Harmony, 2014. bit.ly/mjfluent

40 Bryson, Bill. *The Mother Tongue: English and How it Got that Way.* William Morrow, 1990. bit.ly/mjmothertongue

41 Rubin, Jay. *Making Sense of Japanese.* Kodansha International, 2013. bit.ly/mjmakingsense

42 Lederer, Richard. *Crazy English: The Ultimate Joy Ride through Our Language.* Gallery Books, 1998. bit.ly/mjcrazyeng

43 Willink, Jocko. *Discipline Equals Freedom: Field Manual.* St. Martin's Press, 2017. Kindle. bit.ly/mjdiscipline

44 Willink, Jocko. *Extreme Ownership: How U.S. Navy SEALs Lead and Win.* St. Martin's Press, 2017. Kindle. bit.ly/mjextreme

45 Lamott, Anne. *Bird by Bird: Some Instructions on Writing and Life.* Anchor, 1995. Print. bit.ly/mjbird

46 Smith, Will. *The Charlie Rose Show*, 2002. YouTube. bit.ly/mjytws (Skip to 3:23)

47 Potts, Rolf. *Vagabonding, Vagabonding: An Uncommon Guide to the Art of Long-Term World Travel.* Ballantine Books, 2002. Kindle. bit.ly/mjvagabond

48 Suzuki, Mami. "Everybody Makes Embarrassing Mistakes." *Tofugu.* bit.ly/mjtofugumistakes

49 Heisig, James, *Remembering the Kanji 1: A Complete Course on How Not to Forget the Meaning and Writing of Japanese Characters.* University of Hawaii Press, 2011. Print. bit.ly/mjrtk1

50 Gallimore, R. & Tharp, R. (2004). "What a Coach Can Teach a Teacher, 1975-2004: Reflections and Reanalysis of John Wooden's Teaching Practices." *Sport Psychologist.* 18.2 (2004): 119-137. bit.ly/mjwooden

[51] Pimsleur, P. "A Memory Schedule." *The Modern Language Journal*, 51 (1967): 73-75. bit.ly/mjmemsched

[52] Buzan, Tony. *Master Your Memory*. BBC Books, 2003. Print. bit.ly/mjmastermemory

[53] Gardner, Howard. *Frames of Mind: The Theory of Multiple Intelligences*. Basic Books, 2011. Print. bit.ly/mjmultint

[54] Carrol, Ryder. *The Bullet Journal Method: Track the Past, Order the Present, Design the Future*. Portfolio, 2018. Print. bit.ly/mjbulletbook

[55] Fallon, Sally. *Nourishing Traditions: The Cookbook that Challenges Politically Correct Nutrition and Diet Dictocrats*. Newtrends Publishing, 2001. bit.ly/mjanourish

[56] Burgomaster, Kirsten A., et al. "Six Sessions of Sprint Interval Training Increases Muscle Oxidative Potential and Cycle Endurance Capacity in Humans." *Journal of Applied Physiology*, vol. 98, no. 6, 2005, pp. 1985–1990. bit.ly/mjsprint.

[57] Coyle, Edward F. "Very intense exercise-training is extremely potent and time efficient: a reminder." *Journal of Applied Physiology*, vol. 98, no. 6, 2005, pp. 1983-1984. bit.ly/mjintense

Printed in Great Britain
by Amazon

58534203R00353